CLOWNS AND PANTOMIMES

From a coloured engraving after a drawing by De Wilde
in the Garrick Club

CLOWNS
& PANTOMIMES

BY

M. WILLSON DISHER

BENJAMIN BLOM New York/London 1968

First Published 1925
Reissued 1968
by Benjamin Blom, Inc. Bronx, New York 10452
and 56 Doughty Street London, W.C. 1

Library of Congress Catalog Card Number 68-21211

Printed in the United States of America

DEDICATED TO

Derek

Harry Paulo

Tom Coventry

Harry McClelland

I. M. Jones

Will Simpson

CONTENTS

ILLUSTRATIONS

ILLUSTRATIONS

ix

ILLUSTRATIONS

The illustrations in the text include a selection from " I
Balli " series of Jacques Callot (1592-1635), and selected
prints from a portfolio labelled " Theatrical and Fancy
Costumes " at the British Museum.

A FOREWORD ON LAUGHTER AND EMOTION

    . . . all their plays be neither right tragedies nor right comedies, mingling kings and clowns, not because the matter so carrieth it, but thrust in the clown by the head and shoulders to play a part in majestical matters, with neither decency nor discretion.   SIDNEY.

lucia mia   vernoualla   chebonamisa

BALLI DI SFESSANIA
di Jacomo Callot

SATISFY people's desire for the ridiculous and they will accept your idea of the sublime. That has been the policy of the showman since his trade began. Holiday folk, he knows, want to be both stirred emotionally and amused. If food for mirth be not provided, they may not gape or weep at the time appointed but jeer instead.

Showmanship is based on the study of human nature—undulant and diverse at the best of times—in a fever. Unexcited people may be induced to sit through unrelieved tragedy without smirking. In the same state they accept unadulterated farce without going away in disgust. But on holiday the twofold quality of their needs is not to be ignored. The merrier they are the more they want to be thrilled. The more they are thrilled the more they want to be merry. How he can alternate the sublime and the ridiculous is the test of the showman.

So strong a link between emotion and laughter cannot be accidental. There is, moreover, further evidence to connect the two. Pathology, for instance, indicates that loss of control over the one is accompanied by outbreaks of the other. Likewise, in normal emotional disturbances, internal conflict causes grim laughter—such as the tragedian likes to emphasise. Furthermore, excitable natures are more prone to fun than the stolid, and the statement is as true of races as of persons since the history of mirth is mainly Italian. There is no truth in the academic theory that laughter arises in a mood of detachment. By concentrating on wit, to the neglect of the more palpable causes of laughter, the professors have studied the subject backwards, and come to the absurd conclusion that any kinds of laughter which will not accord with their formula of wit are not laughter. Yet why should we agree that what our eyes or ears recognise as laughter may be something else ?   The professors are wrong not merely because common sense finds them at fault but because they have broken their own rules.   They study in laboratories while they should be delighting in circus tents and music-halls.   In other words, they deduce facts from theories instead of inducing theories from facts.   Their explanations are far too intricate.   What can be said for an authority who could not enjoy the spectacle of two clowns beating each other until inspired with the idea that they were becoming " solid wooden dummies," nor of two others bounding against one another until he thought they resembled " large rubber balls " ?   There is no such nonsense about the showman.   While the unscientific professors have been deriving a maximum of elaborate guesswork from a minimum of experience, he has been methodically providing facts.   Laughter, he knows, can be created in more ways than the professors have noted.   Yet he is sure that the explanation must be simpler than any they have put forward.   Unlike them, he is willing to learn from babes and sucklings.   He knows the tricks that amuse his offspring are essentially similar to those enjoyed by audiences of grown-ups.   More important still, there is a hint of explanation in young laughter.   A baby startled by the bobbing-up of a head behind a chair will catch its breath in fright before realising joyfully whose the face is.   The child, a little older, slithering plates off the ledge of its high-chair, will wait a second in apprehension before chuckling with delight ; or, watching an uncle who growls and walks on all fours, will spend some seconds in open-mouthed wonder before deciding that human quadrupeds are a joke.   That momentary spasm of emotion is to be noted in adults as well.   In fact, the showman's test of a clown is whether he can call forth, as part of the response to his joke, a half-muffled feminine shriek.   Consequently, out of the depth of his practical knowledge of humanity gained in barn or tent, the showman believes that laughter is directly related to emotion.   All opinions agree that it tends to take away fear and anger, tenderness and wonder and so forth.   That is obvious to the showman.   Sophisticated spectators, when the babes in the wood are being covered with the sparrows' shroud of leaves, keep back their tears by actually manu-

xiv

facturing a smile. Such deliberate and purposed laughter is, however, not his concern. Yet it reveals how the spontaneous kind arises. Though the former is ordered by the will within and the latter prompted from without, both are alike. Both occur when emotion is relieved by reason.[1] Of course we seem to laugh at times in spite of reason. That is because the effort to control, say, grief, is apt to succeed unexpectedly.

All opposites, said Socrates, are only to be understood through each other. To know what is ridiculous we must know what is sublime. To know what laughter is we must know what emotion is. There is, however, no safe guide. Neither common speech nor the jargon of the professors is infallible. Yet they agree in giving emotion plurality. They disagree widely, on the other hand, in their classifications. Love and hatred, the psychologist declares, are as distinct from emotion as a nest is from the eggs ; and sympathy is not synonymous with pity but the state of sharing the emotion of others. After such misconceptions have been explained the subject is narrowed considerably. In Mr. William McDougall's " Social Psychology " the primary emotions are limited to seven. According to his theory (but not his terminology) they are : tenderness, anger, fear, disgust, the wonder of curiosity and the feelings of superiority and inferiority. This is a serviceable list, since practically all other emotions are compound forms. There are also those that differ merely in intensity from the seven, or are affected by impotence which turns fear to despair and tenderness to grief. But joy, in all its forms from hope to ecstasy, is distinct. When it is added to the list the eight names are revealed as four pairs of opposites. Furthermore, if they are arranged octagonally their relationship is clear (see page xvi).

What we imply by the word emotion is, to all intents and purposes, that part of the human mind which resembles the minds of animals. It is the mental energy which manifests itself, no matter what the psychologists may say, in love and hate as well as shame, pride and all its other forms. It is independent of conscious reason,

[1] Since this was written J. C. Gregory's " The Nature of Laughter " has demonstrated that relief is an obvious element in all laughter.

and seems to act automatically in response to the stimulus of the senses. It is capable of deciding what action the body should take, of mobilising the blood for particular muscles, and of undertaking all those operations that are known as instincts. The particular nature of such actions depends on the particular nature of the emotion,

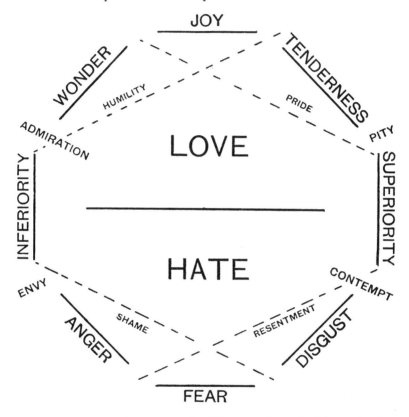

and that again depends on the significance the mind has given to the object perceived by the senses. Yet things that create fear are not necessarily as fearful in themselves as tooth and claw, tempest, fire and flood; nor objects which arouse joy as joyful in themselves as sunshine, food and running water. Emotion is, therefore, directed by the nature of past experience. The dog who shrinks from the cane and gambols at the sight of the ash-stick his master uses on country

xvi

walks, proves that memory supplies the colour which makes the manifestations of emotion divisible into the categories we call anger, disgust, tenderness, wonder and so forth.   But though these may act contrarily to what is willed, they are not entirely unaffected by reason. When emotion is the stronger the instincts have their way.   When the forces are in agreement there is a balance like that in the mind of the playgoer who pities but does not aid a distressed damsel on the stage.   When reason is the stronger emotion is relieved and shatters in laughter.   If the will's effort to control the agitation has only momentary success, or if emotion waxes in one form while it is waning in another, the sound will be the grim, mirthless kind beloved by the tragedian.

Laughter, being thus a gift to mankind not for holiday use alone, has accidentals in its notes.   While reason is imperfect it cannot but be imperfect also.   In consequence, it is confused with cruelty even though there is no limit to the jokes entirely unconnected even with the semblance of suffering.   Though laughter is distinct it is often the measure of a man's indifference to pain, not only in himself but also in others.   When friend buffets friend, anger is aroused only to be dispelled, but if the blow be hard enough to cause pain there will be no laughter unless a spectator consider the injury not serious.   This assessment of suffering has been demonstrated.   During the performance of a comic cyclist a well-intentioned rumour made it known that he had not yet recovered from a broken rib : in consequence, his tumbles were watched in the silence of deep concern.   Of course, the joke of a fall is not always that it has no ill results.   Hatred may increase indifference until real suffering cause laughter, but the failure of sympathy is due not to merriment but to a desire for justice or revenge. Cruelty—which in its positive forms is due to excessive and unchecked emotion, especially joy or fear—takes more delight in sport, righteousness, or the law than in clowns.   In Rome, while the frivolous delighted to hear (so Juvenal complained) how many slaps Mamercus could take, the righteous watched robbers, decked out as Prometheus or Daedalus, eaten alive by bears.   Law-abiding Elizabethans eschewed the playhouse but took their children to see heretics burned

xvii

or traitors hanged, drawn and quartered. To-day cruelty finds satisfaction less in seeing Charlie Chaplin hit a bully (capable of bending a lampost at a blow) with a brick, or silence a mouthing soprano with a custard tart, than in murder trials and the Waterloo Cup.

Purposed laughter is not so distinct. It is the expression of the will to kill emotion. The staunch treat fear in this manner and the cruel smother pity likewise. It is also the sign of a revolt against the oppression of emotion by minds that hunger for relief, a need of human nature well known to the showman. That is why in the history of entertainment tragedy is so often provided with a safety valve. In Athens satyric dramas relieved the gloom of a succession of tragedies. In Rome, as Juvenal mentions, the clown gave a burlesque perform- ance in the interlude of the story of Leda acted by the pantomime Bathyllus. Then the Church adopted the plan. Towards the end of the tenth century the Patriarch of Constantinople, in order to induce Christians to refrain from profane orgies, instituted orthodox orgies. Theophylact is, therefore, the patron saint of showmen, even in prefer- ence to Rahere, prior of St. Bartholomew's, who juggled in his fair and worked miracles in his church. With the Patriarch's blessing holy days became holidays. At Christmas and Easter the faithful took their fill of scurrilous buffoonery at the altars of the sublime. Whatever the priests thought of the desecration of holy places they were, consciously or unconsciously, keeping religion alive by giving rein to the desire for the ridiculous instead of letting it gather strength behind interdicts and bulls. Medieval art, similarly, understands that the mind can only sustain rapture when relieved by spells of laughter. To complain of its incongruity is a failure to give full emotional response to its beauty. The comic in medieval art cannot be ignored. There is, for example, the comic heretic holding his nose in the painting of the raising of Lazurus. There are the gro- tesque Gothic heads that gape, and grin, in stone around the inside of the old Round Church (Lamb's Church) of the Templars. There is the chapter in the story of Aucassin and Nicolette of Torelore where the king lay in childbed while his men-at-arms flung cheeses, baked

xviii

apples, eggs and mushrooms into a stream to see who could make the great splash which would decide the issue of the war. There is a Continental miracle play of St. Christopher wherein the Fool, while the pious giant rests exhausted after carrying the Infant across the stream, takes his wife on his back, steps into the water and drops her midway. There are, similarly, comic Cains, comic Josephs who warn young folk not to marry, and comic slaughterers of the Holy Innocents in the religious plays of all parts of Europe, until the spirit dies under rigid edicts and there comes the Reformation as a (possible) consequence. Had medieval civilisation developed without interruption, Mr. Chesterton believes, our pantomimes would combine the sublime and the ridiculous in "a fashion not attained in any other art, for the miracle plays had begun the miracle." But that miracle was not wholly interrupted. Though the bishops put down the Bishops of Fools, and tried to manage without showmanship, a generation of lay showmen arose with a knowledge of their business that had not been equalled before nor will be again. Their method is expounded by the induction to the most pleasant comedy of " Mucedorus." Comedy enters joyfully to proclaim her intention of making " good gentilles " laugh ; but Envy, whose naked arms are besmeared with blood, insists on having legs quite shivered off and hearing the cries of many thousand slain. " Lamentable tragedies mixed full of pleasant mirth " were what the public wanted, though the court prefered comedy, and sententious authors desired to compose unrelieved tragedy, ignorant that if given horrors alone the people will find their laughter where they will. In truth, Hamlet's portrait were incomplete did he not meet the gravedigger ; the fairies would seem unreal had they dealings only with lovers and not Bottom ; Prospero's isle would be nowhere but for Trinculo of London ; Macbeth's murder might be done in Spain but for a porter to bring his castle to earth. Shakespeare's showmanship is incomparable. His plays are written at such high pressure that laughter is a necessary safety-valve for romance.

Yet before Shakespeare's death the shifting of the appeal from the people to the court separated kings from clowns in the manner Sidney desired. From that time onwards showmanship is a study in itself, outlawed as a trade from the arts of the theatre. As holiday folk are not to be attracted by laughter alone, mechanical magic had to be invented to take the place of the magic of romance. Theophylact invented nothing. The mingling of the sublime and the ridiculous was an unchanging human need. Long after his tradition had been broken, the clown was still required to find surroundings of emotional significance. That is the idea of pantomime. That is how Perrault and our own nursery tales came to be jumbled together with the Commedia dell' arte, music-hall turns, topical allusion, stoutly filled fleshings, sentimental ballads, mechanical devices, patriotic tableaux and advertisements. And that, again, is how the importance of clowns and pantomime has been hid.

Cap. Zerbino. .Scapino.

CLOWNS

THE ANATOMY OF MIRTH

PLAYER.—Ay, but the cheater has learned more tricks of late,
    And gulls the clown with new additions.

SIMON.—Then is your clown a coxcomb; which is he?

PLAYER.—This is our clown, sir.

SIMON.—Fie, fie, your company must fall upon him and beat him : he's too fair,
    i' faith, to make the people laugh.

PLAYER.—Not as he may be dressed, sir.

SIMON.—Faith, dress him how you will, I'll give him that gift, he will never look
    half scurvily enough. O, the clowns that I have seen in my time ! The
    very peeping out of one of them would have made a young heir laugh, though
    his father lay a-dying; a man undone in law the day before (the saddest
    case that can be) might for his twopence have burst himself with laughing,
    and ended all his miseries. Here was a merry world, my masters !

" Mayor of Queenborough " (MIDDLETON).

BaGatrino.   Cap' Spessa Monti.

CLOWNS OF FOURTH CENTURY B.C.

Actors in the Greek burlesques of Apulia. One plays Apollo and the other
two the Centaur Cheiron who comes to Delphi to be restored to sight

From a Mixing Bowl in the British Museum

ONCE the world was without a joke. In these generous days when it enjoys at least seven, a mirthless generation seems more remote than the ice age. Yet where are the jesters in the frescoes of ancient Egypt ? Where the equivalent of Old Bill in the ranks of Greece before Troy ? Where the jest among all the words of Solomon ? In Babylon and Nineveh and Thebes kings gladdened their hearts with dances and minstrelsy as well as wine, but if there seem to be a fool with a jester's bauble inscribed upon their monuments, he will be disclosed as merely a time-beater for the dancers. There is no evidence that the ancientest sort of peoples understood any gibes or blows except those given in earnest.

Laughter was then simpler. Mirth, to Solomon, was the enjoyment of wine and dancing, and merriment his pleasure in the good things of earth. Or else laughter was harsh, not a holiday outburst, but the jarring note of reason struggling with emotion. Abraham laughed to hear a child could be born unto him that is an hundred years old, not because he was amused but because his momentary elation turned to despair. Thersites, who withheld nothing that could arouse laughter, was a bitter mocker, ignorant of the nature of a joke. His sarcasms persuaded the Greeks into a laughing disgust of war until Ulysses, belabouring him till he blubbered, made them laugh back their pugnacity. Bitterness, scorn and hatred are occasionally reflected in laughter now, but before reason grew subtle their notes were never absent. Even Momus, god of pleasantry (to become the deity of clowns), was without lightheartedness. Chaos was his grandfather ; Discord, Death and the Furies his brethren. His pleasantries were to blame Vulcan because he had not placed a window in the breast of man, Minerva because her house, being

5

immovable, might be subjected to an unsalubrious neighbourhood, Neptune because the eyes of the bull were not nearer the horns, and Venus because she made too much noise with her feet. Mockery for mockery's sake is, however, a stage in the cultivation of laughter. Had the gaping mouth of Momus relaxed into an irresponsible grin he would not have been driven from Olympus because of unassuaged disgust. But laughter could not be tempered until the same change had been made in emotion. That was accomplished by the invention of make-believe. Consider the cart that staged the first dramatic performances of Thespis in the sixth century before Christ. Simulation of emotion was not a new thing, for the minstrel, as well as the liar, had practised it. But the power of pretence to isolate emotion from tangible cause and effect was a revolutionary enlargement of human experience. Moved by the evidence of eyes and ears, reason could be subdued by terror and pity, though the danger and suffering were frankly unreal. When the illusion broke, these emotions turned to anger at being tricked, such as inspired Solon to denounce the falsehood of dramatic representations, and magistrates to fine Phrynicus for performances that were too moving. But when familiarity gave play-goers a measure of self-control, the shock of the awakening was unembittered and they laughed. They grew aware that whenever the unreal calls forth the emotional associations of the real without quieting reason, there is mirth. They saw the effect produced deliberately instead of accidentally, by the staging of utter extravagance and impossibility that reached a zenith in what Frere calls Aristophanes' " great lie." They brought the idea of mirth into everyday use, and so made it possible for Menander to create a joke within the serious illusion of the stage—to raise laughter without breaking the theatre's spell. Modern comedy is, therefore, the same mirror as tragedy, except when Jacques walks out of the frame with his " God be wi' you, and you talk in blank verse." The difference to the onlooker between the jokes of everyday life and the jokes of make-believe resembles the difference between a real death and a stage death. At the play reason has enough control—except in the case of the sailor who, in many an anecdote, clambers across the footlights and joins in a scuffle

6

SLAVE

DOLT

GLUTTON

PARVENU

COMIC CHARACTERS OF MENANDER

Roman terra-cotta in the British Museum

—to prevent emotion calling instincts into action.   Similarly, reason is sufficiently strong at the play to rouse laughter at incidents which in real life would be distressing.   In other words, the playgoer's indifference to the spectacle of misfortune, crime and so forth, is increased to a certain though not unlimited degree by the knowledge that what he witnesses is make-believe.   This imperfect sympathy enables the playgoer to see comedy in happenings which he would take seriously outside a theatre.   Laughter has been so skilfully cultivated that to-day there may be some who would never laugh had they never heard of laughter.

If the anatomy of mirth be vivisected without reference to psychology, the primary jokes appear to be divisible into six kinds.   To give each a name would require some philological ingenuity.   They can be indicated, however, by these terms :

Falls.	Blows.	Surprise.
Knavery.	Mimicry.	Stupidity.

On comparison with the primary aspects of emotion as outlined by Mr. McDougall the list forms a parallel which is too instructive to be merely accidental.   Injury suffered arouses pity, and injury dealt anger.   Surprise is a form of fear.   Knavery awakens disgust, and mimicry (as the fowler knows) curiosity.   There remain, on one side stupidity, on the other the feelings of superiority and inferiority : a contact of ideas which brings to mind that one term covers both the folly of the wise and the wisdom of the fool.   But before the ridiculous aspect of these serious things can be inspected, the fact must be considered that jokes have degree as well as kind.   Actually there can be no limit to the number of the degrees, since they are measured by the complexity of the conflict between emotion and reason.   But we make do with a few rough and ready classifications.   Thus the cause of thoughtful laughter—if we can agree to ignore Meredith's specialised meaning for " comedy "—is wit.   Humour denotes the type of joke which seems to follow immediately upon sight or hearing.   Fun is still simpler—so simple, in fact, that such classic instances as the rear view of a pig bring no laughter at all to a mind accustomed to wit.   Horseplay is fun that is felt.

7

Jokes occur in their purest form in what Grimaldi dignified with the name of clownship. There is a temptation to define broad mirth as knockabout humour, which appeals, apart from thuds and bangs, horse-laughs and outcries, to the eye and not to the ear. " The invaluable peculiarity about pantomime wit," somebody wrote in a newspaper about a century ago, " is that it weakens little or nothing by repeating, for a pun tells only once—but it is not so with a poke in the eye." This may be ambiguous, but it is as true in mirth as in serious reality. Jokes that are seen remain effective although they are remembered. Verbal jokes, though quickly forgotten, are stale when heard again. The paradox, however, can be explained. All visual mirth is not everlasting. Victorian clowns, for instance, had mechanisms of pulleys, flaps and labels, which have gone completely out of fashion. Only those jokes which are directly related to the primary emotions remain constantly popular. Clownship, therefore, is to be distinguished by its upholding of the fundamentals of laughter, by its regard for the elemental jokes as if they were the rites of a religion, by its refusal to spoil our delight in rudimentary emotional checks with feats of intellectual skill—which is the difference between the swings and the shooting gallery.

Ciurlo.   Gian Fritello.

FALLS

And if I laugh at any mortal thing
'Tis that I may not weep.   " Don Juan."

All the comic aspects of misfortune are typified by the joke of falls. Its simplest form is the trip over the last step that isn't there. The essence of it is in contrasted degrees of pain and suffering. Signs of distress arouse the onlooker's instinctive concern before he has had time to reason things out. The greater the disproportion of the evidence of suffering to the injury, the greater will, probably, be his mirth. Pain, however, does not necessarily cease to be funny by being real. As pity is increased by liking and decreased by dislikes, the spectator's inclination to laugh is affected by his attitude of mind towards the sufferer. The punishment of Tartuffe would need to be very great to change laughter into consciousness of his pain. The fate of Malvolio, on the other hand, exceeds our insensibility, and Falstaff's downfall in " The Merry Wives of Windsor " is a serious matter. These, however, are complications due to character. Misfortunes, otherwise, become comic when minute or too exaggerated to be credible. This aspect of laughter has already been pointed out. In *Scribner's Magazine* (of March 1922), Mr. William McDougall describes the " biological function of laughter " as Nature's method of curbing the " strong and delicately adjusted " sympathies of mankind.

Misfortunes beneath pity are familiar enough. Falls on that part of the anatomy meant for falls arouse laughter because popular superstition holds that smart impacts may occur here without much harm being done. Professor Bergson's friend, who stumbles to demonstrate how irresistibly ludicrous is a citizen's failure to maintain

9

an attitude of " elasticity and tension " towards life, would deprive the philosopher of data did he not fall in a sitting-down posture. Supposing he fell forward, the Professor's hopes would lie in a silk hat to act as buffer, or in a pair of spotless gloves saving further damage by getting soiled on a wet pavement. Should he fall without an incident of this kind he would ruin the mechanical theory, because nobody laughs at a plain fall. A woman may be so entirely regardless of psychology as to shriek even at a funny fall. She cannot help herself, her sensibility to injuries being greater than any reasoning to prove there is none this time. For a similar reason a pacifist's idea of the humour of misfortune differs from the bruiser's, since black eyes, cauliflower ears, swollen lips, bleeding noses and even broken noses, seem flamboyantly spectacular only when compared with the knock-out. To a surgeon also they may seem of no consequence, and whether he alter his opinion on receiving them himself is another matter. As a rule a man's pity for himself is almost unlimited, and his own pain must be very small before he can laugh at it.

Misfortunes too great for pity (and even for awe) are only represented in real life by the tale of a monstrous series of monstrous crimes told at a distance of time (Richard III.) or place (Mexican revolutions). Of clownship, however, Aristotle could well say, " Those who employ spectacular means to create a sense not of the terrible but only of the monstrous, are strangers to the purpose of tragedy." The fat policeman's characteristic doom is to be flattened to a wafer behind a door. Live dogs are put into machines and sausages run out barking. Pancakes with an outline reminiscently human are left in the wake of crazy steam-rollers or rolled out of turbulent mangles. Observe, however, that each of these monstrosities ends with an assurance that it is entirely incredible. This principle is faithfully observed by the pantomime burglar who is sitting on a chimney which suddenly belches forth crimson flames ; the next moment he puts his head down it and shouts, " Hi, missis, your chimney's on fire."

Another familiar form this joke takes in pantomime is the dummy head. Charlie Poley, the French clown, keeps poking his head through a doorway and gibbering. At last the other man waits for

10

him with a hammer.   Poley thrusts out a wooden reproduction of his head and takes the blow on that.   A century ago a Sheffield clown named Herbert practised a very similar joke.   Harlequin as a night-watchman lay in wait for him to come up a trap.   During one per-formance the wooden head was lost.   Clown put his own head through and received a blow hard enough to stun a normal man.   Herbert bawled out " I'm a dead man !   He's killed me," and went on with his business.   Thus even serious injury becomes comic when suffering is exaggerated.

There has recently appeared a new kind of comic fall.   In a music-hall act called " The Dream of the Removal Man " one of the Briant Brothers renders himself almost, but not quite, inanimate.   When stood upon his feet by his partner he begins to collapse in a coil, and cannot be picked up until he has been unwound.   At first the joke seems entirely new.   On examination it explains itself as a combina-tion of the joke of falls and the joke of imitating a dummy.

Fracasso.   Taglia Cantoni.

BLOWS

Panurge, on his arrival, gave him a pig's bladder well inflated and resounding by reason of the peas that were within it ; moreover a wooden sword well gilt.   RABELAIS.

To distinguish between the jokes of injury and of blows may seem a splitting of hairs. But though the two are often combined, they are just as frequently apart. Comic blows are typical of offensive conduct in the shape of all such gibes, threats and conspiracies, all such attacks upon the person, as cannot maintain the anger their appearances arouse. One of the most disturbing chapters of ancient history, the fate of those who cried out, " Go up, thou bald-pate," gives the contrast of what is comically and what is seriously offensive. Judged impartially, there is no great harm in childish mischief, and a start of annoyance quickly turns to amusement. On the other hand ferocious bears are only humorous to those who believe they never happened.

Onlookers' anger—all that is here considered—is fairly easily turned aside. Thus, standardised insults may be given and received in earnest without becoming serious. Reflections against parentage (always provided an extra " r " is in the word), a tongue put out, the cocking of a snook, the sign of horns (still as popular as ever though seldom, if ever, understood), and allegations concerning the make of a car or jewellery, are funny because an insult offered to all men is not libellous when offered to one. The rule, of course, is not applicable to blows. These are assessed with an eye to the injury—an inversion of the mind of the constable who has to succour the victim and arrest the offender in one move. To see a face slapped, ear boxed, or head smacked, is more likely to be comic than to watch fisticuffs, because

12

palms are not so suggestive of pain as knuckles.   Threats of blows
and blows that miss will almost cause the indignant maternal heart,
angry at the mere idea of violence, to be merry.   Triboullet's bladder,
resounding by reason of the peas within it, is for consummated blows ;
his gilt sword he must use in the manner of the Vice in " Sir
Thomas More," who cries to the saucy great knaves :

> What stand ye here so big in your braves,
> My dagger about your coxcombs shall walk.

Mirth, however, sometimes has more serious weapons.   As you may
see in the vestibule of the British Museum, Thalia holds a cudgel.
It was so industriously handed down from generation to generation that
Steele deemed " under the discipline of the crab-tree " a lucid term to
denote acting in comedy.   In " The Frogs " the fun of Hercules'
club lies in putting it into the hands of Pan, and in " Henry VIII." the
" dozen crab-tree staves and strong ones " are fetched merely to be
broken over heads " off," but in the graceless eighteenth century the
crab stick, chosen for hardness of grain, was vigorously employed in
full view of the audience.   What has caused the playgoers' sudden
callousness ?   The slapstick.   Towards the end of the seventeenth
century Arlequin had introduced into England the double-lath of
castigation, which made the maximum amount of noise with the minimum of injury.   Blows become so popular that Pinkethman and
Bullock must have surpassed Juvenal's Mamercus in the number they
could take.   In nineteenth century Harlequinades a pinch of gun-
powder was placed in the cleft.   After that the craze in London died
down.   At the same time, however, Paris was infected with the *funnism*
of blows.   Clowns at the cirques had to have their faces smacked
constantly.   The results are described by Gustave Frejaville in *Au
Music-Hall.*   The cheeks of the clown, he says, have skin of the
texture of wood, and the eyes are also affected.   But the French
adopted the violence of English clowns before they understood.
Horseplay, no matter how thoroughly copied from the Italians, has ever
been exotic in France, and audiences not familiarised with the comic
possibilities of offensive conduct require a blow to be extravagant
before they will believe it to be a sham.   That was what Jerome K.

13

Jerome found when he took part in a stock company's production of " Dick Whittington " in a fishing village. Of his performance as a clerk, he wrote :

> I pretend to go to sleep, and then the clown, who plays another clerk, catches me over the head with a clapper, and then I wake up and catch him over the head with a clapper, and then he rushes at me and hits me, and I take the nap from him, and then he takes a nap from me (it wakes you up, this sort of nap, I tell you), after which, we both have a grand struggle with the cat. I fell on my head the other night (lucky it wasn't any other part of me), and broke a chair in the course of this struggle. I got an encore for that, but didn't take it. I suppose you might call this knock-about business.

There are, fortunately, other ways of creating a sense of the monstrous. For instance, in their ballet of " The Dying Gladiators," Nervo, after stabbing Knox, frees his Roman sword by planting a foot upon the other's breast and making a prolonged tug.

Fricasso.   Scaramucia.

SURPRISE

THE SERPENT (laughs) ! ! !
ADAM (brightening) That noise takes away fear.
" Back to Methuselah."

Surprise is the result of the sudden, not necessarily of the unexpected. It is a spasm of fear as light as dread is heavy. It is felt when the Jack springs out of the box, when the acrobat lets go the trapeze, and when the screen is pulled down by Charles Surface. It is so clearly discernible as a prelude to laughter that the connection between the two has not had to wait until now to be discovered. " Fear " and " laugh " have ever been spoken of in antithesis. Even dread is not immune from being turned to laughter.

Sometimes the onlooker is made part of the joke. For instance, when Du Calion totters on his ladder the concern of the spectators likely to be struck if he fell is not merely on his account. And should the audience be in no danger, real or imaginary, the thrill of apprehension which is this joke's peculiar characteristic is seldom purely sympathetic. More often than not there is mingled with it the personal dread of hearing a crash or explosion. In consequence, laughter that springs from fear is the loudest of all.

One of the cleverest performances of this kind is given by Charlie Poley. Perched on the top of a high pair of steps fastened to a table with wobbly legs, he sways more and more violently until the structure overbalances. Without haste he reaches out with the crook of his stick to a contrivance hidden behind a side-wing and restores his balance. He repeats the trick, each time more daringly, until every watcher is convinced he will fall. He does so, and steps casually clear just at the right moment. Another example is provided by the clown

15

in Cornalla and Eddie's turn.   He throws a tin pan in the air straight above his head, and bends down to pick up another.   While the audience is expecting him to be hit by the pan in its descent, down comes a clatter of fifty pans.   A clown swinging his bucket of white-wash and indicating the head it will be flung upon, the pantomime cow that quarrels within itself until it breaks in two, and the broker's men moving a rickety dresser loaded with crockery, are all playing on the same stop.

What amusement can be obtained from the fear of destruction is described in Mr. Arnold Bennett's " The Regent."   Two intoxicated waiters bearing towers of plates tottered to and fro in an attempt to mount two insecure chairs and deposit their burdens on the topmost shelf of a dresser.

> One tower safely lodged on the shelf.   But was it ?   It was not !   Yes ? No !   It curved ; it straightened ; it curved again.   The excitement was as keen as that of watching a drowning man attempt to reach the shore.   It was simply excruciating.   It could not be borne any longer, and when it could not be borne any longer the tower sprawled irrevocably and seven dozen plates fell in a cascade.

The other waiter's seven dozen plates fell on the head of a being in a dress suit and an eyeglass, who helped in the smashing.   " Niagaras of plates " surged on the stage.   New supplies were constantly pro-duced from strange concealment, tables and chairs were broken to pieces, and each object on the walls torn down and flung in bits on the " gorgeous general debris," while the audience " shrieked, gasped, trembled, and punched itself in a furious passion of pleasure."

Here the distinction may be drawn between the laughter of surprise and the joke of surprise.   A joke may be suddenly per-ceived without being sudden in itself.   A coming crash of crockery on the other hand needs to be gradually perceived to be thoroughly relished.

KNAVERY

Let us about it : it is honest pleasures
And fery honest knaveries.
"Merry Wives of Windsor."

Whether a knavery is honest or not depends largely on person-alities. Reduce husbands to ciphers, make lovers good-fellows, and you get the age-old joke of stealing what is given—cuckoldry. This joke is always the most difficult to separate from those who enact it, but there are offences so mild or so closely associated with clowns that the average onlooker cannot remain in a state of distaste, disgust or horror, when they are committed. As for theft, certain commodities are deemed anybody's property. Drink is so generally the staple of hospitality that to empty another's glass is mostly amusing. To steal drink by strategy—all the wineskins held by the comic terra cotta figures of ancient times look questionably gotten—is more pleasant than by stealth, because the loser has had his chance. Thus, in "Cyclops," the satyric drama of Euripides, Silenus lays hands on the skinful brought by Ulysses, and tries vainly to hide it while the giant is stretching his bulk on the ground. Then he attempts to sneak a draught by taking advantage of a spurt in the conversation ; likewise by wishing to know how the wine is mixed; likewise by proposing his master's health ; likewise by declaring drink bad for the health. At length he succeeds while teaching Cyclops how, so to speak, to bend his elbow. Very much the same feeling inspired the Elizabethans. Mouse, the clown in long-popular "Mucedorus," is caught with a stolen draught. While the " olde trot " of the ale-house searches his pockets, he " drinketh over her head and casts down the pot ; she stumbleth at it ; then they fall together by the ears."

17

When food is stolen, laughter depends on whether some peculiar association of ideas is stronger than our disapproval. Vegetables have a variety of humorous possibilities : carrots are the symbol of auburn hair, turnips and cabbages denote stupidity, potatoes and tomatoes can be made to rhyme, asparagus is a test of social decorum, onions are eloquent of the results of cutting or eating them. Offal of any kind, sheep's heart, bullock's kidney and horse's lights, are related to a medical consultation. Fish is difficult to handle if not wrapped up. Live creatures, especially lobsters, are troublesome. Bread suggests hunger too strongly for humour, and clowns have to counteract the impression by returning purloined loaves immediately, as missiles, or, copying Grimaldi, use them as boxing gloves. Associations, however, change from generation to generation, and what was humorous in the knavery of the Harlequinades of fifty years ago is less than serious now. Carrots, for instance, have been ousted by bananas.

Mountebanks are never likely to go out of favour, because, by appealing to the vanity of those not yet deceived, they give their knavery an air of sport. Quackery is seldom punished. In John Heywood's interlude of " The Pardoner and the Friar," one of the " many mad plays " this Jester wrote for Henry VIII., the rival vendors of such relics as the " great toe of the Holy Trinity " and the " blessed jawbone of All-Hallows " win the day. For, although they threaten to tear off each other's ears, their blows fall not upon each other but upon the Parson and Neighbour Pratt who try to preserve the peace.

Incidentally, Heywood's interlude, " John John the Husband, Tib his Wife, and Sir John the Priest," makes cuckoldry a joke without dwindling the husband as Wycherley did or beautifying the lover as Somerset Maugham (in " The Circle ") does. The history of morals is in the fluctuations of this joke. Much of the humour that turns on a matter of propriety is, however, due not to the relief of disgust but to shame. Take, for instance, Tubby Edlin's joke when he points to the photo of a hospital ward and explains that he is in the end bed. " But that bed's empty," objects his captain. " I've just gone out for a minute," is the answer. In part that is the joke of stupidity. Mainly, we laugh to find ourselves nearly shocked at what is inferred.

18

MIMICRY

You may laugh at an animal, but only because you have detected in it some human attitude or expression.   BERGSON.

All the arts, said Aristotle, are modes of imitation. All collective mental life, the psychologist has declared, requires it as "the prime condition." It depends on curiosity, an instinct prompted by the emotion of wonder. Perverse imitation may become the caricature, parody, travesty or burlesque of persons. These are forms of the joke of mimicry complicated by the addition of a (possibly serious) gibe. But when there is perverse imitation of the impersonal, mirth is simply thwarted wonder. Professor Bergson offers another explanation. Animals, he says, are funny when they resemble human beings ; yet he does not find the human body funny when it resembles an animal, but in exact proportion as it " reminds us of a mere machine." The theory falls down before a comic clockwork horse and cart.

Imitation causes laughter according to its capacity both to create and dispel illusion. Music-hall impersonators show the principle in all its stages. Nelson Keys will imitate the gestures of Sir Gerald du Maurier exactly, and time them outrageously, which is funny. Another impersonator will be exact in every detail, which seems to be clever. Another will not even pronounce the name rightly, which is funny because the performance is a perverse imitation of impersonation. The mimicry of animals shows the workings of the mind still more curiously. Bransby Williams is not comic when he barks like a dog, but is ludicrous when he moves his mouth like a gold fish. The explanation is that the first, an aural illusion, is complete, but the second, a visual illusion, is not. If Bransby Williams were to go down on all fours when he barks, the ear's evidence would make a merry conflict with

19

that of the sight.   On this principle the Arnaut Brothers' imitations of birds are amusing, though they reproduce the calls exactly.

"Spoof" performances make wonder easily discernible in mirth. Laveen and Cross, dressed as strong men, perform feats of skill which merge the remarkable into the incredible.   The illusion is strong enough to make the simple gasp, and the sophisticated realise that they are marvelling in spite of themselves.   Both types of spectators laugh when Laveen neglects the partner he has been balancing on one finger and leaves him hovering in the air.   The marksmanship of the Grotesque Jovers is similarly arranged.   One clown, "sighting" in a mirror, hits the biscuit by firing over his shoulder ; the Auguste fires his pop-gun into the mirror but the biscuit flies in pieces just the same. Significantly, the magicians whose "disappearing ladies" disappear palpably into tables made like shallow coffins, and reappear perched on visible machinery, are not laughed to scorn as long as the magician has explained convincingly that he is in earnest—stage illusion is a powerful spell.

Expectancy, as the word is generally understood, is a form of wonder.   That, too, can be played upon by the clown.   Van Hoven is the most expert in this way.   His excitement is too great for him to finish a sentence.   He rushes into the auditorium breathlessly and seizes upon small boys who hold lumps of ice and other conjuring properties.   The preparations multiply but are still incomplete when the curtain descends.

STUPIDITY

The passion of laughter is nothing else but sudden glory arising from some sudden conception of some eminence in ourselves, by comparison with the infirmity of others.
HOBBES.

Laughter that springs from the feelings of superiority and inferiority is occasionally, as Hobbes' statement proves, difficult to distinguish from these feelings themselves. The mere mention of a Ford car, an engagement ring bought at Woolworth's, or a home at Wigan is considered a joke. Similarly, an actor playing a rustic part has only to drink tea out of his saucer to arouse shrieks of feminine delight. But, on consideration, it must be plain that this mirth is distinct from the feeling of superiority in the breast of a man who owns a Rolls-Royce towards the less fortunate motorist, or the factory girl who has a real diamond ring towards wearers of paste, and of the girl learned in the etiquette of the tea table towards parents who " don't know any better." Pride and humility turn to laughter when they have been evoked without reason. The Ford car, figuratively speaking, operates both ways. The plutocrat, secure in his possessions, laughs because he needs a more serious challenge before he desires to mention the cost of his own car. The junior clerk laughs because he needs more magnificence to sustain his envy. Similarly, the women who like to see rustics drinking from saucers are a stage removed from the young thing who finds her manners too good for her home. In laughter the glory is very sudden and soon dispelled. Misspelling, mispronunciation and malapropisms are funny, but our neighbour's lack of our knowledge of business or politics is serious.

So far only the primitive fun of the joke of superiority has been indicated. Its humour is exemplified in the story of the village idiot who, given the choice of a penny or a sixpence, took the larger coin. When a busybody advised him to do otherwise the next time, he shook his head—" There'd be no more pennies for me if I did." Here our feeling of superiority is thwarted. Anecdotes of absent-minded professors imply, on the contrary, the relief of feelings of inferiority. Nevertheless, the joke of stupidity can sometimes be enacted by idiot or pedant, since its nature is not always dependent on character. Whether the man who holds up a walking-stick in a shower, in mistake for an umbrella, is a fool or a professor, the humour of it is that he knows what to do yet cannot effect his purpose, and not that he effects his purpose without knowing what to do. The difference is between effort without result and result without effort—or, more generally, between much effort with little result and little effort with much result. Grock combines the two. He throws his violin bow in the air, grasps at it and misses it. He tries again and again without success. Then in a mood of sheer abstraction he accomplishes the trick without thinking.

" Gammer Gurton's Needle " belongs to this category. So that the joke be not missed, the Prologue not only sets forth how

> As Gammer Gurton with many a wide stitch
> Sat piecing and patching of Hodge her man's breech,
> By chance or misfortune, as she her gear toss'd,
> In Hodge's leather breeches her needle she lost.

but tells the end of the story :

> Suddenly the needle Hodge found by the pricking,
> And drew it out of his buttock where it was sticking.

so that the audience may know the commotion of search, suspicion, accusation and conflict to be much ado about nothing. In modern humour its counterpart is Tom Sawyer's burrowing expedition, which breaks through the floor of the shed just after the negro " prisoner " has walked out. Dan Leno reproduced the idea in " The Babes in the Wood " by climbing on to a stable roof (in order to poison a horse) because " no real burglar ever goes through a door." In anecdotes it is typified by the yokel who turned a sign-post the wrong way to deceive the Zeppelins, and by the professor fleeing before an express

22

down a railroad track, and crying " Thank heavens, a branch line at last."   Sometimes the joke of the feeling of inferiority and the joke of wonder combine—just as the emotions themselves combine to form admiration—as in the latter stages of Van Hoven's performance or in the efforts of a clown who pulls strenuously at a rope until a tiny toy lion appears.

Thus, to nullify positive virtues, as persistence, ingenuity and concentration, is as common a joke as any.   The opposite joke, to be found in the wisdom of folly or the effectiveness of sloth, is rarer.   Will Fyffe, however, provides a happy example in the character of a half-witted poacher who always has a pheasant's tail-feathers sticking from his pocket in order to make the keepers tired of being outwitted.   And there is also the once popular song of " Billy Muggins," who never went out to enjoy himself but stayed at home (his landlady made it worth while).   Shakespeare's " material fools " are living examples of how it profits a man to lose his wits, but he does not illustrate the theory in action though the reverse joke inspires many of his comic scenes.

.   .   .   .   .   .

Joy has been omitted from the anatomy of mirth not because no laughter can be so obtained but because the joke of joy belongs more to the study of Saturnalia.   It provides mirth, however, in exactly the same way as other aspects of emotion, since unsustained joy is as comic as unsustained fright.   This is the joke a clown exploits when he stands before the footlights for several minutes smiling inexplicably, or exhibits a face rapt in delight at some trivial occurrence.   A typical joke of joy is the blissful but very humble meal, such as bread and cheese in a spotted handkerchief.   Many comedians, especially Will Evans, practise it to-day ; but the classical example is " the incomparable Robert Cox," who ate bread and butter delightfully at the Red Bull during the Commonwealth.   The same laughter is aroused throughout the exhibition of Charlie Chaplin's film of " The Kid," not only at the remarkable meals but at the clown's delight in making sundry humble utensils for the use of his adopted child—a chair, for instance, with a hole cut in the seat.

CLOWNSHIP

Dɪᴄᴀᴇᴏᴘᴏʟɪs.—Well, dear Euripides, if you could but lend me
A suit of tatters from a cast-off tragedy . . .
O Jupiter, what an infinite endless mass
Of eternal holes and patches.   Here it is,
Here's wherewithal to clothe myself in misery.
Euripides, now, since you've gone so far,
Do give me the other articles besides
Belonging to these rags, that suit with them,
With a little Mysian bonnet for my head.
For I must wear a beggar's garb to-day,
Yet be myself in spite of my disguise,
That the audience all may know me . . .
Why, bless me, I'm quite inspired (I think) with phrases
I shall want the beggar's staff, though, notwithstanding.

Aristophanes (Frᴇʀᴇ).

Meo squaquara · Pasquariello Truonno

Langlois.

"FUNNY things happening to unfunny people," says Mr. James Agate, "become unfunny, while ordinary things happening to comic personages put on comicality." Separating the joke from the clown is, indeed, rather like cutting off neither less nor more than a pound of his spirit. What he does or what happens to him, if it arouse any feeling at all, is funny because his irresponsibility and the thickness of his hide are advertised. Put the king in his place and every flourish of a flapstick is, according to whether he is thrashed or thrasher, a treason against majesty or a fearful sign of royal displeasure, if not insanity. Mirth is largely a matter of appearances. The onlooker must see here and now the incongruity between semblance and reality. If not forewarned his judgment may err and allow his tenderness to warm over the burial of the office boy's fictitious grandmother, or his laughter to increase over a damaged spine. Comic and serious are outwardly so finely divided—the space between has not the length, breadth or place the poorest of Euclid's creatures possess—that a sign is needed to show when a joke is a joke. That sign is the clown.

According to Dr. Murray's dictionary the word originally meant "clod, clot, lump" and, like other words, was applied in various languages to a clumsy boor, a lout. The changes of meaning this and some related words have undergone tell the history of clowns. Once the idiot was an object of awe. Afterwards he was given a seat at lords' tables because he could make merry gentlemen laugh : thenceforward " silly," which had meant blessed, expressed amused contempt. Folly became profitable. The quick-witted coveted the place of the half-witted and obtained his privileges without shame. That is the origin of the jester,[1] the " material fool " whom Shakespeare

---

[1] Dr. Doran's "History of Court Fools"—based to a certain extent on Flögel and other laborious seekers after humour—is an exhaustive treatise on jesters.

dubs clown, because in his day the servant licensed to abuse had become confused with the mummer subjected to abuse. But the real stage clown is different in origin. The country lout was not dressed in livery and given a seat at lords' tables. The only share he took in the profession of mirth was to inspire comic actors to mimic his ways. Then, as the name of fool stuck to the jester long after he had ceased to resemble the half-wit, so the name of clown was kept by comedians. When lords hired players, the jesters were merged into the companies. Consequently the terms fool and clown became interchangeable. Thus Touchstone is dubbed clown, though his cry of " It is meat and drink to me to see a clown " at the sight of William shows the distinction. General use has now given the preference to " clown " —not necessarily Clown of the Harlequinade—and, therefore, clown-ship, a Jacobean expression of mockery before invested with the pathos of Grimaldi's farewell, is the best label for all that makes a clown : his state and his art.

When the first actors mounted the cart of Thespis their faces were raddled with the lees of wine. The obvious intention was to mark them off from ordinary men. Concealing the features of the citizen helped the illusion that he was a hero or a god. At the same time the smears, by advertising his unreality, checked the illusion of passion from becoming too moving. That was the origin of the masks necessary in tragedy when the actors were at a great distance from the audience. That was also the origin of the " make-up " necessary in all circumstances to clowns : " mask," in fact, comes from the Arab word, maskharat, for clown. Sooted cheeks in Ancient Rome, red noses for devils in the Middle Ages, masks in the Commedia dell' arte, bismuth and rouge in the English Harlequinade, flour in old French farces, and burnt cork in the nigger-minstrel shows, all indicate the advantage of a covered face. Colley Cibber came to the same conclusion when in 1702 he saw Pinkethman attempt to play Harlequin in " The Emperor of the Moon " without the " unmeaning mask of a black cat." The actor

could not take to himself the shame of the character without being concealed —he was no mere Harlequin—his humour was quite disconcerted ! his con-

TARLETON

From a Harleian MS.

ARLEQUIN

From an etching in Riccoboni's "Théâtre Italien"

science could not with the same *effronterie* declare against nature, without the cover of that unchanging face, which he was sure would never blush for it ! no ! it was quite another case ! without that armour his courage could not come up to the bold strokes that were necessary to get the better of common sense.

Tarleton could clown without a mask, but he enjoyed the advantage of a flattened nose that had only to be shown between the tapestries at the back of the stage to raise delight. Similarly Hippisley relied on the scar of a burn on his face.[1] Perhaps he received it in the days when he was a candle-snuffer. (Possibly he was the lion in the opera of " Hydaspes " whom Steele described as " a candle-snuffer, who being a fellow of testy choleric temper, overdid his part, and would not suffer himself to be killed so easily as he ought to have done.") Anyhow, his burn was so successful that when he proposed to bring up his son for the stage, Quin commented, " It is high time to burn him." The story is instructive because it points to the purpose of the clown's mask. Unlike the actor's disguise, which made him into another being, it served merely as a disfigurement. The sooty mime's fun was not the fun of the knaves and butts of the New Comedy at Rome in the same century. Instead of representing a comic character he had to be himself in spite of his disguise. His familiar manner made his every day reality known to the audience ; his fantastic face made him a creature of the imagination. He was thus in himself a standing joke. Furthermore, being neither wholly real nor unreal, his experiences could be regarded neither as actual nor make-believe. Therefore, if he were pricked he would not bleed, if he were poisoned he would not die, if he suffered he was not in pain. That boast of being something more than human explains the pathos latter-day minds see in the clown. To become apparent in spite of the conceal-ment of the pigment, his pain cannot be less than terrible. The clown who dies in his mirth-paint gives an added terror to the spectacle of death. As a child Mr. Chance Newton felt this shock at the time

[1] When British troops took over the theatre at Bonn in 1919 they had a clown who seemed to talk with his tongue in his cheek. A surgeon considered the cist causing this unilateral swelling was dangerous. The operation was fatal to mirth.

he was a sprite in a pantomime.   The clown, William Buck of Surrey fame, did not appear.   The sprite, sent to call him, found him dead— he had snuffed the bismuth of his white make-up into his brain.   Sub-stituting suicide through unrequited love for accidental poisoning two or three authors have made much of similar " situations " on the stage.

Motley serves the same purpose as the mask.   The fool's was a livery crowned with the vainly valiant cockscomb and children's bells, to take meaning out of his offence.   The clown's served the same end by copying the tatters of the lout, exactly as the garb of Dicaeopolis did when he set out to mock the warrior without losing hold of his wartime audience's sympathy.   At length patches and livery were merged in one design.   Then history had to repeat itself.   The dress of a poor man's tragedy was again borrowed, and again became motley.   Now the process begins again.   In fact, whenever the clown's costume is elaborated out of recognition, the conscious mirth-maker finds inspiration anew in the unconscious mirth-maker.   When Harlequin's patches had become a pattern of coloured lozenges,[1] the clown of the English Harlequinade was invented as a tatterdemalion. After his rags had become frills, the black-faced scarecrow, called Jim Crow, appeared.   When nigger minstrels wore white collars and red-and-white striped trousers, the comedian was born with a red nose (not because the medieval devil and Elizabethan Jew had red noses) and with patched trousers (not for any other reason than that patches were funny in everyday life).   Before Grock gave a sort of regularity to the costume, Auguste of the cirque wore old, ill-fitting garments— partly, perhaps, because French minds are amused at the masquerade of London streets, where the poor have no costume but the discarded garments of the rich—mainly for the reasons Dicaeopolis put forward. Charlie Chaplin follows suit, and, being singularly articulate, he finds philosophic reasons for doing so :

[1] Though probably he was, like other Italian masks, as some Callot engravings show, once a ragged fellow, there is just a doubt whether his lozenges were originally coloured patches as Riccoboni, Goldoni and others have led us to believe.   A French print of an earlier date than this theory shows Arlequin as a smart valet with neither patches nor rags.   Probably, however, it represents not the Italian clown but a French imitation.

That costume helps me to express my conception of the average man, of myself. The derby, too small, is a striving for dignity. The moustache is vanity. The tightly-buttoned coat and the stick and his whole manner are a gesture towards gallantry and dash and "front." He is chasing folly and he knows it. He is trying to meet the world bravely, to put up a bluff, and he knows that too. He knows it so well that he can laugh at himself and pity himself a little.

Compare this picture with Arlecchino when his lozenges were coloured patches bedecking rags. His hat, being ornamented with a rabbit's tail, was dignified like the equally beggarly " derby." His bat, like the twirled cane, was for show. He had a moustache to caress. He was dull and unhappy as well as perky—qualities reflected in the blank gaze Chaplin gives a policeman. Both gradually learned how to use stupidity as a stalking horse for artful designs.

So far the resemblances between clowns of all ages are simple to explain. Their nether garments, however, are rather puzzling. Originally, trousers were clown's wear. As the word, both in French and English, means " trussed," the garment probably began as pieces of cloth tied round legs with thongs. In any case, trousers have proved as persistent as rags. They were the distinctive garb of the actors of Greek burlesque, and reappeared in the Commedia dell' arte. In Elizabethan England they were worn by yokels and by Tarleton, Shakespeare's Yorick,

> When he in pleasant wise,
>   The counterfet expreste
> Of clowne, with cote of russet hew,
>   And sturtops with the reste,

and he introduced breeches into fashion :

> When Tarlton clown'd it in a pleasant vaine,
> And with conceits did good opinion gaine
> Upon the stage, his merry humor's shop,
> Clownes knew the clowne by his great clownish slop.

" Slops " or " slivings " were at first confined to mirth. For the Court revels " viii paire of sloppes parted the one legge of the said blewe clothe of gold and the other of greene cloth of silver " were

31

ordered.   They became typical of the stage clown until, in the time of James I.,

> . . . present fashion sayes
> Dick Tarlton's part gentleman's breeches playes :
> In every streete, where any gallant goes,
> The swaggering slop is Tarlton's clownish hose.

Pantaloons, derived from the Venetian Magnifico, were a fashion wherein English gallants aped the French towards the end of the seventeenth century.   The *caleçon* was also not unconnected with the Harlequinade.   When Camargo came from Paris to dance in " Harlequin Sorceror," critics declared she showed " more in dancing than any lady whatever."   She had to elaborate her lingerie in consequence.   She did not invent the *caleçon*, for it is mentioned in the shop scene of *Arlequin Lingère du Palais* at the Hôtel de Bourgogne in 1698, but she is supposed to have been the first to change its sex.   Since then " sloppes parted " have, in one form or another, become folly's hallmark stamped on all the world.

Resemblances between clowns are, obviously, not evidence of mystic connections between present and past.   The entangled theorists who, following Riccoboni, piece together scattered references in ancient authors until they see the complete Harlequinade fore-shadowed in Augustan Rome, were reduced to absurdity when a very industrious traveller named Clarke decided that

> we see Harlequin, upon the modern stage, as Mercury, with the *herpe* in his hand, to render himself invisible, and to transport himself from one end of the earth to the other ; wearing, at the same time, his *petasus* or winged cap ; and being accompanied by Columbine, as Psyche, or the soul ; an Old Man, who is Charon ; and a Clown, Momus the son of Nox.

Speculations of this kind need know no limit.   Look at the scenes from burlesques on Greek vases and the Harlequinade can be paralleled in various ways.   Zeus is very like Pantaloon, Hercules very like Clown, his club very like the red-hot poker, and so on until so many resemblances have been noted that we recognise in ourselves the gullibility of Polonius.   Wild as such guesswork is, it has as much justification as the theory of direct connection between the Commedia dell' arte and the characters—Maccus (the Fool), Bucco (gobbler),

32

Pappus (daddy) and Dossennus (sharper)—of the fables of Atella acted in Rome. Once again the frame of mind of Polonius is observable. Because a mimic praised by Cicero was named Sannio he is declared to be the forerunner of the Zanni, though Arlecchino and Brighella came fresh from Bergamo in the cinquecento. Remote references to the sooted faces, rags and bare feet of the mimes are offered as descriptions of his person and proof of the Zanni's descent from his loins. References to the part of Maccus in the Atellanae have been attached to a bronze figure of a hunchback [1] discovered in Rome in 1727. Riccoboni, who first imagined the resemblance, offered his supposition as evidence that Maccus was Polichinelle, though Pulcinella, the first of the line of Punch, lacked the humped breast and beaked nose common to the ancient statue and modern puppet. George Sand went further. With a fervour that might identify them both with Richard Crookback, she declared the figure to be undoubtedly the " Polichinelle of the Atellanae," whom she could see from afar as " a sort of Thersites popular in the struggle with the oppression of slavery and ugliness." In this way there is nothing to prevent Alichino, a devil of the " Inferno," becoming an incarnation of the Zanni, and the scurra (first the term for a gallant, then for a scurrilous clown, and then for a soldier of the guard) the ancestor of Scaramouche.

Dispassionate inquiry reverses all such theories. Clowns maintain their distinctive characteristics despite, not because of tradition. All Greek and Roman comedies, the medieval religious plays, the Commedia dell' arte and the English Harlequinade certainly possess definite types in common. Yet these are the very types that are manifestly not borrowed but spontaneously created afresh. The clowns that can be traced from country to country, from century to century, retain only their names and lose their characteristics. Thus Arlecchino, the butt, changed to Arlequin, the knave, then to Arlequin, the parodist in every shape imaginable, to Arlequin, the swain of

---

[1] Probably the Augustan equivalent of the stuffed Pekingese under a glass case. Not only were misshapen dwarfs popular pets in Rome, but there is a case on record of a dead *morio* being modelled for remembrance. Joe Boganny's midget boxers are his descendants.

Marivaux, to Harlequin the magician, adventurer and dancer, and finally to a symbolic character. Pierrot, before he became mystic and pale as the moon, was a butt or a knave. Clown, who also began as a butt, changed to knave, then to bully, and then to a symbol of pathos. Auguste of the cirque, another butt, is imbued by Grock with the romance of a thwarted musician. Charlie Chaplin begins as a half-wit, grows into an artful dodger and threatens to develop the theme of a clown's unrequited love in a serious cinema tragedy. Every clown that has basked long enough in the world's love has grown too small for his boots, taken wings and flown into fancy. And at each metamorphosis the world has to hatch another from a clod.

The more he changes the more the clown is the same. Take away all the vestments and ritual that proclaim his calling, still his every word and act reveal his relationship with the clot and the lump. There is no necessity to invest him in motley if there be virtue in his looks naturally, if his body be blown up like Triboullet's bladder, or his face resemble " a perpetual triumph, an everlasting bonfire." There is, moreover, no special need of these if he be openly and palpably irresponsible, and therefore as immune as a lunatic from all the laws of morality and justice. But our mood depends not a little on the knowledge that he is a fool as well as a knave, a butt as well as a bully, that he is these things equally and therefore undeserving of anger or pity.

That comic giant cannot be brought to his full stature many times in the world's history. Even the mixture of the warlike and unwarlike, cheating and gulled, in the disposition of Dicaeopolis, is unlike true clownship, because his irresponsibility is the cloak of good citizenship. Falstaff is the true breed. He can express the spirit of the clown in a phrase :

I call thee coward ? I'll see thee damn'd ere I call thee coward.

He talks motley, acts motley, lives motley. There was no decency in carrying him to the Fleet, nor in condemning him to the buck-basket and the beating that poetic justice would reserve rather for jealous husbands than clown lovers. But he died saying the flea stuck on

34

GROCK

From a photograph supplied by the London Coliseum

CHARLIE CHAPLIN

From a photograph supplied by the Charlie Chaplin Film Co.

Bardolph's nose was a black soul burning in hell—which is as good a death as a clown could die.

Even Grimaldi's girth of laughter was not comparable to Falstaff's. In other times the stage has had to dismember the clown spirit and be content with the antics of his separated members. But the parts together are never as great as the whole. Though the jokes of the full-sized clown are endless, the fun of the lesser types is mainly confined to the old play of " The Cheaters and the Clown." It had that title when performed before the Mayor of Queenborough, who, exasperated by the dupe's folly, took the part himself, only to have his purse stolen and a peck of meal flung in his face.

Sometimes the butt and the knave are in one body. Charlie Chaplin and Turlupin combine the two. Davus did likewise. His tricks were always successful. But once, tempted to speak the truth, he was immediately carried away to punishment. Again, in the Wakefield Nativity Play, Mak suffers for his sheep stealing in spite of his device of disguising it as his bairn. His wife swears to the shepherds,

> I pray to God so mylde,
> If ever I you begyld,
> That I ete this child.

But one of the shepherds, having asked leave to kiss the infant, cries out,

> Will ye se how thay swedyll
> His foure feytt in the medyll ?
> Sagh I never in a credyll
> A hornyd lad or now.

Though Mak's wife explains her child has been taken by an elf and misshapen he has to suffer for his sins by being tossed. Similarly with the knave in Skelton's moral of " Magnyfycence," for Crafty-conveyance becomes the butt of Fancy and Folly, who lay him a wager that Folly will laugh him out of his coat. After Folly has made " semblaunt to take a lowse from Crafty-conveyance shoulder " the dialogue runs :

> FANCY.—What hast thou found there ?
> FOLLY.—By God, a lowse.
> CRAFTY.—By cockes harte, I trowe thou lyste.
> FOLLY.—By the masse, a spanyshe moght with a gray lyste.
> FANCY.—Ha ha ha ha ha ha ha.

35

CRAFTY.—Cockes armes, it is not so, I trowe. (Here Crafty-conveyaunce
    putteth of his gowne.)
FOLLY.—Put on thy gowne agayne, for nowe thou hast lost.
FANCY.—Lo, John a bonam, where is thy brayne.

Butt and knave as a pair are the customary formula of knockabout
humour. They appear together in the designs on Greek vases. In
" The Acharnians " they are represented by the Theban who barters
good cheer for nothing better than a trussed informer, and the
Megarian who gets a good price for his daughters by swearing they
are pigs. In the comedies of Rome there is Milphio, who is thrashed
for making love too well on his master's behalf, and Syrus who seems
to be the origin of Figaro.

Devil and Vice are the historic pair of the medieval stage when
that valuable adjunct to clownship, the topical allusion, became popular in references to thin brewings. Likewise, the repetitive " gag "
was employed. Says Hodge in " Gammer Gurton's Needle " to
Diccon, " Did not the devil cry, ' ho, ho, ho ' ? " and then to Gammer
Gurton, " O the knave cried ' ho, ho ! ' he roared and he thundered."
In " Wily Beguiled " it is written, " I'll rather put on my flashing red
nose, and my flaming face, and come wrapped in a calf's skin and cry
' Ho, ho, ho.' " And Ben Jonson gives us a Satan who cries,

    Hoh, hoh, hoh, hoh, hoh, hoh, hoh, hoh.

Hasse, who writes of the early drama in France and Germany, describes how Satan, horned, tailed and hoofed, carried off his victims in
a wheelbarrow, but was often exhibited as marching off in the character
of a poor, stupid, outwitted imp. Payne Collier discloses that the
English devil's shaggy appearance led him to be mistaken for a dancing bear, while his " bottle-nose " was derided. The Vice would
ask him for a piece of his tail for use as a fly-trap, and cause him to
roar and cry under castigation. That the Vice and the Devil kept
company for many years is proved by " The Playhouse to Let " (1662),
in which one player exclaims :

    . . . till the nation be more civilised,
    Your Fool and Devil may be entertained ;
    They'll get money ; none but very choice
    Spectators will vouchsafe to see a Play
    Without 'm.

Brighella, the schemer, and Arlecchino, the butt, are the most famous pair in Italian clownship. Another case is cited by George Sand, who states that in the Neapolitan farces one Polichinelle is base and doltish, and a second daring, thieving and quarrelsome.

Thus clowns remain steadfast without the aid of tradition. But the changing needs of human nature are ever exerting an influence. The old man, a secondary type of dupe, has come and gone. In Menander, Terence and Plautus, he was constantly deceived by his children or tricked out of his hoarded wealth; in Italian pieces and the English pantomime Pantaloon took his place. Now the increased consideration paid to old age has killed him. The butt to-day is young. Generally he is an athletic tumbler. In recent pantomimes at the Lyceum, Drury Lane and Covent Garden, one of the Egberts had no other share in existence except injuries. His partner, whether actually exasperated or merely argumentative, struck him on the mouth, kicked him or flung him across the stage to vent his wrath or illustrate a theory. Though preferring to avoid blows wherever possible, he accepted them as natural to his station in life, blinked, stood up when told to, and collapsed the next second because of yet another blow. Albert Fratellini suffers misfortunes gladly. He is hit on the head violently, but continues to smile although a large crimson bump swells visibly on the spot and bursts with a report.

Other types of clown are comparatively unimportant. These are the gluttons, sycophants, parasites and hypocrites who are embodied aspects of his character. There are those who represent his pretensions—Miles Gloriosus and the Pedant. They appear in the various guises Cowley mentions in his declaration that

> A cowardly ranting soldier, an ignorant charlatanical doctor, a foolish cheating lawyer, a silly pedantical scholar, have always been, and still are the principal subjects of all comedy taken by their severest professors.

The bully has made some attempt to keep his individuality. But even as a cabotin of wood, whose brutalities give no offence, he too has learnt to stoop to cunning, unlike his ancestor, bold Polichinelle, who was unafraid even of the terrible corporal of the guard.

37

SATURNALIA

Our comedians think there is no delight without laughter, which is very wrong; for though laughter may come with delight, yet cometh it not of delight, as though delight should be the cause of laughter; but well may one thing breed both together. Nay in themselves, they have as it were a kind of contrariety: For delight we scarcely do, but in things that have a conveniency to our selves, or to the general nature. Laughter almost ever cometh of things most disproportioned to ourselves and nature.

SIDNEY.

Couiello.   Bello sguardo.

A Fidler

A Milk Maid on May Day

A Iack Foole of a Play.

Merry Andrew

One that crieth Wafers after Candle light in Paris.

An Antick or Foole of a Shew

FOOLS OF THE SEVENTEENTH-CENTURY FAIRS

From engravings in the Author's Collection

WHAT gives the clown love as well as laughter is our recognition of his spirit within our own. Whether we are capable or not of seeing ourselves as the comic butts and knaves of life, we are all well aware of our clownship in relation to joy. Few men, outside the band of saints and martyrs, are capable of sustaining rapture. Its exhilaration is a tyranny that has to be relieved; the only escape is to become a servant at the court of the clown, even if there be no better way than wearing paper hats and exploding crackers.

That is the explanation of Saturnalia. The instinct of joy is to gambol in all seriousness. But when the emotion is checked, the ecstatic dance of David before the Ark changes to a sacrilegious mockery of all the solemn rites of thanksgiving. Rulers are dethroned, priests unfrocked, and fools set in their places. The servant becomes the master. Men wear skirts and women trousers. Virtue is spurned and unchastity honoured. Drunkenness is a virtue and sobriety a crime. Sleep is for the day. Harmony is cacophony, and " a reasonable good ear in music " is betokened by Bottom's demand for " the tongs and the bones." These customs, several of them actively observed nowadays in the night clubs of London, have been known from the earliest ages. Yet the professors are still puzzled at resemblances they deem inexplicable between the Saturnalia of races not in touch with one another. In many communities,[1] Jewish and Moslem as well as Pagan and Christian, there have been Lords of Misrule after the pattern of the king of the winter festival at Rome, whose only care was, to quote Sir James Frazer, " that the revelry should run high and the fun grow fast and furious." These revels are supposed to have begun in outbreaks of serious joy. In the case of the Bacchanalian

[1] The *Marshallik* of the Jews in the Middle Ages provided ribaldry at wedding and other feasts much after the fashion of the Roman *mimus*, who at funerals mimicked the ways of the dead.

orgies, the reaction from the sublime to the ridiculous is vividly revealed. Professor Gilbert Murray, describing how the religion of Dionysus, God of Intoxication, found its climax in the Orphism of the sixth century B.C., states :

> Ascetic, mystical, ritualistic and emotional, Orphism easily excited both enthusiasm and ridicule. It lent itself both to inspired saintliness and to imposture. In doctrine it laid especial stress upon sin, and the sacerdotal purification of sin ; on the eternal reward due beyond the grave to the pure and impure, the pure living in an eternal ecstasy—" perpetual intoxication," as Plato satirically calls it. . . . It seems possible that the savage Thracians, in the fury of their worship on the mountains, when they were possessed by the God and became " wild beasts," actually tore with their teeth and hands any hares, goats, fawns, or the like that they came across.

Those are the symptoms of excessive joy. How different are the results when reason turns it to laughter is told in the Bacchanalian chant of Dicaeopolis ;

> Leader of the revel rout
> Of the drunken roar and shout,
> Crazy mirth and saucy jesting,
> Frolic and intrigue clandestine ! . . .
>   With my neighbour's maid, the Thracian,
> Found marauding in the wood ;
> Seizing on the fair occasion,
>   With a quick retaliation
> Making an immediate booty
> Of her innocence and beauty.
> If a drunken head should ache,
> Bones and heads we never break.

Very much on the same lines were the May games of Merry England when, after the feasts, maids were lured into the woods where maids never more came out. Mauchline Holy Fair, whose " famous laughin' " is extolled by Burns, was not at all dissimilar :

> How monie hearts this day converts
>   O' sinners and o' lasses !
> Their hearts o' stane, gin night, are gane
>   As saft as ony flesh is.
> There's some are fou' o' love divine,
>   There's some are fou' o' brandy ;
> An' monie jobs that day begin,
>   May end in Houghmagandie
>   Some ither day.

Parallels could be multiplied.   In fact, whenever there is feasting to break the monotony of winter or to celebrate harvest or crown a victory or honour a god, joy will tend to bubble over to the glorification of clowns.   An account of the Armistice rejoicings in London could be so worded as to fit a festival of ancient Egypt, Augustan Rome or medieval Europe.   At the festival of Diana of Bubastis, which Herodotus recorded, the men and women danced about to the sound of the tabor, threw aside their garments and cried aloud to the onlookers, provoking them with injurious language.   In the medieval Feast of Fools, Christians leapt and danced through the church like madmen, sometimes stripping themselves quite naked during the performance, and provoked the priests with filthy rites at the high altar.   On the four days and nights of Armistice rejoicings, groups at street corners threw their limbs about and provoked the godly and the police with the song of " Knees up, Mother Brown."   Battalions paraded the streets led by amateur clowns and bands consisting of tin cans or the gongs that sounded the alarm in gas attacks.

The throwing aside of garments, which was practised very successfully at Bartholomew Fair in the time of *The Spectator*, and now, being forbidden in public, inspires the card game of " Strip Patience," is linked with the desire to change clothes.   Costers who swop hats on Bank holidays are not merely observing a local custom.   Similar bartering, only on a larger scale, occurs at private parties in cities from Paris to Philadelphia where " coster " is an unknown word. Centuries ago the May Games were played by men dressed up as " maymarions," whose jest is repeated in the Christmas pantomimes of the present.   Reversals of sex are only another form of the inversion of rank and the debasement of holiness.   The comic ecclesiastic is an age-old figure of fun who will survive " The Private Secretary." He began when the clergy burlesqued their own office.   Hasse decides that the Feast of the Fools was prompted by the Easter story, " a tale containing all sorts of merry jests at the expense of the great apostles, the lesser saints or Satan, which the priest on Easter morning used to relate from the pulpit in order to excite Easter merriment." When buffoonery was first allowed in the church the clerics took part,

43

but when the orgies increased in vigour they stood aside in protest while their place was taken by Bishops and Archbishops of Fools, wearing spectacles with orange peel in the place of glasses, playing dice and eating pudding on the altar, and burning an old shoe (or worse) in the censer. That was mainly the Continental custom. In Scotland there were Abbots of Unreason, and in England (as an Act of Parliament describes) children were

> stranglie decked and apparayled to counterfeit priests, bishops and women and to be ledde with songes and dances from house to house, blessing the people and gathering of money ; and boyes do singe masse and preache in the pulpit.

Stage historians class these customs as origins of the theatre. Dramatic disguise, however, is for the players to become the men and women whose clothes and titles they assume. Saturnalian performances, on the contrary, rely on the absence of illusion—on the incongruity of the man being the opposite of what he half appears to be. On the stage there is a sharp distinction between the actor's pretence to be Sir Oliver Mar-Text and the disguise of Sir Topas worn by Olivia's clown. Similarly, the boy who played Rosalind did not create the joke of the reversal of sex until he, paradoxically, wore man's apparel as Ganymede, after the audience had agreed that he was feminine. There seems to be a curious side-light on this in " Bartholomew Fair," when Zeal-of-the-Land Busy objects to the players because " the male among you putteth on the apparel of the female and the female of the male." As English actresses were then unknown, the Puritan conscience may have been outraged more violently when Olivia donned the hose of a page or Falstaff put on the skirt of the old woman of Brentford, than by the boys who passed agreeably well for heroines or the men who mimicked the ways of ancient ladies.

There was probably little illusion about the real sex of the old women in our early drama. The wife of Noah, whom Chaucer alludes to in the lines :

> The sorwe of Noe with his felaschipe
> That he hadde or he gat his wyf to schipe,

is sister to the dame of pantomime. She is so in the Chester play of the Flood. " Wife, come in," says Noah, adding, " Thou art ever

44

froward," whereupon she tells him to get " a new wife." Her sons fetch her aboard ; " Welcome," says Noah ; she fetches him a smack. Shrews in Tudor plays are very similar. In " Tom Tiller and his Wife " (1551) her name is Strife. Taylor, to befriend Tom, borrows his jacket and stick. As soon as Strife calls him knave he beats her (under the pretence that he is her husband) unmercifully. When she bewails that she can " neither stand nor sit " Tom's remorse causes him to confess, whereupon she revives and almost kills him outright.

There are mightier manifestations than these of the Saturnalian spirit in the English drama. In Shakespeare it is so potent that even the sobriety of modern acting cannot always overcome its gaiety. More frequently than not, however, it is quenched. Like Christopher Sly, we have become unable to note the difference between a " commonty " and " a Christmas gambol or a tumbling trick." But Shakespeare drew the distinction :

> I see the trick on't ; here was a consent,
> Knowing aforehand of our merriment,
> To dash it like a Christmas Comedy.

Plainly enough, " Twelfth Night," " A Midsummer Night's Dream," " As You Like It," and " The Tempest " are not meticulously exact reproductions of life at court or countryside, as stage undertakers would have us believe. Nor are Caliban, Touchstone and Bottom— parts created when the clown had a large say in the management of the companies—of minor importance. Here is the richest riot of turbulent irresponsibility. It is fancy taking flight directly away from reality, away from the deer-keepers at Charlecote to the lions and serpents and palms of Arden, away from Bankside to the sea-coast of Bohemia, away from all convention to a society where Jacques can quarrel with Rosalind for speaking blank verse, and where the end of life is a dance and a song.

Christmas festivities, in Shakespeare's days, lasted from the end of October to Shrovetide. The universities, as is set forth in the records of the Christmas Prince at Oxford, were diligent in their observance of " Ye Saturnalls." The Inns of Court, likewise, gave delight to sovereigns with their festivities. But the revels at White-

45

hall were the most lavish of all.   Since the first Tudor king, mirth became more and more, to quote Misrule in " Impatient Poverty,"

Beloved with lords and ladies of birth.

The Saturnalian nature of the revels is testified in many episodes, but particularly in licensed plundering.   In the time of Henry VIII. the gentlemen of the court considered themselves privileged to seize what they would of the properties, and broke the heads of the guards who tried to resist them.   In Elizabeth's reign, when a fox was let loose in the court and hunted by dogs on the leash, " harness garnished with silver " was provided for the maskers, who kept it " against the will of all the officers."

James I. fully maintained the traditions of laughter-loving Elizabeth.   He had plays at Court " every night, both holidays and working days," and indulged further in overmuch liquor and many masques.   The " Masque of Christmas " of Ben Jonson and Inigo Jones, presented at Court in 1616, is notable for its resemblance to the celebrations the same spirit produces to-day.   Christmas, " attired in round hose, long stockings, a close doublet, a high-crowned hat, with a brooch, a long thin beard, a truncheon, white shoes, his scarfs and garters tied cross, and his drum beaten before him," opens the performance much in the style of Clown.   After complaining that they have tried to keep out " Christmas, old Christmas, Christmas of London, and captain Christmas," he cries : " I have seen the time you have wish'd for me, for a merry Christmas ; and now you have me, they would not let me in : I must come another time ! a good jest, as if I could come more than once a year ! "   A summons brings in his ten sons and daughters, led in a string by Cupid in a flat cap and a prentice's coat.   They include several members of the clown's court, notably Mumming, whose " masquing pied suit, with a vizard " suggests Harlequin.   There is also Misrule, in a great yellow ruff ; Carol, in a long tawny coat ; Minced-Pie, like a fine cook's wife ; Gambol, like a tumbler, with a hook and bells ; Post and Pair, with a pair-royal of aces in his hat ; New-Year's Gift, in a blue coat, serving-man like, with a collar of gingerbread ; Wassel, like a neat sempster and songster ; Offering, with a porter's staff in his

46

hand; and Babycake, in a fine long coat, biggin-bib and muckender. Even Widow Twankey is added to the number when Lady Venus, of Pudding Lane, widow of a smith in Do-Little-Lane, supplies the comic relief after the fashion of the good woman in " The Knight of the Burning Pestle." She warrants that her Cupid is " as well as e'er a playboy of 'em all," and declares that " Master Burbage has been about and about with me, and so has old Master Hemings, too ; they have need of him."

Her Cupid wore the fleshings of the principal boy who took a long time to develop. Yet boys in women's clothes gave way to women in boys' clothes directly after the Restoration. At first actresses donned male attire only to speak an epilogue or when a masquerade was introduced into the play. The possibilities, however, were soon seen to be too pleasant for neglect. Nell Gwynne in her boy's clothes Pepys deemed " mighty pretty," and Mrs. Bracegirdle inspired Anthony Aston to write :

> Genteel comedy was her chief essay, and that, too, when in man's clothes, in which she far surpassed all the actresses of that and this age. . . . She was finely shaped, and had very handsome legs and feet ; and her gait, or walk, was free, manlike and modest.

After the great fire, the King's company, whose playhouse had been burned down, tried to make good their loss by announcing performances of Beaumont and Fletcher's " Philaster " and Tom Killigrew's " Parson's Wedding," to be acted entirely by women. Evidently the idea was a success, for it was repeated often ; in 1668 we find Pepys writing, " Knipp's maid comes to me to tell me that the women's day at the playhouse is to-day, and that therefore I must be there to increase the profit." Later, Mrs. Reeve, after a performance of this kind in 1672, spoke an epilogue by Dryden which began :

> What think you, sirs, was't not all well enough ?
> Will you not grant that we can strut and huff ?
> Men may be proud ; but faith, for aught I see,
> They neither walk, nor cock, so well as we,

and continued with a few provocative references to legs which, she presumed, were " no ill sight."

47

Peg Woffington's boast that as Harry Wildair she deceived half the men, is classical (and so is Quin's retort, " It may be so, but, on my conscience, the other half can convince them to the contrary "). After Peg " breeches parts " were commonplace. In fact, when Miss Catley played Macheath in " The Ladies' Opera " in 1781 the piece was a failure, and led a critic to declare for all time that " the appearance of ladies without petticoats is no novelty." The test, however, was not altogether fair. Catley was petite. And in this age we know that an actress with such a figure will not do for a principal boy. Not long afterwards the point was proved. When Madame Vestris made Macheath her first masculine part at Drury Lane, the enthusiasm of the town could only be expressed in such lines as :

> What a breast ! What an eye ! What a leg, foot, and thigh,
>   What wonderful things she has shown us !
> Round hip, swelling sides, and masculine strides,
>   Proclaim her an English Adonis.

From that time not only were her " representations of the other sex " the most popular, but an opera to be fashionable had to have an actress for the hero. Vestris added Don Giovanni, Apollo and Young Malcolm (Rossini's " Lady of the Lake ") to her rôles, moving critics to delight by gambolling about the stage in a scarlet jacket and white trousers. As Giovanni she had been preceded by Mrs. Gould, whose masculine habits won her the name of " Joe " Gould. And of the opera " Aladdin " at Drury Lane in 1826, we read that Miss Stevens' Aladdin was a " most feminine " performance, and " the more delightful from that very circumstance." About the only noteworthy protest against the breeches convention came from Byron. While " still black and blue from the squeeze on the first night of the lady's appearance in trousers," he railed against " degenerate Britons " who

> smile on Italy's buffoons,
> And worship Catalani's pantaloons.

The real origin of the principal boy was the fashion in burlesque for what Planché called the " outré and ridiculous," which led in time to blonde wigs, very curt tunics, fleshings and high heels. Vestris did

48

not set the vogue.   When Planché wrote for her a fairy extravaganza with a principal boy part it was not till the Christmas of 1852.   Then, in his " Good Woman in the Wood " at the Lyceum, Miss Elington was Prince Sylvan and Vestris merely Dame Goldenheart.   From that time to this the " novelty " has passed rapidly away.   And it is heretical of Mr. Chesterton to declare that " When the young girl in tights was introduced into the hero's part, we destroyed at a blow the fine, romantic sense of the fairy tale."   The public are too orthodox to accept that view.   For the season of 1913-14 the hero of " The Sleeping Beauty Reawakened " at Drury Lane was a baritone.   The experiment was maintained in " The Sleeping Beauty Beautified " and " Puss in Boots," but on the Boxing Day of 1916 the management compromised by finding an actress with the manner of a hero (Madge Titheradge), and then chose a frankly feminine " Lord Fairplay " in " The Babes in the Wood."

Meanwhile the Dame part has come to be played by women occasionally.   But Nellie Wallace has retained the traditions belonging to men, from the rag-bag furs to the striped stockings and peculiar underwear.   She is a woman dressed as a man who is dressed as a woman—a duplication of reversal's mirth.   Other female clowns, however, are not so considerate towards tradition.   The youthfully pert " comedienne " of musical comedy is much too much the bright young woman of everyday life to suggest the licence of festival.   In every way Saturnalia is flickering out under the snuffers of propriety.   First music-hall audiences were forced to be strictly sober.   Then the carnival spirit, which led to the battles royal with balls of wool between audiences and choruses, was dowsed.   Night clubs and cabarets now try, vainly enough, to revive the impulse towards liveliness—with paper hats.

As for the jazz band, there is no remarkable novelty here.   One of the entries in a masque seen by Charles I. was " Mock music " provided by five persons, " One with a Violl, the next with Taber and Pipe, Knockers and bells, Tongs and tray, Gridiron and shooing horne."   In the eighteenth century the tongs were unfashionable, but the gridiron attracted the attention of a musician who, said *The*

Spectator, " added two bars to give it a greater compass of sound." The animal noises now made by bandsmen were anticipated by the braying of an ass in a *concert ridicule* given by the Italian comedians in Paris. The imitations of a squeaking pig that delight us delighted ancient Rome.

MONSTERS

BOTTOM.—Masters, you ought to consider with yourselves, to bring in (God shield us) a lion among ladies, is a most dreadful thing. For there is not a more fearful wild-fowl than your lion, living; and we ought to look to it.

SNOUT.—Therefore another prologue must tell he is not a lion.

BOTTOM.—Nay, you must name his name, and half his face must be seen through the lion's neck, and he himself must speak through, saying thus, or to the same defect; Ladies, or fair ladies, I would wish you, or I would request you, or I would entreat you, not to fear, not to tremble : my life for yours. If you think I am come hither as a lion, it were pity of my life. No, I am no such thing, I am a man as other men are ; and there indeed let him name his name, and tell them plainly he is Snug the joiner.

" A Midsummer Night's Dream."

Mestolino.   Guatsetto.

ONCE Mr. Chesterton saw two amateurs under a tablecloth act a cow. "Compared with such truly pantomime patchwork," he commented, "the elaborate and expensive London pantomimes are as dull as the freak dinners of millionaires. And they are dull for the same reason ; because they can afford to do anything. They do not have to cut their cow according to their tablecloth."

The real reason is more involved. As the pantomime Mr. Chesterton saw was performed at Beaconsfield the amateurs were not more compelled to cut the cow according to the tablecloth than the London managements. Most probably they preferred the amateurs, because a real cow, whatever humorous possibilities it may possess in a field, excites curiosity, not merriment, on the stage. Similarly, the more realistically a cow is acted the greater are the chances that the performance will be taken seriously. The cow, like the lion, has emotional significance. One person may fear her, another be disgusted by her, another elated by comparing her slowness with his own (imagined) grace, another feel tenderly disposed. Stage illusion is capable of making even the tablecloth arouse these emotions if the amateurs do nothing definitely uncowlike. What destroys the illusion and upsets emotion, is an assurance, accidental or deliberate, that the actors are "no such thing." Bottom lays down a law that Bernard Shaw, in "Androcles and the Lion," has seen fit to obey.

Animals' skins inhabited by human beings remained a serious convention for centuries. The joke, like many others, began as sacred ritual. Greek historians mention combats between Apollo and the dragon before the time of Thespis. Historians of the Middle Ages describe how the good folk of Messina, to commemorate the Madonna's mercy in sending a corn-laden camel to the city at a time of famine,

53

instituted a procession whose place of honour was taken by two lusty youths in a camel skin.   Historians of the church reveal how the ass joined the sacred to the absurd.   He was, from the first, particularly associated with clowns.   Even the Greeks, who inherited the Egyptian veneration of animals, linked him with laughter, for on a bowl of the fifth century B.C., a donkey[1] with comic ears, draws the cart of comedy. Christianity, though recognising the sign of the cross on his back, held festival masses that both honoured and ridiculed him.   Balaam's ass was commemorated by a procession where he was represented in wood with a man inside to supply the voice ; the ass of the flight into Egypt by choristers who sang his praises and imitated his bray in the responses ; the ass of Palm Sunday by the wooden effigy of an ass drawn by a live ass.   On the Feast of St. Stephen the deacons brought an ass in cope and mitre to the altar.   Why he should raise laughter is natural, considering that his stupidity is more apparent than real. He is always funny, unlike the mule, the pig, the goose, the duck and the monkey, who are only funny in unusual surroundings.   On the other hand, doves, pigeons, dogs, horses, camels, lions and elephants are objects of wonder on the stage.   So are most of the other creatures that came out of the ark, though bears, cats (more particularly when dead), rabbits and gold-fish incline to mirthful associations.   In " Rejected Addresses " the clown's reliance on animals, observable in Whimsical Walker at the present day, is remarked on :

> Amid the freaks that modern fashion sanctions,
> It grieves me most to see live animals
> Brought on the stage.   Grimaldi has his rabbit,
> Laurent his cat, and Bradbury his pig.

The donkey has been ridden by so many clowns that there is no need to name them.   He has been equally popular in effigy, notably the hobby-ass used by Grimaldi in his famous song of " Me and My Neddy," and the Blondin Donkey, who walked a plank painted to resemble a tight rope, a favourite of twenty or thirty years ago.   In

---

[1] Authority says a mule.   Reference is made to the Greeks' mule-cars and their expression " jesting from a car."   But the humorous associations of the mule, apart from his alleged ambition to be an ancestor, are derived from the ass anyhow.

54

fact, the donkey invented the pantomime animal. Being funny in himself, he was funny when imitated by two men in his hide even while such representations were still a serious dramatic convention.

Except for the hobby horses, common in May games and the processions of Lords of Misrule, the familiar monster who possesses human brain and feet but a head and tail of the brute creation, supplied, for three centuries, the wonder that is now supplied by the Zoo. When first introduced into court revels the idea was greatly admired. At the disguisings at the marriage of Prince Arthur and Katharine of Arragon, there was

> a Castle, right cunningly devised, sett upon certaine wheeles and drawne into the said great hall of fower great beasts, with chaines of gold. Two of the first beasts were lyons, one of them of gold and thother of silver: one of the other was a hart with guilt hornes, and the second of the same was an Ibeke, which every each of the which fower beasts were two men, one in the forepart, and another in the hinder part, secretly hid and apparelled, nothing seene but their leggs, and yet those were disguised after the proportion and kinde of the beasts that they were in.

When the disguisings were replaced by another Italian fashion, namely the masque, they continued to be regarded in all seriousness. Bacon gravely declared that " baboons and turquets " were suitable antimasques, and recommended that the chariots of challengers in jousts and tourneys should be " drawn with strange beasts ; as lions, bears, camels, and the like." In the Whitehall accounts of Elizabeth's Master of the Revels you may read of a " Monster XXs," of " Mosses and yong Okes for Wylde men," " dishes for devells' eyes," and " Past and paper for the Dragon's head." In the play of Predor, " ffyshes Counterfete—vz Whiting, Playce, Mackerell, etc.," were used, and in another hounds' heads were made for the actors of dog-headed Indians. When the children of Westminster gave " Paris and Vienna," 42s. 6d. was paid for

> x dozen of Kydde skynnes together with the workmanship done upon the Hobby horses that served the children of Westminster in the triumphs (where parris won the christall sheelde for Vienna, at the Turneye and Barryers).

To turn from the Court revels to the public plays of the Elizabethans is to find further evidence that animal clownship had not become

deliberately practised.   There may have been many a Snug the joiner
to provide unconscious humour, but the beast was intended to be
taken seriously.   Middleton's Mayor of Queensborough, who loves
a clown, replies to the players' boast that they have a play wherein they
use a horse, " Give me a play without a beast, I charge you."   The
bear in " Mucedorus," though the clown says, " Sure it cannot be a
bear, but some devil in a bear's doublet," is put in not for fun but
dramatic effect.   In " The Tempest " Trinculo and Stephano are
hunted by " divers Spirits " in the shape of hounds—an apology for
human actors' inability to look like ordinary hounds.   If stage animals
were comic the actor no more intended it than Snug or the mummers in
" Vowbreaker, or the fayre maid of Clifton," who promise to be a " fiery
dragon " and " a thundr'ing St. George as ever rode on horseback."

With the rise of burlesque at the end of the seventeenth century
the convention was ridiculed.   While Italian opera retained Snug to
play the lion heroically, the Italian comedians in Paris began the process which in the course of time drove human quadrupeds out of
drama.   In *Arlequin Mercure Galant*, produced at the Hôtel de
Bourgogne in 1682, Arlequin enters on an ass which, he explains to
Pan, can perform tricks and play the harpsichord.   When Pan mounts
it falls in two.   In *Ulisse et Circe*, 1691, the enchantress changes
the Doctor into an ass (except for his face), Pasqueriel into a pig and
Mezzetin into a cat ; they imitate the movements and cries of these
creatures, and are led by a girl with a pan of food, calling " Petits,
petits, petits."   In *Arlequin Misanthrope*, 1696, the hero leaves
human society to walk in a wood where he delights in saluting a stag,
cat, dog, fox, lion, camel and elephant.   In other pieces Jupiter's
eagle and Pegasus appear, but not with human occupants.   A snail
takes part in another play, and a whale with saddle and bit in another.
There is also a fish whose species is in doubt ; while the others are
debating what sort it is, Arlequin, who is inside, says, " I am a fish of
honour." [1]

[1] "Man of honour" was to Dominique, the Arlequin, what " Yes, I don't think "
was to music-hall comedians in 1907-10.   One of his jokes was to prepare to
commit a nuisance on the stage.   When remonstrated with, he replied that
as a man of honour he could do no wrong.

56

ANIMALS OF THE COMMEDIA DELL' ARTE

Though these pieces were not seen in London, the new critical spirit towards stage conventions affected London audiences. Evidence is provided by No. 13 of *The Spectator* concerning Nicolini Grimaldi's combat with the lion in Hydaspes. "There is nothing," it says, "that of late years has afforded matter of greater amusement." The lion has been "changed upon the audience" thrice. The first was a Candle-snuffer, a fellow of testy choleric temper who would not suffer himself to be killed so easily as he ought to have done ; the second was a tailor, too sheepish except for a rip he gave to Nicolini's flesh-coloured doublet " to make work for himself " ; the third a country gentleman whose temper was a " happy mixture of the mild and the choleric." This was related to show what were the reigning attractions of the politer part of Great Britain. The hint was taken by Rich, who brought out at Lincoln's Inn Fields in 1716 Leveridge's mock opera based on Peter Quince's performance of " Pyramus and Thisbe." Three years later, in " Harlequin-Hydaspes ; or, the Greshamite," there was a comic lion who strutted about to the sound of the trumpet to impress several people on horseback. But the history of the pantomime lion is best told by quoting from a letter appearing over his signature in the *St. James's Chronicle* in 1782. Replying to a charge of acting bashfully in the scene of Sir Ashton Lever's Museum in " The Choice of Harlequin," at Covent Garden, he says :

> Know, Sir, that I was created by the late Mr. Rich, and introduced in Pyramus and Thisbe, about the year 1716 ; was taught to sing by old Leveridge, and travelled with the rest of my owner's menagerie to Covent Garden in 1732, where I contributed to the entertainment of many a laughing audience. All persons, however, who were the avowed enemies of Pantomime, were mine of course. The Tragic Muse commissioned the surly house dog to tear off my ears, and her comic sister encouraged an audacious nest of kittens bred in the wardrobe, to strip the honours from my mane and tail. Even the purveyors to Harlequin were hostile to me. A careless scene-shifter knocked out my right eye, and the best of my teeth were drawn to supply the mouth of a mastiff, appointed to catch Pantaloon by the leg, and stop his pursuit after his fugitive daughter. In short I have been so often plundered, and refitted, that, like the Royal Sovereign Man of War, scarce a bit of my original fabric remains. Being lately called out into service, my renovations consisted of a fresh skin, a pair of glass eyes, a tongue of scarlet cloth, and a clean set of grinders. Till this winter, when I appeared, I was

57

always looked on as a majestic representation of my species, nor hitherto had the stage exhibited any rival to my acknowledged dignity. But guess at my surprise and mortification, when I first discovered that an animal, twice as big as a dozen of me was appointed my associate. This creature too was not only out of his element, but is allowed to be almost twice as large as his original in Leicester Square. I kept myself at a distance from the spectators, that by avoiding notice I might escape the disadvantages of comparison. Let me add, that I am not the only discontented being on the present occasion ; for I have heard our scene painters one and all declare that this cursed hippopotamus, by his unnatural bulk, destroys the effect of Mr. Catton's architecture, as well as of his tigers, etc., so faithfully delineated from nature.

Meanwhile the stage menagerie had been rapidly growing. The dragon was the favourite. Before being adopted by the stage it was a customary attraction of the fairs. Elkanah Settle, looked upon in his prime as Dryden's rival, ended his professional career in Mrs. Mynn's booth at St. Bartholomew's where, in the droll called " St. George for England," he acted in a dragon of green leather of his own invention. In Young's epistle to Pope there are further details :

> Poor Elkanah, all other changes past
> For bread in Smithfield dragons hissed at last,
> Spit streams of fire to make the butchers gape
> And found his manners suited to his shape.

In the opera of " Rinaldo and Armido " at the Haymarket in 1711 the heroine's coach was drawn by two dragons, directed in the spitting of fire and smoke by a boy who " flashed out his rosin in such just proportions and in such due time " that *The Spectator* hoped he would one day be a most excellent player. The first pantomimes had much to do with dragons according to Pope's description in the " Dunciad " :

> All sudden, gorgons hiss and dragons glare
> And ten horn'd fiends and giants rush to war.

and this vogue led to the burlesque in Carey's " Dragon of Wantley " at Covent Garden in 1737. Though a copper structure he was akin to clowns, his ravages being confined to swallowing all the coffee, toast, and butter of the Squire's breakfast, and his death due to a kick in the rear that caused him to cry, " Oh, oh, oh ! the Devil take your toe." In " Orpheus and Eurydice " at this theatre three years later a serpent " so lively as to frighten half the ladies " was described by a critic as

> a piece of machinery, that enters, performs its exercise of head, body, and tail in a most surprising manner, and makes behind the curtain with a velocity scarcely credible.   It is about a foot and a half in circumference of the thickest part, and far exceeds the former custom of stuffing a bag into such likeness.   It is believed to have cost more than £200, and when the multitude of wings, springs, etc., whereof it consists are considered, the charge will not appear extravagant.

This expensive endeavour to make audiences gape instead of employing clownship to make them laugh is typical of the mismanagement of shows to the present day.   In the eighteenth century, however, pantomime animals were still in advance of their time.   For instance, of the scene in " Harlequin Sorcerer " where the hero changed himself into an ostrich to gain an interview with Columbine, a newspaper said the transformation " had a very good effect upon the audience ; but perhaps would have had a much greater, did not one discover that by the extremities it is Harlequin."   Yet, as the bird was indecorous in its behaviour, the scene was probably intended to be funny.

The serious convention was admirably satirised in *The Adventurer* (1752), where a scene for " a most sublime Pantomime " on the subject of Hercules is laid bare.   For the opening the undertaker has prepared " a couple of pasteboard serpents of an enormous length, with internal springs and movements for the contortions " which will far exceed " that most astonishing one in Orpheus and Eurydice." The Nemaean lion is to drop from an oiled-paper moon, be slain, and provide a " tawny-coloured hide made of coarse serge, with the ears, mane, and tip of the tail, properly bushed out with brown worsted," for Hercules.   By the art of machinery the Hydra will exhibit a successive regeneration of double heads, " till a hundred or more are prepared to be knocked off " by one stroke of a cork club.   The wild boar of Erymanthas

> has nothing in its belly but a wadding of tow, and a little boy who is to manage its motions, to let down the wire jaw, or gnash the wooden tusks ; and though I could rather wish he were able to grunt and growl, yet as that is impossible, I have taught the urchin to squeak prodigiously like a pig.

The hind of Maenalus has to be omitted because no common buck can be taught to run slow enough to be caught, but a whole flock of the birds of Stymphalus's Lake have been formed of leather covered with ravens' feathers, with wires so disposed as to make them flap out the candles. Cows' hides stuffed with straw will furnish the Augean stables ; the bull which breathes out flames has caught fire at rehearsal but is now fitted with an iron lining ; the noted ox with six legs and two bellies is to represent the cannibal oxen ; and the vulture of Mount Caucasus " shall vie in bulk, beauty and docility, with the so much applauded stupendous ostrich."

Despite ridicule, the property animal continued in serious regard. At the beginning of the nineteenth century there was a machinist of Drury Lane named Johnstone who was famous for the construction of wooden children to be tossed over battlements, straw heroes and hero-ines to be hurled down a precipice, wickerwork lions, pasteboard swans, and all the birds and beasts of a theatrical menagerie. In his " Random Records " Colman sets forth the story how this expert smug-gled himself into Covent Garden to see a rehearsal of " Harlequin and Padmanaba." There was an elephant :

> The friend who sat next to Johnstone jogged his elbow, whispering " This is a bitter bad job for Drury. Why the elephant's alive !—he'll carry all before him and beat you hollow. What d'ye think on't eh ? " " Think on't ! " said Johnstone in a tone of the utmost contempt. " I should be sorry if I couldn't make a much better elephant than that at any time."

That he was as good as his word is evident in the parody of Coleridge in " Rejected Addresses." As the performance of " Blue Beard " referred to was equestrian, the property beast had to survive contact with real horses :

> Johnson, the machinist,
> Of former Drury, imitated life
> Quite to the life. The elephant in Blue Beard,
> Stuffed by his hand, wound round his lithe proboscis
> As spruce as he who roared in Padmanaba.

His fame is only equalled by George Conquest, who made the Grecian Theatre, in the City Road, famous for monkeys, eagles, bats, dwarfs, giants and a host of other property monsters. In " Hokee Pokee, the

Mr Grimaldi & Mr Norman on the Epping Stand, from the Popular Pantomime of the Red Dwarf

GRIMALDI's LEAP FROG. *in the Grand Pantomime of the Golden Fish.*

JOSEPH GRIMALDI'S IDEA OF SPORT

From prints in the Author's Collection

Fiend of the Fungus Forest ; or the Six Links of the Devil's Chain,"
performed there in 1878, he played the demon Hokee Pokee, who had
glittering fans which opened and closed, attached to his limbs.   He
changed into a vampire bat with glaring eyes and monstrous wings,
and then into a porcupine with quills (the costume was said to consist
of two thousand five hundred pieces) that moved up and down.   Drury
Lane brought realism and mechanism to the limit of costliness.   Giants
for " Jack the Giant Killer " were recruited in the Basque country
among the farmers who spent their lives on stilts.   Special " dressing
rooms "—still called " the elephant's hole "—were built for real, live
elephants, and three of them were employed in " Sinbad " (1906)
merely to walk on in the last scene.   Choruses were disguised as
everything in heaven or the earth beneath or in the waters under the
earth.   How little impression these made is apparent in the story of
the galleryite who, noting the scarlet lobsters in a fish ballet, shouted
out, " Gus, you've *boiled* the bally lobsters."

That was the tradition which killed pantomime.   The lesson of
Grimaldi's boxing match with a man made of vegetables—a burlesque
this of Mrs. Shelley's terrible tale of the monster Frankenstein made
by a student out of dissecting-room relics—or his duet with a mammoth oyster that had been crossed in love, or his game of leap-frog
with frogs, or his hunting exploits on a property horse, was insuffi-
ciently heeded.   There were comic animals in Mid-Victorian pantomimes, of course.   The Paynes in " Ali Baba," for instance, had a
donkey who brought away a bag labelled " Halfpence " from the
robbers' cave and hid it in a cradle.   Yet though the humorous
possibilities of such monsters were not altogether neglected, they were
eclipsed by the scene-shifter's rocs or menagerie elephants.   Some of
the traditional tricks of the pantomime beast were forgotten and had
to be " invented " anew.   At least, that is the interpretation we have
to put on Pierre Mariel's claim that the Fratellini first broke an
animal in two.   His story is that they heard of a mishap to a property
elephant which had quarrelled inside itself while a clown was trying
to give a burlesque of trainers.   The effect when fore and aft parted
company was comical enough, but the clown discharged them for

spoiling his prearranged entertainment.   Thereupon Paul and Albert Fratellini were inspired to give an *entrée* as an elephant in a state of internal strife, while François imitated a trainer who tried to conceal his chagrin with professional smiles.

No pantomime animals, however, have ever surpassed in fame the Blondin Donkey and the performing horse of the Griffiths Brothers. Pogo first became famous at the time of the campaign against the exhibition of animals on the stage.   The Griffiths Brothers took great care to make it known that their horse had been trained only by kindness, but the leaders of the movement would not be appeased.   When invited to the Coliseum they drew up a protest with four signatures against " silly tricks and contortions behind the footlights," adding that " such indifference to the feelings of the spectators and would-be spectators—*and* animals—will however inevitably reap its ' own reward.' "   Yet, as Miss Lutie (the trainer) now emphatically informs her audiences in her introduction to each performance, Pogo made the King and Queen shake with laughter at a Royal Performance given at the Coliseum in December 1923.   " As you know," Miss Lutie concludes, " their Majesties would not laugh at a performance that contained the slightest suggestion of cruelty."   Here an inanely mild horse's head, with a lock of flaxen hair falling between its ears, appears in the wings.   Then, in marked contrast to the docility of the face, a turbulent body dances on to the stage.   According to the position of the legs, Pogo expresses utter irresponsibility, care-free joy in life, defiance towards authority, dismay at the sight of an obstacle, or sheer bellicosity towards Miss Lutie.   Every now and again the head goes round to consider or dispute with its stomach, and occasionally the forelegs and the hindlegs exchange kicks.   But, except when both actors stand upright, Pogo is an entity and almost a horse.   The secret lies in the exact concatenation of the movements.   Apart from such deliberate incongruities as the quarrels and differing methods of taking the jump, the legs act as though controlled by one mind.

The Griffiths Brothers and Miss Lutie are father, son and daughter.   Fred Delaney, the elder, was born at Corfu in 1856.   His father, a sergeant in the 96th Regiment, apprenticed him to a circus proprietor at the age of five.   Since then he has performed in music halls, " legitimate " plays, pantomimes and circuses in all parts of Europe, in America, Australia, Africa and Asia.   When at St. Petersburg in 1876 he made friends with a member of the Hanlon-Lees. The next year, when he was in Italy and the other in Austria, they were free of contracts and decided to join their fortunes.   In 1885 they became the Blondin Donkey.   Next they presented the wrestling lion, a quick-change burlesque and a strong man skit.   In 1887 they began, in " Puss in Boots," a succession of pantomime engagements at Drury Lane.   Fred's partner died in 1901, and the younger Delaney took his place.   Sixty years' experience has produced a monster whose rival does not appear in all the records of the mimicry of clowns.

Ratsa di Boio.   Smaraolo cornuto.   63

HARLEQUIN'S INVASION

Most modern wits such monstrous fools have shown,
They seem not of Heav'n's making, but their own.
Those nauseous Harlequins in farce may pass ;
But there goes more to a substantial ass :
Something of man must be exposed to view,
That, gallants, they may more resemble you . . .
From each he meets he culls whate'er he can,
Legion's his name, a people in a man.
His bulky folly gathers as it goes,
And, rolling, o'er you, like a snowball grows.
His various modes from various fathers follow ;
One taught the toss, and one the new French wallow.
His sword-knot this, his cravat that designed,
And this the yard-long snake he twirls behind.
From one the sacred periwig he gained,
Which wind ne'er blew, nor touch of hat profaned.
Another's diving bow he did adore
Which with a shog casts all the hair before ;
'Till he with full decorum brings it back,
And rises with a water-spaniel shake.

DRYDEN.

Cap: Grillo.　　Cap: Bonbardon.

Scaramouche

Scaramouche imite a Son aage   Et Sa figure, et Son visage
Les caracteres les plus forts: Ont d'inimitable ressorts.

Chez N Bonnart, rüe St Jacques   Avec privil.

HOW Arlequin became naturalised in England is a tale with a moral. There is, in fact, no more significant figure in the dramatis personae. No other character has made so many appearances on the stage. No history of the theatre is coherent without taking him into account. His conquest of the London stage was due to the neglect of the Elizabethan tradition of thrills mingled with laughter. He is the symbol of the drama's failure to fulfil humanity's needs.

" It is peculiar to Italy," says Schlegel, " that from the earliest times its people have displayed a native talent for a merry, amusing though very rude buffoonery, in extempory speeches and songs, with accompanying appropriate gestures." As her influence spread at the Renaissance, Italy's " vain delights " set the fashion in the courts of England and of France. While the tales of Boccaccio were inspiring Chaucer the disguisings of Italy were being copied by the nobles and the king. When a new device sprang out of the Florentine pageants of allegorical figures wearing masks, Whitehall again followed suit as Hall's " Chronicles " tell :

> The king with XI others were disguised after the manner of Italie, called a maske, a thing not before seen in England.

Profane plays were the next vogue, beginning with " Supposes " and " Jocasta," Gascoigne's translations of Ariosto's comedy and Dolce's tragedy, which were presented at Gray's Inn in 1566. Then it was the turn of the Commedia dell' arte to conquer the taste of the town. They had, despite occasional setbacks brought about by the French Puritans, definitely established their fame in Paris. They also secured the patronage of Elizabeth's Privy Council, who in 1573 prayed the Lord Mayor " to permit liberty to certain Italian players." But there was at once apparent the opposition which was to last a century.

The Privy Council, marvelling that he "didst not at their first request," had to pray the Lord Mayor again. Whether the second letter were more successful than the first is doubtful, but an entry in the Revels' Accounts for 1574 concerning the "hier of iij devells' cotes and heades and one olde manne's fries cote for the Italian prayers at Wynsor" may mean that they received from the court the welcome denied them by the city. In any case, the Privy Council granted another licence four years later to Drusiano Martinelli, and, whatever happened in this particular instance, the Italian players became well known to England. As early as 1582 there was mention of "The comedians of Ravenna who were not tied to any written device," and Thomas Heywood refers to "Zanyes, Pantaloons, Harlakeans, in which the French, but especially the Italians, have been excellent in this country." Nashe spoke of "that famous Francatrip' Harlicken" of Bergamo, and Day of "an Italian Harlaken come to offer a play." Also, Shakespeare embodies the lean and slippered age of man in Pantaloon, besides making Bottom proffer a Bergomask dance, which calls to mind that the author of "Epictetus' Man" scorned the country dances of "a Zanie or Pantaloon."

Here is evidence in plenty that the Commedia dell' arte was well known to the Elizabethans. It also bears witness that the Italian players failed to establish themselves because they were held in contempt by people who, though they might go "any whither, so the clown have a part," were thoroughly content with their own clowns, familiar fellows who not only acted, piped and danced, but would come out upon the stage and challenge them to bouts of homely repartee. How many they had may be reckoned by the parts written for them in Elizabethan plays. Though Sidney objects to their "scurrility, unworthy of any chaste ears, or some extreme show of doltishness, indeed fit to lift up a loud laugher, and nothing else," there is Shakespeare's evidence that Richard Tarleton, who practised at the time this was written, was a fellow of infinite jest, of most excellent fancy. And though Shakespeare may be judged to refer to William Kempe in the strictures of the First Quarto "Hamlet" concerning a clown who "keeps one suit of jests:

HARLEQUIN AS FOOL TO THE "INFALLIBLE MOUNTEBANK"

From an Eighteenth-century print in the British Museum

> Cannot you stay till I eat my porridge ? and, you owe me
> A quarter's wages : and, my coat wants a cullison :
> And your beer is sour : and, blabbering with his lips,
> And thus keeping in his cinkapase of jests,
> When, God knows, the warm clown cannot make a jest
> Unless by chance, as the blind man catcheth a hare,

—yet "that most comical and conceited Cavaliere Monsieur du Kempe" was called "Jestmonger and vice-gerent general to the ghost of Dick Tarleton," and was the original Dogberry. It was in his time too that Middleton wrote :

> Some talk of things of state, of puling stuff ;
> There's nothing in a play to a clown, if he
> Have the grace to hit on't ; that's the thing indeed :
> The king shows well, but he sets off the king.

Kempe was succeeded by Thomas Greene, manager of the Red Bull, whose fame was such that a favourite comedy was printed with his name in the title as "Greene's Tu Quoque."

Native humour being thus plentiful, the Harlequinade obtained no engagements on the Elizabethan stage. In the stage directions of "Dead Man's Fortune," which is supposed to date from 1593, one of the characters is described as "the panteloun," but the name was then used to signify any old dotard. His companions were ignored. Columbine was deemed a common courtesan ; for one thing, she was played by a woman, and, for another, her name had a sinister sound. The wild flower was first named columbine because it suggested doves clustering. To the Elizabethan mind, however, its horn-shaped nectaries suggested cuckoldry—"That thankless flower grows not in my garden," says a character in Chapman's "All Fools." But there was a better reason for the turning away of all foreign mummers. It was given by Nashe in "Pierce Penniless" (1592). "Our scene," he said,

> is more stately furnished than ever it was in the time of Roscius, our repre-
> sentations honourable, and full of gallant resolution, not consisting like theirs
> of Pantaloun a Whore, and a Zanie, but of Emperors, Kings and Princes.

As he was not a clown to set off a king, the only employment Harlequin

had here was that of a mountebank's man. In "Britannia Triumphans"
at Whitehall in 1637 there was an " entry " of a quack doctor,
who, while distributing recipes to " two pale wenches presenting their
urinalls," was attended by a Zany and a " Harlekin."   In two plays
of the Restoration he was introduced in the same rôle.   " I am poor
Harlequin," he said, " by the learned I am called Zane, by the vulgar
Jack Pudding.   I was late fool to a mountebank."   Probably he had
continued in this rôle during the Commonwealth, when, according to
Kirkman, drolls were acted on quacks' stages by " mountebanks'
zanies," as well as by " several strolling players, fools and fiddlers."
In his preface to a collection of snippets from Shakespeare, Beaumont
and Fletcher, Jonson and other contemporaries, Kirkman declares
that these were the farces performed ; but, as he was intent on selling
his book to those who dealt in " drugs, potions and balsoms," he is a
questionable historian.   In other respects, however, his account of
how the clowns drew their auditors " under pretence of rope-dancing,
or the like," seems trustworthy :

> I have seen the Red Bull Play-House which was a large one, so full,
> that as many went back for want of room as had entred ; and as meanly
> as you may now think of these Drols, they were then Acted by the best
> Comedians then and now in being ; and I may say, by some that then ex-
> ceeded all now Living, by Name, the incomparable Robert Cox, who was
> not only the principal Actor, but also the contriver and Author of most of
> these Farces.   How have I heard him cryed up for his John Swabber, and
> Simpleton the Smith ?   In which he being to appear with a large piece
> of Bread and Butter, I have frequently known several of the Female Spec-
> tators and Auditors to long for it ;   And once that well-known natural Jack
> Adams of Clarkenwell, seeing him with Bread and Butter on the Stage, and
> knowing him, cryed out, Cuz, Cuz, give me some, give me some ; to the great
> pleasure of the audience.   And so Naturally did he Act the Smith's part,
> that being at a Fair in a Countrey Town, and that Farce being presented,
> the only Master Smith of the Town came to him, saying, well, although your
> Father speaks so ill of you, yet when this Fair is done, if you will come and
> work with me, I will give you twelve pence a week more than I give any
> other Journey-Man.   Thus was he taken for a Smith bred, that was indeed
> much of any trade.
> And as he pleased the City and Country, so the Universities had a sight
> of him, and very well esteemed he was by the Learned ; but more particu-
> larly by the Butler of one of those Colledges, who liking his Acting, and
> finding that those Representations were defective for want of a Prologue

CLOWNS OF THE COMMONWEALTH

From Kirkman's "The Wits or, Sport upon Sport"

he being a dabler in Poetry, would needs write one, part of which I remember to be thus.

> Courteous Spectators, we are your Relaters,
> Neither Tylers nor Slators, nor your Vexators,
> But such who will strive to please,
> Will you sit at your ease,
> And speak such words as may be spoken,
> And not by any be mistaken, Catera desiderantur, etc.

Although I question not but the University afforded good wits, and such as were well skilled in Poetry, yet this was the best our Butler was infected with, which Robert Cox did speak, not as a Prologue at the beginning, but as a Droll in the middle of what he then acted.

Thus were these Compositions liked and approved by all, and they were the fittest for the Actors to Represent, there being little Cost in Cloaths, which often were in great danger to be seiz'd by the then souldiers ; who, as the Poet sayes, Enter the Red Coat, Exit Hat and Cloak, was very true, not only in the Audience, but the Actors too, were commonly, not only strip'd, but many times imprisoned, till they paid such Ransom as the souldiers would impose upon them : so that it was hazardous to Act any thing that required any good Cloaths, instead of which painted Cloaths many times served the turn to represent Rich Habits.

At the fairs Harlequin came in contact with Punchinello, a much favoured puppet at the time of the Restoration, who was, according to a Smithfield ballad, shown thrice to the king. His name was a household word for " all that is thick and short," observed Pepys, when mightily pleased to hear a fat child called Punch. Thus at Southwark and Smithfield the foreign motley was welcomed. On the stage, while even the shreds of the Elizabethan tradition remained, Harlequin was resisted. But showmanship was a dying art. Instead of playing to the public, the actors were now in fact as well as in name servants of the king, mere courtiers and sycophants. The change affected the clown most of all. In 1662 the prologue of the tragedy of " Thorney Abbey, or the London Maid," was spoken by the Fool, who declared, " The poet's a fool who made the tragedy to tell a story of a king and a court and leave a fool out on't." Incidentally, he revealed how completely the tradition had been lost by adding that " in Pacy's and Sommer's and Patche's and Archee's times, my venerable predecessors, a fool was always the principal verb," for these are the names of court jesters quite distinct from stage clowns.

No heed was given to the warning. The King and the Court, knowing all there was to know of kings and courts, wanted to see themselves raised to the sublimely heroic, above the ridicule of clowns. Though there were many comedians of repute, including Angel, Nokes, Jevon and Haines, they were ill-provided with parts. Etherege's " The Comical Revenge ; or, Love in a Tub," was boisterous enough, and there was horseplay in plenty elsewhere notwithstanding the vogue of elegant wit. But the fools of fashion were not saturnalians—they were not beloved, as the clowns these same actors performed at the fairs. Once, declares Sparkish in Wycherley's " The Country Wife," authors were " contented to make serving-men only their stage-fools : but these rogues must have gentlemen." It was not a social advancement all the same. The Elizabethan clown may have been a serving-man, but he was a serving-man sitting in his lord's chair. The fool of the Restoration was a whipping-stock for the gallants. The poets of the London stage were seeking to emulate French models, but were unable to bring themselves to adopt Molière's clown. Scapin, descendant of Davus and ancestor of Figaro, will not flourish on English soil. Our notion has ever been that a serving-man may be as outspoken as he will, but not cunning without forfeiting sympathy. Therefore, the poets were in a dilemma. For a makeshift they invented the ass, who satisfied nobody except on the notorious occasion when Nokes, playing before King Charles, his sister the Duchess of Orleans and her Court, made himself like a " dressed-up ape " by imitating the French fashion for short-tailed coats and broad waist-belts. Which put the King and *his* Court to an excessive laughter.

The London stage was exposed to foreign invasion at the moment the Italian troupes were most formidable. Tiberio Fiurelli, the greatest Scaramouche[1] of all time, who had had the honour of having his clothes ruined by the infant Dauphin while nursing him from squalls to delighted laughter, who could make an audience laugh for a full

[1] Angelo Constantini, the Mezzetin of the Italian troupe, published *La Vie de Scaramouche* in 1695 and a translation appeared in London the next year. In this Fiurelli is described as short-sighted, deaf in his left ear, and withered in one shoulder. " As for his inclinations, he was extremely mistrustful, covetous and passionate ; he had a lively imagination, he spoke but little, and had much

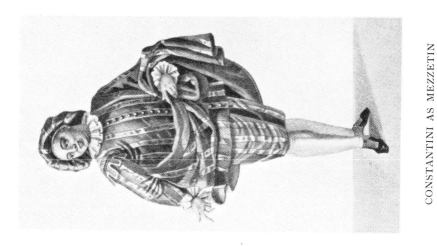

CONSTANTINI AS MEZZETIN

FIURELLI AS SCARAMOUCHE

From "La Galerie Théâtrale", 1873

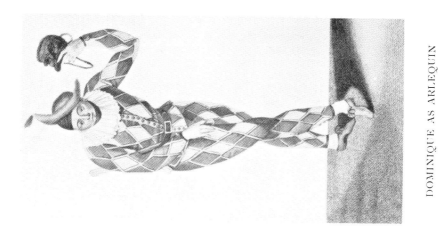

DOMINIQUE AS ARLEQUIN

quarter of an hour at his grimaces of fear, was acting in Paris and his fame spreading through the civilised world. The same year that Charles II. was crowned, a traveller spoke of Scaramuzza's genius for " distorted countenances and postures." About ten years later this reference to him occurred in Wycherley's " The Dancing Master " :

MONSIEUR DE PARIS.
Ay, ay, the French education make us propre à tout. Beside, cousin, you must know, to play the fool is the science in France, and I didde go to the Italian academy at Paris thrice a week to learn to play de fool of signior Scaramouche, who is the most excellent personage in the world for dat noble science. Angel is a dam English fool to him.

HIPPOLITA.
Methinks, now, Angel is a very good fool.

MONSIEUR DE PARIS.
Nauh, nauh, Nokes is a better fool, but indeed the Englis are not fit to be fools : here are ver few good fools. 'Tis true, you have many a young cavalier who go over into France to learn to be de buffoon ; but, for all dat, dey return but mauvais buffoon, jarnie !

HIPPOLITA.
I'm sure, cousin, you have lost no time there.

MONSIEUR DE PARIS.
Auh, le brave Scaramouche !

In 1673, exactly a century after the first known venture of the Commedia dell' arte across the Channel, Fiurelli came to London. Immediately his name became part of the English language as a term of abuse far more effective than " Fool " or " Clown," and his costume all the rage in masquerades. His success was even more disastrous to the English companies than the competition of the puppets. The actors of Drury Lane, only able to " act by fits and starts, like drowning men," sought refuge at Oxford, where Dryden poured out his grievance against the Italians in epilogues :

A French troop first swept all things in its way ;
But those hot Monsieurs were too quick to stay :

---

difficulty to deliver his words ; but in recompense, nature had endowed him with a wonderful talent to express by the postures of his body, and the grimaces of his face, whatever he had a mind to say." Though gluttonous, he was a most active player. He was still acting at seventy, but to the end was noted for his upright carriage.

> Yet, to our cost, in that short time, we find
> They left their itch of novelty behind.
> The Italian merry-andrews took their place,
> And quite debauched the stage with lewd grimace :
> Instead of wit, and humours, your delight
> Was there to see two hobby-horses fight ;
> Stout Scaramoucha with rush lance rode in,
> And ran a tilt at centaur Arlequin.
> For love you heard how amorous asses brayed,
> And cats in gutters gave their serenade.

The compliment of imitation was not long withheld. At first it was slight—in Shadwell's " Virtuoso " (1676) Sir Formal attends the masquerade " in Scaramouche's Habit " and there is a dance by a Scaramouche and six clowns. But an emergency created a complete English Harlequinade. Both the London theatres in 1677 prepared translations of *Les Fourberies de Scapin*. Dorset Gardens was first in the field with Otway's version. Drury Lane was therefore unwilling to stage Ravenscroft's. As a last resource he copied the methods of Fiurelli, entitled his piece " Scaramouche a Philosopher, Harlequin, a Schoolboy, Bravo, Merchant and Magician," described it as " A comedy after the Italian manner," and offered this explanation :

> The poet does a dangerous trial make,
> And all the common roads of plays forsake,
> Upon the actors it depends too much,
> And who can hope ever to see two such
> As the famed Harlequin and Scaramouche
> This well he knew. . . .
> Yet rather chose in new attempts to fail,
> Than in the old indifferently prevail.

Ravenscroft's Scaramouche, however, is not the Miles Gloriosus we might expect. Instead, he is a pantaloon-like parent—Fiurelli had left London with many varying ideas of the braggart in black—and the " coward ignorant and bold " of the piece is Spitzaferro. Scapin has become Harlequin, stupid but mischievous, who begins by singing out of tune, making legs and making thrusts, to aggravate a master of singing, dancing and fencing. When brought to account he fights with his wooden sword and then runs away. Next he finds the

" talkative doctor " standing " in a posture leaning his ear, as listening to what Scaramouche will say " while " Scaramouche does same to him." Harlequin fetches a drum, " stands betwixt them and beats louder and louder " ; then " hits each a pat with his sword on the buttocks." Halfway through the plot a school scene is introduced :

> The scene draws, and discover Harlequin among a company of little children at school, all gabling together in a school-tone ; the mistress sitting in the middle in a great chair, with a great rod and a ferrula sticking upright at either corner of the back o' the chair. Harlequin snatches a piece of bread and butter out of one of the children's hands ; the child falls a crying.

When the Mistress leaves them Harlequin sits in her chair, " takes the rod and plays with it ; pulls out an apple, and sits and sings with his mouth full," while the children applaud. But because he becomes dictatorial they " throw books at him, and pull him to come out." The Mistress returns. Finding first that his hands are dirty, and secondly that he cannot say his alphabet without a fault, she commands, " Come put your head through the back of this chair . . . Come down, down, I say . . . So, children, one of you untruss his points quickly." Thereupon Harlequin " puts his head through the back of the chair, lifts it up, runs about the room with it hanging round his neck ; all the children take rods, and, with the Mistress, run about the stage whipping him." Because of this ordeal he asks Scaramouche to make him a philosopher. His next disguise is " in the habit of a bravo, with a huge sword, and a girdle stuck round with pistols and daggers, which are discovered by his cloak falling off ;—and rosy-cheeks with great whiskers." In the end he is caught for chastisement, but " slips out of the gown as they hold him by the arms, goes behind them, and hits each two or three times o'er the head—they strike at him and buffet one another."

Harlequin was played by Jo Haines, who began as a dancer in France, but got into trouble for impersonating an English peer. He escaped to England and set up a booth, where he acted the droll of " The Whore of Babylon, the Devil and the Pope " in Bartholomew Fair. That being after James II. was crowned, he only avoided punishment by pleading, so Anthony Aston tells :

75

That he did it in respect to his Holiness; for, whereas many ignorant people believed the Pope to be a beast, he shewed him to be a fine, comely old gentleman, as he was; not with seven heads, and ten horns, as the Scotch parsons describe him.

About the time of Ravenscroft's piece, he again fell into mischief. Hart had commanded him to play a senator in " Cataline's Conspiracy." Feeling slighted at having to be a " super," Haines put on a Scaramouche dress, a large full ruff, whiskers from ear to ear, and a long Merry-Andrew's cap. With a short pipe in his mouth and a little three-legged stool in his hand, he followed Hart on the stage, set himself down behind him, and began to smoke his pipe, laugh and point at him. Hart, whose " exactness and grandeur " were upset, turned him out of doors.

Whatever its success, Ravenscroft's example was not followed immediately. When Harlequin and Scaramouche next appear, in the second part of Aphra Behn's " The Rover; or the Banished Cavaliers," staged at the Duke's Theatre in 1681, they are the attendants of a mountebank, and an insight is given into their duties at the fairs. Harlequin stabs himself and " falls as dead," but revives when the mountebank empties his elixir into the wound. The only suggestion of the Italian comedians' influence is in the scene where the suitor of a giantess disguises himself as a giant, and comes to grief in this manner :

Hunt being all doublet, leaps off from another man who is all breeches, and goes out; breeches follows stalking.

But the Harlequinade soon won definite signs of popularity. Mountford's Italianised version of Marlowe's " Dr. Faustus " was several times acted at the Duke's Theatre about 1685, and frequently revived during the next half century. The parts of Wagner and Robin are played by Scaramouche, and the Clown and Dick by Harlequin. They meet in a street scene, where Harlequin raps at a door and strikes Scaramouche who opens it. The Pope's feast is changed into a haunted banquet. They conjure up the devil, who sends them " the giant which St. George destroyed "—since then rotting in the earth—to do their bidding. After Scaramouche has got upon Harlequin's shoul-

76

ders to salute the ambassador infernal, the giant remarks " I can divide myself to serve my friends," breaks in two and commands his breeches to be his page.   He conducts them to a feast.   Then " The upper part of the giant flies up, and the under sinks, and discovers a woman in the room."   They kiss her : " Woman sinks, a flash of lightning." The table "removes," then "flies up into the air," they are "hoisted up to the table," then the table flies down, and they are let down to the table.   When Harlequin takes off the lid of the pasty " a stag's head peeps out, and out of the pot of fowl flies birds."   Harlequin and Scaramouche fall over their chairs.   For want of oil and vinegar Harlequin fetches a lamp and a chamber-pot.   The bread " stirs," the table sinks amid a flash of lightning, bottles fly up and chairs rise. Harlequin and Scaramouche are caught fast when they sit down. Several Devils black the faces of both, and then squirt milk upon them. After a dance they both sink.   At the end the Doctor's limbs " all torn asunder by the hand of hell " come together to provide dance and song.

Direct imitation of Fiurelli's performances was the next method. This was tried by Aphra Behn, who in 1687 made an English version of the *Arlequin Empereur dans la Lune* performed in Paris for the first time in March 1684.   That it may have been performed previously in England is suggested in these lines in the last part of " Hudibras," published in 1678 :

> But what, alas ! is it to us,
> Whether i' th' moon men thus or thus
> Do eat their porridge, cut their corns
> Or whether they have tails or horns ? . . .
> Can they make plays there that shall fit
> The public humour, with less wit ?
> Write witty dances, quainter shows,
> Or fight with more ingenious blows ?

In any case, Aphra Behn is unconscionable in saying that she took from the Italian piece " which, even as it was, was acted in France eighty odd times without intermission," no more than " a very barren and thin hint."   The tricks performed in Paris by that most famous of Arlequins, Giuseppe Domenico Biancolelli, are the same as those set down for Jevon. There is the same plot of an astronomer with a pretty daughter, and a similar pretence, to win his consent to her marriage, that the Emperor of the Moon has descended to earth. But while the *lazzi* of the original bear on the story the by-play of Aphra Behn's version is inconsequential. Arlequin's disguises as an apothecary, a farmer and a baker, were intended to satisfy the desire of the astronomer to marry his daughter to an honest tradesman. Harlequin and Scaramouche repeat his tricks—his chair which becomes an apothecary's shop, and his calash which changes into a baker's cart the moment the officer in charge of the tolls turns his back—just for the fun that is in them. The scene where Harlequin tries to commit suicide, first by stopping his mouth and nose with his hands and then by tickling himself, is also copied direct. The story ends with a transformation scene. The astronomer is taken to a disused gallery in his own house in order to meet the Prince of Thunderland. Then :

> The scene in the front draws off, and shews the Hill of Parnassus ; a noble large walk of trees leading to it, with eight or ten negroes upon pedestals, ranged on each side of the walks. Next Keplan and Gallileus descend on each side, opposite to each other, in chariots, with perspectives in their hands, as viewing the machine of the Zodiac. So music plays still.

After the Doctor has been induced by the Prince to give his consent to his daughter's wedding to her lover, Harlequin and Scaramouche enter as mock heroes in helmets to fight at barriers. Scaramouche throws his opponent in a duel resembling that described by Dryden, then takes off his helmet to receive the prize. The trick is revealed, but the Doctor, seeing the error of his ways, reaffirms his consent. In the original, Arlequin (himself the lover) is divertingly baulked, and renounces his claims to the heroine, even her cat and the bugs on the walls of her house.

Though an artless imitation of a witty original, Aphra Behn's version lived the longest of all Harlequinades. It was especially popular at the beginning of the eighteenth century, as letters to *The Spectator* prove. There is one, for instance, from William Screne, who had acted " in the hangings in the Emperor of the Moon," had twice performed the third chair in an English opera, and rehearsed

78

the pump in the " Fortune-Hunters." Ralph Simple, tired of being " one of the finest flower pots in the same opera where Mr. Screne is a chair," requested that, upon his promotion, he might " succeed him in the hangings with my hand in the orange-trees." Next comes the scheme of a projector for the collection of all the strange animals, etc., in town into one piece, and an imaginary response from the actors of Drury Lane, who wish to help the scheme by parting with everything that does not contribute to the representation of human life. In consequence, " The hangings you formerly mentioned are run away ; and are likewise a set of chairs, each of which was met upon two legs going through the Rose Tavern at two this morning." The piece was frequently revived as a " speaking-pantomime " until 1777.

Before the end of the century Columbine and Clown had joined Harlequin. They were brought on the stage by Peter Motteux in " The Novelty," a piece, acted at Lincoln's Inn Fields in 1697, which consisted of " A Short Pastoral, Comedy, Masque, Tragedy and Farce," the last being after the Italian manner, because the author had " seen most of the things that were misliked, much applauded when Acted by Harlequin and Scaramouche." But in the farce, " Natural Magic," their places are taken by " Pasquarel " and " Nicholas a Clown "—" There's Nicholas your farmer's man ! He's a stout fellow." The rest include the usual pair of romantic young lovers, Pantalone (an old miser), Mezzetin (his man), and Colombina (the heroine's maid), besides " Men personating the Devil and his sub-jects." The horseplay is clumsily copied from Italian examples. Imitating the celebrated trick of Fiurelli who (in *Colombine Avocat*) was struck with fear when the guitar he held was played by Pasquariel crouching behind his chair, Motteux directs that " Pas-quarel " shall slip into a chair just before Pantaloon and play his guitar similarly. The ending is a transformation scene to trick the miser into consenting to his daughter's marriage, after the manner of " The Emperor of the Moon."

Thus, because the native drama had not supplied the clown with a " sympathetic part " important enough to satisfy himself and the audience, Harlequin was ardently welcomed by all except the tragedians.

79

Jevon excelled even Haines in the part. Then came William Pinkethman, known at the fairs as " Pinkey." He was in his " most shining circumstances," says Steele, when beating William Bullock or receiving a beating from him. Of this pair he also tells :

> Mr. Pinkethman devours a chick with great applause ; Bullock's talent lies chiefly in asparagus. Pinkethman is very dexterous at conveying him-self under a table ; Bullock is no less active at jumping over a stick.

Both exhibited their talent at Smithfield in " Pinkeman's Medley," where they presented spectacles of sieges enlivened by the antics of Harlequin. As he was a master of grimace and of vaulting, Pin-kethman realised that his destiny was the fairs. At first he went to May-fair, but when it broke in 1709 he moved his " ingenious strollers " to Greenwich. Steele declared that two of the heathen gods and goddesses which were to descend in machines got into trouble—Mars breaking his landlord's head and Diana being " taken in the act of fornication with a boatman "—but the next year Greenwich was stated to be the place where " he has erected his home."

The English Harlequinades of the seventeenth century were but dim shadows, in their byplay as well as in their wit, of the scintillating inventions of the Italian troupe in Paris from 1682 to 1697. Their performances at the Hôtel de Bourgogne were inspired by a delight as fresh as that of the nursery in all the objects, common or uncommon, in the world. Most of the tricks of the modern pantomime can be traced to them. Their zoology has already been described. Their geography was equally extensive, ranging from Turkey and Egypt to China, and from fairyland to hell. Their comic realism is still more remarkable in anticipating devices of contemporary pantomimes. Take, for instance, shops. In *Arlequin Lingère du Palais* the scene consists of a draper's next to a place of refreshment. Arlequin, standing between, is dressed half as a woman and half as a man. He presents each profile in turn to Pasquariel, and then showers blows upon him under the pretext that the *lingère* and the *limonadier* are fighting. In *Le Marchand Duppé* the scene is a shop where assistants are rolling stuffs on a counter (as they do in " Dick

SHOP SCENES OF THE COMMEDIA DELL' ARTE

From Gherardi's "Théâtre Italien"

Whittington "). In the *Francoises du Banqueroutier* Arlequin appears as a barber who holds a customer down with a foot on his stomach. In *La Foire de Saint Germaine* he accepts goods from every stallholder, and is grieved when they ask him for money. The kitchen was not so popular, but in *Le Tombeau de Maitre André* a tun forms the base of a mausoleum consisting of cooking utensils, and in *L'Opera de Compagnie* the palace of Armide is made of household chattels with a chimney at the back where fowls are roasting on the turn-spit. In *La Magie Naturelle*, Arlequin, for striking a miller, is fastened to one of the wings of a mill and left whirling round. The device of a real head in a picture occurs in *Colombine Avocat Pour et Contre*, and in *La Fausse Coquette* Arlequin is deluded by a screen, one wing showing Colombine as a lover and another Mezzetin who sings to the accompaniment of a flute.

Besides introducing novelties of this kind they developed the old tricks of horseplay. In the *Grand Sophie* Arlequin and Pasquariel collide and sit down suddenly. In *Le Bel Espirit* one enters with a hump on his back, the other with a hump in front, and when they go to make reverence the humps come sharply in contact. In *Arlequin Lingère*, when Arlequin orders the arrest of Scaramouche four statues round the chimney seize him and clap the mantle over his head to serve as the stocks. In *Arlequin Protée* Arlequin is a housebreaker who throws various goods out of the window to Mezzetin, including a baby and a cheese. In *Arlequin Homme à Bonne Fortune*, this pair rob an old man of his clothes by pretending to help him catch an imaginary scorpion which, they say, is crawling over him, ready to sting. Very few tricks were left undiscovered or untried by the company at the Hôtel de Bourgogne. Even the interruption from the auditorium, much used in contemporary revue, was thought of by them—but in a more boisterous fashion. Mezzetin, when he clambered on the stage, impersonated " Parterre " by wearing several heads and several catcall whistles.

In the eighteenth century their horseplay was gradually refined into parody. When they appeared in the Haymarket for the season of 1726-7 their pieces had lost their spontaneity. " Harlequin Prince

in a Dream, German Baron, Flying Physician and Pretty Marget "
(which resembles the induction to " The Taming of the Shrew "),
"Argentina; or, the Sorceress," and "L'Honorato Poverta di Rinaldo;
with Harlequin Guardian to his Master's Family and Defender of his
Castle " were laboriously ingenious.   In Paris the Italian and the
French companies were chiefly engaged in lampooning one another
at this time, and Arlequin, said Holberg, had " not much higher pretensions than the Punch of the strolling mountebanks."   He also
established himself in Germany [1] early in the eighteenth century so
thoroughly that, according to Holcroft, " neither tragedies nor comedies were performed, to the perfect satisfaction of the spectators, in
which Harlequin was not allowed to mingle his ridiculous and often
indecent buffooneries."   Both in France and England he suffered
many changes.   At the fairs he was long retained as the mountebank's
man, but otherwise ceased to be a clown.   Marivaux turned him into
a pretty simpleton and London pantomimes into a romantic magician.
In Italy, however, he remained a comic country servant in the nineteenth century.

[1] There was a Harlequinade in the modern English version of *Der Bestrafte
Brudermord, oder Prinz Hamlet aus Dännemark,* staged by Mr. William Poel in
1924.   In the text, however, there is no mention of Harlequin, Columbine or
Pantaloon.   The original scene is the age-old joke of the gull and the cheater
acted by Phantasmo, the court fool, and Jens, a country clown.

ARLEQUIN AT AN ITALIAN CARNIVAL OF 1820

From an engraving in the Author's Collection

GRIMALDI

As if a bright picture of King George, heaven bless him! wasn't better than all the worn out coins of all the outlandish Emperors in the world; but as times go, I may be an Emperor; my comical phiz be stuck on a farthing, and somebody be fool enough to give a ha'penny for it—

> For folks curiosities love to see,
> And, as I'm a curiosity, come to see me.
>
> Tol lol . . .

Of what use is Mercury without heels, or a Venus without a head? Then they prefer a Cockleshell to a Cockle, and an Alligator's toe to a Pig's foot! What's a dried Scorpion to a dished Lobster, a stuffed Snake to a stewed Eel, or a rusty Pike to a Pike with a Pudding in its belly? Then a mummy; O, that's all very well, because, as the Irishman said, it teaches one how to keep people alive an hundred years after they're dead—that is a curiosity.

GRIMALDI in the museum scene of " Fairlop Fair; or, the Genii of the Oak," Sadler's Wells, Easter, 1812.

JanPotage

F. de Wit Exc   1

IF to be loved by a whole nation in his lifetime and to live in all men's fancies a hundred years after is a true sign of greatness, then Joseph Grimaldi has a right to be reckoned among our famous men. Though no attempt, beyond the restoration a few years ago of the headstone of his grave on Pentonville Hill, has been made to honour his memory, his name is as illustrious as a living actor's. His portraits, still numerous in printsellers' stocks, are evidence of a popularity no pretty boy or girl of the stage of to-day can rival. He is spoken of by a generation which cares not a great deal for clownship. And occasionally there is a touch of hero worship in the mention of his name. A month or two ago an inquiry for Grimaldi prints in a little shop in Seven Dials brought forth the sharp correction, " D'you want a portrait of *Mr.* Grimaldi in his professional clothes ? "

There must, obviously, be reason for the enduring glamour of his name. A French writer believes it is because Dickens edited his *Memoirs.* But that apocryphal book gives little or no idea of Grimaldi in the days of his clownship, " a fowl in one pocket and sauce for it in the other." Boz's explanation was not that the task was impossible : there were so many who knew how rich his humour was, he feared " any attempted summary " of his peculiarities might be deemed an impertinence. The excuse suggests that Dickens had not seen Grimaldi. Those who had were not so constrained. Their testimony, eked out with facts from the annotations of the *Memoirs,* from old prints, playbills, scrapbooks, and newspapers, provides a glimpse of the greatest of all clowns that makes his fame understandable. He was rightly called " The Michael Angelo of buffoonery." To compare even the relics of his motley with the living bloom of modern clownship is to realise that the critics who hailed him as a genius were not exaggerating. The whole gamut of laughter was his. All the

85

ancient jokes found in him their best exponent, and he made many of the new ways they have run in until our own time.

Where did Clown spring from ? " Tradition," according to some authorities, declares that his make-up is inherited from the medieval stage devil. But that devil has a lineage of his own. He was popular before the Commonwealth in other plays besides " Dr. Faustus," although sometimes merely a part offered to small boys who, in payment, would see the play for nothing. At the fairs of the seventeenth century he took a favoured place in the hustling of the Pope ; he also appeared in Harlequinades and operas. Pantomime renewed his popularity but changed him in time to Sulphuro, the Fire Fiend, and then to the Demon King. Nor are the clowns of Shakespeare the forebears of Clown. They were the " Jack Fools of the Play " who disappeared at the Restoration, and their motley has now become the dress suit of the music-hall raconteur. Only one part of Clown's costume is a genuine antique. That is his " falling bands " or bib. Neither Tarleton nor Kempe wore it, for the foppery was of rather a later date. But the frontispiece of Kirkman's *Drolls* shows it on three types of fools—the one who cries " Tue quo que," the simpleton and Sir John Falstaff. These characters, says Kirkman, acted at Bartholomew Fair during the Commonwealth. Afterwards their place was taken by the Merry Andrew, one of " those circumforaneous wits," *The Spectator* said, " whom every nation calls by the name of that dish of meat which it loves best," such as the Dutch Pickled Herrings, the French Jean Pottage and the Italian Macaroni. In this fashion the Merry Andrews were called " Jack Puddings," a name which lends itself to the exploit of one who, having got into trouble with the authorities, walked through the Fair holding a neat's tongue and a black pudding. To all questions he replied :

> Mind neither Good nor Bad, Nor Right nor Wrong :
> But eat your Pudding, Slave, and Hold Your Tongue.

The most celebrated Merry Andrew was William Phillips, who wore a bibb or ruff that was part of the conventional costume of the fools of the fair until, following the fashion set by the Parisian *forains* at the beginning of the eighteenth century, they one and all became Scara-

86

JEMMY WARNER OF SADLER'S WELLS

From a mezzotint in the British Museum

mouche or Harlequin. Whether the droll were " The Siege of Be-
thulia, containing the ancient history of Judith and Holophernes,
with the Comical Humours of Rustego and his man Terrible " or
" Jephthah's Rash Vow, with the comical Humors of Captain Bluster
and his Man Diddimo," the comic parts were dressed in the Italian
motley. The only place free from their influence was Sadler's Wells,
where " Honest Friend Thomas " was both clown and waiter. In
Garrick's time, the clown of the Wells was Jemmy Warner, notable as
Falstaff and Sancho Panza, who kept to the costume of the Merry
Andrew. But the clown of the pantomimes at Drury Lane and Covent
Garden had no costume. Nicholas, the first trace of Clown in a
Harlequinade, was a farmer's man. One of the earliest pantomimes
was a mimic scene between a Scaramouche, a Harlequin and a Country
Farmer. The clown of pantomime was merely a rustic servant and
only a minor character until 1727, when a pantomime called " The
Miser " was changed into " Harlequin's Triumph " to give a leading
part to Harlequin's servant, the clown. Himself and the miser's
wife were discovered " very loving together," and when he tried to
escape through a window the sash fell so that a suitable part of his
anatomy was available for beating. Often he had such a name as
Clodpate or John Trot, and that he was dressed simply as a stupid
yokel is shown as late as 1772 in a " 6d. plain, 1s. coloured " folder
called " The Witches ; or, Harlequin's Trip to Naples." He was
generally the ragged servant of Pantaloon until pantomime traditions
underwent a radical change. This was happening during the second
half of the eighteenth century, because of the performers from Italy
and France who came to London for good on account of the great
demand for frivolous entertainment. Previously the clown had
been an actor—Hippisley, Spiller and Macklin played the part—but
it was now handed over to members of the company who came under
the category of ballet.[1] Dancing, however, was only one of several
accomplishments each of the newcomers possessed. They were, as a
rule, capable of playing any part in a pantomime though they often

---

[1] Including such performers as the carrot-swallower who is reputed to have
delighted George III.

specialised in one particular capacity. Thus, Johannot and Decastro were known as comic singers ; Le Petit Diable and Pietro Bologna as rope dancers ; and Laurent, Dubois and Delpini as Pierrots. Their Pierrot, a comic butt, took the clown's place as servant to Pantaloon. For instance, in " Harlequin Teague ; or, the Giant's Causeway "— at the Haymarket in 1782—Columbine was left in charge of Pierrot. " Here," wrote a critic,

> was presented one of the best pantomimical scenes that we ever recollect seeing ; the relighting of one candle, as he is putting out the other, was both new and well conceived—but Pierrot is not so successful in guarding as in catching, for Harlequin entering with a dark lanthorn, fastens the covering of the couch over his head, and carries off Columbine.

Pierrot's costume of ruff, jacket and trousers, gradually merged into Jemmy Warner's costume of ruff, jacket and breeches. There was a long struggle whether the trousers should be long or short before they finally became the baggy drawers of a pilferer, but Jack Pudding's love of bright colours was adopted without much hesitation.

The founder—and, in several cases, tutor—of the new school of pantomime was Signor Giuseppe Grimaldi. Some say he was the son of Nicolini Grimaldi, the opera singer, but the name has belonged to many Italians, of high birth and low, and Joseph said his grandfather's Christian names were " John Baptist." Some say he was Queen Charlotte's dentist, because this personage was " Signor Grimaldi, Surgeon Operator for the Teeth of Martlett Court, Bow Street," but not one of the various addresses of the *maître de ballet* coincides with this. His first appearance in London was at Covent Garden as Pantaloon in " Orpheus and Eurydice " to the Harlequin of Rich. How he left this employment is told by Angelo, the fencing master, whom he taught dancing :

> Rich, the manager of Covent Garden Theatre, who was ever ready to catch at anything that was novel, or of pantomimic tendency, listened with rapture to Grimaldi, who proposed an extraordinary new dance : such a singular dance that would astonish and fill the house every night, but it could not be got up without some previous expense, as it was an invention entirely of his own contrivance. There must be no rehearsal, all must be secret before the grand display in, and the exhibition on, the first night.

Rich directly advanced a sum to Grimaldi and waited the result with impatience.   The *maître de ballet* took care to keep up his expectations, so far letting him into the secret that it was to be a dance on horse shoes, that it would surpass anything before seen, and was much superior to all the dancing that was ever seen in pumps.   The newspapers were all puffed for a wonderful performance that was to take place on a certain evening.   The house was crowded, all noise and impatience—no Grimaldi—no excuse ; at last an apology was made.   The grand promoter of this wonderful, unprecedented dance had been absent over six hours, having danced away on four horseshoes to Dover and taken French leave.

In 1758 he was back in London, performing perilous, acrobatic dances at the Haymarket.   If the stories about his life in France have any foundation in fact, he had left the Continent because of a lurid scandal concerning his blood-relationship to the grotesque creature who passed as his wife.   His character, in any case, was remarkable enough.   When engaged at Drury Lane in the October of 1758 he soon established his reputation off as well as on the stage.   Among other exploits, he persuaded a fellow performer to have a face printed on a peculiar part of his frame and to exhibit it privately to Garrick. The story may be untrue, and so may the others told of him ; all the same the pun of " Grim-all-day," a jest when said of his son, held a true word when applied to him.   But his peculiar character was seen in a more attractive light on the stage.   He made his first appearance at Drury Lane in a dance called " The Millers," presented between the first and second acts of " Richard III."   He entered asleep on a ass which was stolen from under him, and he betrayed a joy like that of Sancho at its recovery.   That he was regarded then purely as a dancer is shown in the criticism :

> Grimaldi is a man of great strength and agility.   He indeed treads the air.   If he has any fault, he is rather too comical.

and also in his appointment as *maître de ballet* to Drury Lane, Sadler's Wells and Astley's.[1]   In Garrick's pantomimes he played several parts.   He was Harlequin in " Fortunatus " and in " Robinson Crusoe ; or, Harlequin Friday."   But Pantaloon, which he represented in " Queen Mab," was a character he soon became noted for.   An

[1] At the circus he trained the children.   If any misbehaved he imprisoned them in cages which were drawn up to " the flies."

article written by " The Mouse in the Green Room " in a newspaper of January, 1777, gives this account of an imaginary encounter between him and Garrick's famous scenic artist :

> The Painter and Ballet Master have had a terrible quarrel. Signor de Grimaldi drew his fiddle-stick upon Monsieur de Loutherburg—upon which the last, with a brush of red oaker, gave a diagonal line across Pantaloon's face, which looked as if he had cut his head into two parts—the Frenchman retired and left the Italian with his mouth open, as we have often seen him in a Pantomine. As they are both sprung from great families, it is expected this affair will not end so comically.

He was the clown in several pantomimes. In " Harlequin Junior ; or, the Magic Cestus " (1784), a performance notable for the transformation of the Bank of Paris into a gas balloon, he became, on entering a hothouse, a fine, large watermelon ; in another scene he changed into a goose whose " affected airs in displaying his tail in the peacock style, set the house in roars of laughter." His prowess as a pantomime composer included the invention of the once celebrated skeleton scene and of the Cave of the Petrifaction which struck stiff everyone who entered.

When Signor Grimaldi was appointed to Drury Lane he had already reached an age when the strenuous life of the old pantomimics generally began to tell. Yet his constitution was such that it was not until 1770, when he was nearly sixty, that there were signs of his strength failing. In that year he fulfilled, besides his Drury Lane duties, engagements in three pantomimes, " Harlequin's Adventure by Night," " Cupid's Frolick " and " Imprisonment of Harlequin " at Sadler's Wells. In 1771, however, he gave up his work at the summer theatre, though he danced there in 1782 at the benefit of Signor Placido. He appeared at Drury Lane at Christmas 1785 as Clodpate in " Hurly Burly ; or, the Fairy of the Wells." In 1788 he died at the age of seventy-five, but his fame outlasted him. For several years later, when his son's name was appearing on the bill of Sadler's Wells, Mercerot, Laurent, West and Williamson were advertised by Astley as " the only pupils of the celebrated Signor Grimaldi, and the greatest combination of pantomime talent in town."

Joseph Grimaldi was born on December 18, 1778, in the Parish

GRIMALDI DAY AT BREAKFAST

GIUSEPPE GRIMALDI AND MRS. BROOKER

From a print in the Burney Collection of Theatrical Portraits

of St. Clement's Danes.   He was English by birth.   His mother was Mrs. Brooker.   His real name was Brooker.   In appearance he was decidedly English.   The portrait in the National Portrait Gallery may suggest a " dark and saturnine " Italian face, recalling the story of the depressed patient who, told to go and see Grimaldi, answered, " But I am Grimaldi."   That story, however, was told of Carlin and possibly of others aforetime, and that portrait was painted when the exhaustion that is the fate of most infant prodigies was overcoming him.   In the heyday of his clownship he was another man.   Someone has said of Dr. Johnson that his personality lives because he realised John Bull in the flesh.   But he is only the half of John Bull.   Grimaldi, whom the public loved to see as " a hearty English squire," was the other half.   Apart from coloured prints in the exaggerated manner of the Regency cartoonists, Grimaldi is drawn with a large fat face, round as a full moon, plump as a Dutch cheese, seeming all the rounder and plumper because of his short, muscular body.   His smile began at the corners of his round eyes, set below well-arched eyebrows, in saucers above his fat cheeks ; his mouth when closed was not unduly large, though his lips were full-shaped.   His expression was engagingly frank ; his voice rich and many toned.   Here is the man who acted true-born English Bob Acres to the immense satisfaction of audiences all over the country.   Here is the man who, at Sadler's Wells, appeared as Sir John Bull before an audience inebriated with the glory of being British-born—for this was the time of the Napoleonic wars—and sang to them

> John Bull is my name
> None my spirits can tame,

with other British sentiments such as the virtue of laughing and growing fat.   " His exuberance of animal spirits," it is written, " was really miraculous—what a rich ringing laugh !—the very voice of merriment."   All that was droll in human action he could portray— all the workings of our nature in everyday occurrences.   No one could be at a loss like Grimaldi.   The hopelessness of one who knows not what to do next he hit to a nicety—he always appeared to be " a grown child, waking to perception, but wondering at every object he beheld." He won praise merely on account of his amazement and awe of Harlequin, his amorous glances at Columbine, and his winks at the imbecility of the doting, and the dandyism of the young, lovers. He would stand with his nose screwed on one side, his eyes nearly closed, though twinkling forth his rapture, and his tongue vibrating in his capacious mouth in the very fullness of enjoyment. " His chin too," it was said, " he had a power of lowering, we will not say to what button of his waistcoat, but the drop was an alarming one," and on any sudden surprise he seemed to move his ears by merely drawing down his lower jaw. His legs, with a stride of " four steps across the stage," were described as " eloquent " by a worshipper who exclaimed, " Speech would have been thrown away in his performance of Clown ; every limb of him had a language."

Typically English parts frequently appear in the record of his career. They dominate a list of bewildering variety. Animals, hags, old men, ogres, spirits, heroes, drunkards, gluttons and savages are a few of the creatures he represented. As a tragedian he was likened to Edmund Kean—the only contemporary actor to rival him at the height of his genius—and as a comedian his style resembled Munden's because of " The roll of the eye—the drop of the chin— the elongated respiration." Bearing this in mind it is interesting to recall what Lamb said of Munden :

> Who like him can throw, or ever attempted to throw, a preternatural interest over the commonest daily-life objects ? A table or a joint-stool, in his conception, rises into a dignity equivalent to Cassiopeia's chair. It is invested with constellatory importance. You could not speak of it with more deference, if it were mounted into the firmament. A beggar in the hands of Michael Angelo, says Fuseli, rose the Patriarch of Poverty. So the gusto of Munden antiquates and ennobles what it touches. His pots and ladles are as grand and primal as the seething pots and hooks seen in old prophetic vision. A tub of butter, contemplated by him, amounts to a Platonic idea. He understands a leg of mutton in its quiddity. He stands wondering amid the commonplace materials of life, like primeval man with the sun and stars about him.

That would epitomise all that has been said of Grimaldi were it not for the initial question. But that doubt may be waived while there is no evidence that Lamb saw the clown even in their childhood. His second pantomime was Sheridan's " Robinson Crusoe "—" Crusoe, man Friday, and the parrot, were as good and authentic as in the story "—and he must therefore have seen Signor Giuseppe. But, though the *Memoirs* declare that Joseph " made his first bow and his first tumble " in this piece, the statement cannot be trusted.

Nevertheless, he began his career not long after. " At a very early age—before that of three years—I was introduced to the public by my father at this theatre," he said at Sadler's Wells. Accepting this statement, his first appearance occurred there on the Easter Monday of 1781, when " Master and Miss Grimaldi " were among the dancers. According to the *Memoirs* he had to fulfil engagements " at two theatres on the same evening " during 1782, but this is a fiction of the same type as that in his infancy he fell forty feet without worse injury than a broken collar bone, and that, through the breaking of a chain, he was flung into the pit without any injury at all. Equally uncertain is the story, told on another authority, that in 1790 he was a dancer at the Dog and Duck, a music-hall in St. George's Fields. But there is no doubt that in 1792 he was given the part of a dwarf at Sadler's Wells in " The Savages ; or, Harlequin Wanderer." From this time his name was constantly billed. He played a *sans-culotte* in a spectacle of the French Revolution, Lacquer in a Chinese Pantomime, and Slang in " The Spirit of the Grotto." Then he was given a share in a glee in " Venus's Girdle," and then an opportunity to act in Charles Dibdin's " The Talisman ; or, Harlequin Made Happy." As the Hag Morad, whom magicians discover by moonlight, he had to sing,

Every ill my thoughts employ
And Man's disaster be my joy,

whirl on to the stage in a " necromantic box," intone a long recitative of temptation to Abudah, who replies, " Monster, begone," and repeat the exploit until the genius of Virtue, on the point of changing Abudah into Harlequin, sings him out of the plot with the words, " False hag, away." Already, though no more than seventeen, and still styled Master Grimaldi, he appeared among the first five members of the company. The others were King, manager and Harlequin ; Dibdin,

93

shareholder and Pantaloon; Dubois, a veteran clown of so much importance that when his wife died in the December of 1796 the Drury Lane pantomime was postponed; and the " ever sportive, elegant and flexile Mrs. Wybrow," a Columbine who gave various and scientific displays with the broadsword when she went to the New Royal Circus a year or two later.

Throughout his career Grimaldi's versatility was remarkable, but his range of parts was never wider than in his early years at Islington. In " The Mountain of Miseries; or, Harlequin Tormentor," based on Addison's moral allegory, he was an Old Man in Love. That was at Easter 1797. At Whitsun there was, according to the custom of the Wells, a new programme. Charles Dibdin, returning to " The Tales of the Genii " for the plot, provided " Sadak and Kalasrade; or, the Waters of Oblivion," and the sons of Sadak were " Mr. Grimaldi and Miss Sims," the latter a very handsome brunette who thus anticipated the first principal boy. Before the season ended in the autumn he had appeared as a French prisoner in " Britain's Defenders; or, a Fig for Invasion," also as a Danish chief —who, disguised as a pilgrim, enters and opens the gates of " the manor " where the Saxons are besieged—in " Alfred the Great; or, the Danish Invasion," a historical ballet of action that wound up with a view of the Royal Exchange. In 1798 he appeared in " The Monster of the Cave; or, Harlequin and the Fay," and " Blue Beard, Black Beard, Red Beard and Grey Beard." In 1799, when D'Egville was clown at the Wells, his name was absent from the bills. With the return of Dubois to play Gobble, eating clown, in " Peter Wilkins; or, Harlequin in the Flying World," in the spring of 1800, Grimaldi came back to pantomime as Guzzel, drinking clown, and as Marcus in " Boadicea." In the summer pantomime, " Chaos; or, Harlequin Phaeton," he accompanied Dubois's singing of a mock Italian air, on the salt box mentioned in the verses written in his honour by the Smiths:

> Our gallery gods immortalize thy song;
>   Thy Newgate thefts impart ecstatic pleasure;
> Thou bidst a Jew's harp charm a Christian throng;
>   A Gothic salt-box teem with Attic treasure.

94

Sadler's Wells was offering him full scope for the inherited comic genius he was richly developing.   Each programme of the boisterous holiday house consisted of a burletta, grand spectacle and pantomime, with various songs, dances and feats of strength or agility as well. Though they were prohibited by Act of Parliament from uttering words, this difficulty was easily overcome.   In " The Talisman," for instance, the words of " The Picter Shop "—sung by Robert Dighton who ended in poverty while "The Picter Shop" was becoming a famous Grimaldi song—are followed by " patter " which he " chaunts out."   Grimaldi also practised the art of pantomime tricks.   There is a manuscript in a hand similar to his, hidden in a scrapbook at the British Museum, referring to the changing in " Chaos " of a pot of beer into a woman without a head—described in the announcements as the " comparison between a pot of beer without a head and a good woman "—and offering to transform a post-chaise into a wheelbarrow on the same principle.   The chaise is to be merely a " profile," but when the door opens a piece of hanging canvas is to give the appearance of substantiality.   On entering, Pantaloon is to stand in a wheelbarrow.   When he undoes a brace the upper part of the chaise will be hauled up while the lower sinks through a " cut " in the stage into the " cellar," leaving the wheelbarrow exposed.   This method perhaps explains how a quack's pill was changed into a duck, and a drum into a temple, as the bills proclaimed.

Grimaldi had learned his trade in a good school.   Though the authors of the *Memoirs* may dispute his indebtedness to Dubois, there can be no reasonable doubt that the years he spent with the old clown must have transferred virtue from experience to youth.   In like manner Grimaldi taught others, including Hartland and Bristow, who were of his own generation.   Even Kean, who recited " Rolla's celebrated address from the tragedy of Pizarro " at the Wells when he was " Master Carey, the Pupil of Nature," sat at the feet of Grimaldi ; at least, he is credited with having learned his desperate crawling fight in " Richard III." from the performance given by the clown of eighteen years at Drury Lane.   In " Lodoiska," as in several of the romantic dramas of the Theatre Royal, Grimaldi was one of the chief

95

combatants. When the castle burst into flames he would be fighting desperately on a parapet ; then, rushing amok through the enemy, he would leap over a high balustrade to the stage and encounter fresh foes. He fought, crawling along the ground, in contortions that suggested injuries from the fire. Probably he had learned swordsmanship from Mrs. Wybrow or the Frenchmen who acted " The Four Valiant Brothers " at the Wells in his boyhood. In " St. George the Champion of England " in 1802 he gave with young Bologna " two of the best combats, with Broad Sword, Battle Axe, etc., ever exhibited on the stage." They also fought in " Ko and Zoa ; or, the Belle Savage," the serious piece in the Wells programme of 1803, when Grimaldi played the desperate Ravin who, time after time, tries to seduce or abduct Zoa from Ko. His representation of the Red Indian's death agonies moved a critic to write : " We do not believe the finest tragedian of the day can produce any finer effect or portray a more faithful picture."

Yet at every Clerkenwell performance Grimaldi excelled in clownship as well as tragedy. At the last pantomime of Dubois before he changed his summer engagements by going to Astley's, Grimaldi and Davis joined with him in the celebrated trio of " Royal Reasons for Roast Beef." In " Egyptian Laurels," also in 1801, Grimaldi sang " Dermot O'Dooley's description of Egypt " before playing Alexander to young Bologna's St. George. He was famed for a " comic ditty on Fashionable Transparent Dresses," which a manuscript in his writing (in the possession of Messrs. Maggs of Conduit Street) reveals as the second verse of " A'nt I the pink of the go " :

> You'll own that my style is quite high
>   So transparent my dress you may see through it
> The lady's all wear such and cry
>   Curse you now don't look at me through it
> I wonder what lady's can mean
>   Who in dress so transparent their body's tie.
> I blush like a Maid of Fifteen
>   To see 'em it quite shocks my modesty.

" Dead or Alive ; or Patchwork Pranks " in " Goody Two Shoes ; or, Harlequin Alabaster " was another of his popular songs at this time.

96

His dances were equally renowned, especially his " comic dance with Nobody, Somebody, and Everybody." He began the vogue of the burlesques of ballerine—to become the speciality of Wieland and Flexmore.

Among the many parts he played in 1803 was Rufo the Robber in the burletta of " Red Riding Hood," supplying comic relief to a wolf much given to singing patriotic songs (in one case disguised as a British tar with a wooden leg). In " Jack the Giant Killer " he was dwarf to the giant Comoran—Belzoni, the " Patagonian Sampson," six feet seven inches in height and capable of supporting eleven persons on an apparatus fixed round his waist. In " Wizard's Wake ; or, Harlequin's Regeneration," he was first Sir John Bull, who fights Citoyen Françoise at the Gates of Calais, and then an intoxicated clown with song, " Flower of Brimstone." Some of the parts he played in the years following deserve mention. In " New Brooms " he was again Sir John Bull. In the serio-comic pantomime of " Philip Quarl ; or, the English Hermit," he took the name part and protected a damsel in distress from blacks and pirates. In the grand military pantomime spectacle of " The Old Man of the Mountains ; or, A Tale of the Eleventh Century," he was Gorthmand the Cruel, who kills Jews, Christians and Turks because he has " No religion at all "—an echo, this, of the inscription Signor Grimaldi chalked on his door during the anti-popery riots. He intends to marry the heroine and sacrifice her lover in a cauldron of fire, but when Richard Coeur-de-Lion and Saladin storm his castle he jumps into the cauldron himself.

Likewise, at Drury Lane Grimaldi was many things besides the Clown. In the ballet of " Robinson Crusoe," staged in the autumn of 1800, he " discovered great cleverness " in the name part ; in the dramatic spectacle of " Blue Beard " his swordsmanship was the chief attraction ; in " A Bold Stroke for a Wife " he played Aminadab. But he did not enjoy here the fervent worship of Clerkenwell. Drury Lane was not suitable for the pantomime of the Regency type. " Magic quickness and variety," then regarded as essential, were incompatible with a stage so vast. Pantomime failed frequently and was replaced by spectacles which smothered clownship. Grimaldi's song in " Cinderella " (1804), for instance, was deemed by a critic to be of " too base a metal," although it was a merry jingle based on the (then) creditable pun of glass slippers and cracked understandings. His reputation was established, but not too securely.   There was a dispute over the terms of his agreement, and in the autumn of 1805 he left the theatre.   Thomas Dibdin found him looking for a job and induced Covent Garden to engage the best clown ever seen on the stage.   " When I say the best," comments Dibdin, " I do not except his father, whose *vis comica* I perfectly well remember."

There were several reasons for his spectacular success at Covent Garden.   That theatre, for one thing, was admirably suited to pantomime.   Moreover, it had, in Thomas Dibdin, a brain accustomed to what he dubbed " the everlasting dream of traps, flaps, daggers of lath and parti-coloured jackets."   It also had in Farley—who began his career at Covent Garden in 1782 as a call-boy of eleven years—a master of the art of acting in dumb-show.   It had the services of the younger Bolognas to take the place of Pietro Bologna, who had, with Dubois, come to the end of his tether the year before.   It also badly needed a clown, since the day of the school of Signor Grimaldi was almost done.   Joseph alone could step into the shoes of Dubois, for he had learned all the old man had to teach.   He straightway took up the part of the bear-suckled hero of " Valentine and Orson " that his old master had made famous and in his " eloquence of gesture " surpassed the original.   Orson was his most difficult part according to the *Memoirs*, and between the acts he would " sob and cry aloud " through his sufferings from " violent and agonizing spasms."   This story, however, probably belongs to his repetitions of the part several years later.

That Christmas Thomas Dibdin and Farley were allowed to try an experiment in Grimaldi's favour.   Instead of the topographical splendour of former years, a piece without any finery was to be exhibited.   It was " Harlequin and Mother Goose ; or, the Golden Egg."   Grimaldi's part was Squire Bugle, " a rich widower of repulsive manners," who attempts to steal Colinette from the arms of Colin. But his scheme is foiled by Mother Goose, whom he had condemned

98

to the ducking-stool.   In revenge she raises the ghost of his first wife, and gives to Colin the goose that lays the golden eggs.   Colinette's avaricious father, however, will not agree to the marriage of the young lovers unless the bird is cut open.   Colin consents, Mother Goose appears, and all the characters are changed into the creatures of the Harlequinade.   Grimaldi is caught gloating at the sight of a meal by Harlequin, who sends the table into " the flies."   Clown, in conster-nation, walks underneath and around where it stood, looks up and sees it, gives a shout of surprise, seats himself when it descends, only to find himself rising with it, chair and all.   After Pantaloon has been simi-larly sent aloft, Harlequin dines with Columbine.   While the servants are cutting down Pantaloon, Clown pelts them with plates.   Panta-loon cuts a pie ; out walks a duck ; Clown makes off with it.   They enter a farmyard and are chased out by the bees.   They throw a basket over a postman ; a blackamoor's head comes out ; Clown hits it with a board ; the board breaks in two ; they disguise themselves as Pandean Minstrels and gain admission to Vauxhall Gardens. Meanwhile the chase of the lovers has been continuing—at one point they escape by substituting themselves for the figures striking the chimes of St. Dunstan's, Fleet Street—until Mother Goose changes them all back to their original shapes, and, while a submarine palace is being " set," makes a speech with a line for Grimaldi's benefit :

> You soon restored to person house and lands
> Shall like a hearty English squire shake hands.

There is no need to read between the lines to discover that the virtue of " Mother Goose " was Grimaldi pure and simple.   His " hearty English " humour in pocketing a duck or in the way he put on a cocked hat, made his managers a fortune of £20,000—" more rather than less," says Dibdin.

From the golden egg of the magic goose the Clown was hatched. Grimaldi's career until this Christmas of 1805 may be regarded as the novitiate of his Saturnalian priesthood.   Once he had been accepted as the supreme clown he could concentrate his genius on elaborating the portrait of mankind reversed.   All the types of clowns met in him. By him, as by Falstaff, minds were entirely relieved from the intolerable tyranny of emotion, and made the discovery that morality is an arbitrary thing. In all the praise of Grimaldi the same impulse is discoverable. " If," said W. J. Thoms (of *Notes and Queries* fame),

> If his drollery had at times a smack of vulgarity, a breadth of colouring, the smallest spice, as it were, of that ruder mirth in which our grandfathers delighted, he did so varnish it over with his irresistible humour, that the veriest prude looked on and laughed, without once dreaming it essential to hide her enjoyment behind her fan.

The critics were roused by the realisation that sins are bloodless and sinners flesh and blood. What, they say in effect, are principles worth compared with human souls ? The laws of property melt in the warmth of our love for Clown ; cowardice is a mere physical fact, to be dispassionately regarded, not despised ; annoying habits, even amounting to a love of physical violence, are not to be resented when springing from excess of the joy of life ; and so forth. Not, of course, observations of much use in running the world. But clownship is not workaday. What are holidays for if not to give a broader, more genial, more human, view of the infernal struggle for existence ?

There is no virtue that could not be found in the everyday Grimaldi. He was almost unbelievably modest—he spoke of theatre managers as his kind masters—though he revelled in the love of his audiences. He was forgiving unto seventy times seven, and brave amid continual tribulation. He was earnest and sincere ; sympathetically credulous ; full of homely sense and sentimentality, flavoured with a smack of homely sententiousness which comes out in all his writings, but particularly in his notebook of *Toasts and Sentiments* (dated 1807), where he writes :

> May our conscience be sound, tho' our fortune be rotten.
> The harvest of life ; Love, wit and good humour.
> May the Lovers of a glass never want a Bottle.

and as simple-hearted a man as ever breathed. On the stage, however, he possessed every vice imaginable. He was " a thief, a coward—a most detestable coward, cruel, treacherous, unmanly, ungenerous, greedy, and the truth was not in him." As for flattery, noble lords were told not to quarrel for superiority in this respect, for " Joe Grimaldi could outglose them all." He delighted in beating the watch and

100

in playing pranks upon his master. He hypocritically feigned con-
dolence for the very misfortunes he had caused. He thieved with
" delicious sang-froid." After a self-approving chuckle he would
give a contemptuous look, half pity, half derision at his dupe, and
then show great caution to escape discovery. He was

> the very *beau ideal* of thieves—robbery became a science in his hands—you
> forgave the larceny, for the humour with which it was perpetrated. He
> abstracted a leg of mutton from a butcher's tray, with such a delightful
> assumption of *nonchalance*—he threw such plump stupidity into his coun-
> tenance, whilst the slyness of observation lurked in his half-closed eyes—he
> extracted a watch, or a handkerchief, with such a bewitching eagerness—with
> such a devotion to his task—and yet kept his wary eye upon the victim of
> his trickery—he seemed so imbued with the spirit of peculation, that you
> saw it in him, merely as a portion of his nature, and for which he was neither
> blameable nor accountable.

His audiences were forced to doubt whether honesty were not a kind
of prejudice. If he took up a red-hot poker to anybody " we never
could interfere though it were to save our own father." For all his
sins, multiplied up to murder, the children

> loved him, yearned for him, wanted to share in his doings ; felt a little volcano
> raging within us whilst he was perpetrating his atrocities. " He'll be found
> out ! " and we clasped our tiny hands till the nails cut into the palms ; no,
> he's safe, and away goes the monstrous booty into that leviathan pocket of
> his, that receptacle of all sorts of edibles, and occasionally of kettles full of
> boiling water, and even lighted candles.

But when he was found out there was equal delight in his ludicrous
agony during the beatings duly given him by all the pantomime personages in turn. He was deemed the most assiduous of all buffoons
because of the rough trials he submitted his head and hide to. Serious
tumbles from serious heights, innumerable kicks and incessant beatings, were a matter of frequent occurrence, but seemed, to his audience, to leave him every night " fresh and free for the next night's
flagellation."

Fortunately some of his sufferings were purely mimic. There
was a scene in a glass factory, in particular. While he is learning the
art of blowing, two red hot globes come out of the mouthpiece of the
tube and fasten one on each cheek to his great terror. He recovers

and renews the pursuit of Harlequin, who jumps into the furnace, where the genius of fire protects him, but Clown who follows him is set alight and makes a great fuss before the blaze is put out. Another of his tricks was staged among the housetops, where he sings, to the accompaniment of cats, of his love for Molly Milestone, until he grows so warm that his room is set on fire. He also had an amusing way of trying to put out a blaze he had started himself.

Because of his " practical satire " he won the title of " Hogarth in action." Whether he had to rob a pieman, open an oyster, imitate a chimney sweep or a dandy, grasp a red-hot poker, devour a pudding, take snuff, sneeze, make love, mimic a tragedian, cheat his master, pick a pocket, beat a watchman or nurse a child, his " extravagantly natural " manner moved spectators of " the most saturnine diposition " to laughter. When he begged a tart, his simple " May I ? " caused one spectator to declare the look and action to be one of the finest pieces of acting he had ever seen. In " drag parts " his way of wearing skirts was commended, particularly Moll Flagon with her cutty and bottle in General Burgoyne's " Lord of the Manor," and his " Jeudy, or Punch's Wife " in " Harlequin and Asmodeus." Even during the O.P. riots at Covent Garden, when no actor could be heard, his dumb show performance of Scaramouche in " Don Juan " was un-interrupted. Practically the only pronounced failure of a piece which had his aid was " The Marquis de Carabas, or Puss in Boots " in the spring of 1818. With Grimaldi hiding his light under the disguise of a Tom Cat, the shortcomings of the play so annoyed the audience that they pulled up seats, flung missiles at the lamps, and tore the curtains until the manager promised its immediate withdrawal.

There was " an infinite variety " in his love-making, from his mincing gaiety when addressing a dandizette to his boisterous freedom with a fishwoman. If he only drew a cork it was, said a critic, " the commentary upon the face of someone of our acquaintance; if he took physic, the moment he poured it out we knew it was salts." He cari-catured ballerine and jugglers, especially the Indian sword-swallowers, whom he imitated with a blade of immense size. His fun with oysters was proverbial. Besides a duet with an enormous specimen

102

supposed to have been " crossed in love," he held a minor Colchester feast. The first he opened made a complaining noise. " Ah, poor thing," he said, " I'll put you out of your misery," and swallowed it. When the second made a similar appeal to his humanity, he gulped it and remarked, " Well, I can't make fish of one and flesh of t'other." Gluttony was among his most esteemed vices. One of his parts was Munchkow, who could eat and drink more than wicked fairies thought possible. He would swallow a tray of tarts at a gulp and great quantities of carrots and turnips. His stupidity, too, took remarkable forms. In " Harlequin in his Element ; or, Fire, Water, Earth and Air," which followed " Mother Goose " at Covent Garden, Grimaldi was sent out with a drink for the watchman. Clown, finding him asleep, drinks it himself. For a drunken frolic he strips off the constable's hat and coat and dons them himself. Then he returns to the bottle. But he cannot get the neck to his lips, even by using one hand to hold his mouth open. A happy thought inspires him to hold the watchman's lantern by his cheek, and so he " effects his wished-for purpose." Shutting the watchman in his box he parades the street, arousing everybody with his rattle, until the watchman comes out, " transformed into an old woman," and knocks him down.

As pantomime at the theatres in town was merely an afterpiece, contemned among the hypocritical as intended for nurserymaids and children, Grimaldi was not sought out as Hazlitt sought out Kean. Yet his portrait is to be found in the works of the essayists of the Renaissance of Wonder. Though his name is not mentioned by them, he is described in detail by Leigh Hunt. In his essay on pantomime he mentions that the pursuers of Harlequin took the steam coach. The idea was tried in " Harlequin and Friar Bacon ; or, the Brazen Head " at Covent Garden in 1820, when Grimaldi engineered its explosion. Here is a reason for believing Leigh Hunt's Clown to be Grimaldi. The other reason is the obvious resemblance :

> He, the cunning rogue, who has been watching mid-way, and now sees the coast clear, enters in front,—round faced, goggle-eyed, knock-kneed but agile to a degree of the dislocated, with a great smear for his mouth, and a cap on his head, half fool's and half cook's. Commend him to the dinner that he sees on table, and that was laid for Harlequin and his mistress.

Merry be their hearts : there is a time for all things ; and while they dance through a dozen inns to their hearts' content, he will eat a Sussex dumpling or so. Down he sits, contriving a luxurious seat, and inviting himself with as many ceremonies as if he had the whole day before him : but when he once begins, he seems as if he had not a moment to lose. The dumpling vanishes at a cram ;—the sausages are abolished ;—down go a dozen yards of macaroni : and he is in the act of paying his duties to a gallon of rum, when in come Pantaloon and his servant at opposite doors, both in search of the glutton, both furious and both resolved to pounce on the rascal head-long. They rush forward accordingly ; he slips from between them with a " Hallo, I say " ; and the two poor devils dash their heads against one another, like rams. They rebound fainting asunder to the stage-doors ; while the Clown, laughing with all his shoulders, nods a health to each, and finishes his draught. He then holds a great cask of a snuff-box to each of their noses, to bring them to ; and while they are sneezing and tearing their souls out, jogs off at his leisure.

So far Grimaldi has been shown as the clown, in excelsis, of convention. His peculiar genius, however, is revealed in the invention of what was, to all intents and purposes, a new joke. It may be given the name of " construction." In one way it resembles the joke of mimicry, and relies on the curiosity that tempts passers-by to linger round any work-man with a job in the street. On the other hand the emotion aroused by the making of any object, be it a tower of toy bricks or an epic, is wonder merging into joy and worthy of a category of its own. Like all emotion, it is carried by sympathy from the mind where it generates to the minds of bystanders. Grimaldi developed the new joke along the lines of the old-fashioned pantomime " trick " of transformation. He was adept in such contrivances. He had ingenuity to produce some new thing but did not despise the old. That Italian device of a dismembered body which is joined together and revives was tried by him in a scene where Harlequin was chopped up in a cauldron, nailed limb by limb against the wall, and restored to life. Similarly, his transformation of butts, pots and barrels in an alehouse garden into soldiers, which he reviewed mounted on a barrel and clad in sauce-pan lids and dish cover, was merely a humorous adaptation of the magic of the early eighteenth century. He had, however, more elaborate effects than these. In a shopping scene, he stole the beadle's hat, a milliner's box, a salmon's head, and a pair of boots, and made an effigy

GRIMALDI's Bold Dragoon *in the Popular Pantomime of the Red Dwarf*

Drawn & Etched by W. Heath GRIMALDI's TANDEM *in the Comic Pantomime of the Golden Fish*

GRIMALDI'S JOKES OF CONSTRUCTION

From prints in the Author's Collection

of them in delight—until scared to see it come to life at a wave of Harlequin's wand. In " Mother Goose " he stood a broom upright so that the bristles were level with his mouth, fixed a tin bath to the pole, grasped a brush and a wooden ladle—and was a one-man band. Another time he clothed the corpse of Pantaloon in a bearskin, a swan's feathers, an ass's head, and brought the strange beast to life. Or he would force a mop-stick through a cheese, place the ends in the hands of Pantaloon lying prone, pile cheeses on his back, and wheel him off by the ankles as a wheelbarrow. Still the idea developed. When peace was flaunting flamboyant uniforms through the town he burlesqued the uniform of the Hussars, though a row of genuine officers," covered *de cap à pied* with chains and cat skins," was occupying the stage box. A newspaper critic describes the performance :

> The scene changed to a street, with a furrier's shop beside a blacksmith's. A Hussar officer, in all the extravagant and foolish finery of the corps, passed thundering by. The spirit of imitation instantly took possession of the clown, and, not unwisely, judging that the secret lay in the dress, he determined to be a hero and a Hussar in his own person. A pair of red pantaloons, which he put on before the audience with the happiest display of blushing modesty, was the only thing which he condescended to borrow of his model : two black varnished coal-scuttles formed his boots, two real horse-shoes shod the heels, and with jack-chains and the help of large brass dishes or candlesticks for spurs, equipped his legs in an uniform almost as clattering, unwieldy and absurd as the most irresistible of our whiskered propugnatores. A white bear skin formed his pelisse, a muff his cap, and a black tippet finished his toilet, by giving him a beard, whiskers and pendent moustaches.

Rough treatment of the Army was not always tolerated, as Grimaldi found when he changed a lobster into a soldier by boiling. All his " constructive " jokes, however, were irresistible. This principle also inspired a serenade :

> See how he stands looking at the window, at which hangs a bonnet ; his back is toward you ; but it tells the tale—the lady within is to be won. Look how he bends towards the balcony—Romeo in red and white : see how mincingly he puts forth his foot, and passes his hand over his garments ; he must woo in another shape ; he turns round in utter bewilderment ; anon a boy passes—he plays at marbles with him, first for money, then for his jacket ; he wins it, a dandy passes—he abstracts his coat tails ; a miller—he steals a sack : he has stolen yonder chimney pot, and made a hat ; taken that dandizette's shawl, and converted it into a waistcoat ; the sack becomes

white ducks ; the tails render the jacket a coat ; a cellar-door iron ring forms an eye-glass ; and he moves, an admirable caricature of the prevailing fashion of the day.

When the " straw ridicule " was the fashionable " embellishment of a lady's hands " he travested the vogue by changing a working woman into a dandizette, with a cabbage net for veil, a horse-mushroom for parasol, a fruit basket for bonnet, and a rush-pannier for the ridicule. He formed a panharmonicon, which brayed horrible discord, out of a bird organ and a few Bartholomew-fair trumpets ; also a carriage with Cheshire cheeses for wheels, a coal-scuttle for the body and a broom for the axle-tree. " But what use is it," asked an admirer, " to mention these things ? It was the style in which he joined and sub-joined them—looked, studied—(what a brown study was his !)—and then rushed, in triumphant joy, when a new idea flashed over the extent of his countenance." When *The Mirror* after his retire-ment, published some verses [1] called " Joseph's Lament," these tricks were among those he sighed to repeat :

> Ne'er shall I build the wondrous verdant man,
>   Tall, turnip headed,—carrot-fingered, lean ;
> Ne'er shall I, on the very newest plan,
>   Cabbage a body ;—old Joe Frankenstein.
> Nor make a fire, nor eke compose a Coach,
>   Of saucepans, trumpets, cheese, and such sweet fare.
> Sorrow hath ta'en my Number ; I encroach
>   No more upon the chariot, but the chair,
> Gone is the stride, four steps, across the stage !
>   Gone is the light vault o'er a turnpike gate !
> Sloth puts my legs into his tiresome cage,
>   And stops me for a toll,—I find, too late !
> How Ware would quiver his mad bow about
>   His rosin'd tight Ropes,—when I stopped a dance :
> How would I trick the Pantaloon's good gout
>   And help his fall—and all his fears enhance.

Every species of trouble, from petty annoyance to tragedy, was Grimaldi's fate. His hobbies—fly-collecting or pigeon-breeding—

---

[1] Possibly they were his own, as he had a fondness for rhyming. Messrs. Maggs of Conduit Street still possess a MS. copy of the verses in his hand which may be regarded as evidence of this.

were spoilt by burglars or some such interference. His love was thwarted by the death of his first wife soon after their marriage and the wildness of his only son. Nor was clownship always his consolation. " Shabbying " was tried even at the Wells to divorce his public from their allegiance. The money he made was soon lost, and after he had taken a share in the Clerkenwell house in lieu of part of his salary the profits turned to a loss. This occurred in 1821 when his health first began to fail. Four years later it broke beyond hope of recovery. That occurred in 1825, when he was forty-seven, and his son, J. S. Grimaldi, had just begun a career so full of promise as to make his father think the premature old age that was upon him not too devoid of hope. His own zeal and the exorbitant demands of clownship had given him no chance to recover. Yet why had he not dispensed with the dancing, falling, leaping and somersaulting ? He had but to show his face to make laughter. His introductory " How are you ? " was irresistible. His power over the audience was a spell. In 1807, while he was playing truant, his place at the Wells was taken by Bradbury, a clown who wore nine pads—one on the head, one round the shoulders, one round the hips, two on the elbows, two on the knees, and two on the heels of his shoes—in order to throw himself about like one possessed. When Grimaldi came back Bradbury was about to receive his benefit. Far from bearing any ill will Grimaldi agreed to appear. Directly he " poked his nose on at the wing " a noise like the roar of artillery sounded through the house. When the curtain fell Bradbury led him to the lamps and made his farewell bow for that season. The rush to see Grimaldi grew year by year ; in fact, at the opening performance at Easter 1818 the crowd was so eager that the foremost in the gallery were forced over the balustrade into the pit, and a youth who fell was trampled to death. In the midst of the uproar Grimaldi came before the curtain and there was quiet. In spite of aquatic spectacles representing the naval exploits of the time, and many other spectacular effects, his personality was the most impressive part of the show. Imagine, say, the Easter of 1809. The programme has many marvels to gape at, but in " Fashion's Fools ; or, the Aquatic Harlequin " there is to be a new song called Odd Fish. Feet apart, knees together, he stands before them like a human scirtopod about to leap. Then he croaks :

> Your mirth to increase I've a wish,
>   And you'll own my endeavour 'tis daily,
> So I'll sing you a song of odd fish,
>   If you won't think the subject is scaly.
> Town's full of sweet souls and sour crabs,
>   And enough fools to flounder in reason,
> And as Billinsgate beauties are dabs,
>   That's a pretty place in the sprat season.

There are yells and screams and shouts of laughter while the chorus of " Tolderol," etc., is taken up. Verse follows verse. At the end, before the chorus opens, Grimaldi's face grows even more confidential. He motions for silence and begins :

> Mr. Muggins was the man to give it mouth over a marrow pudding, and travel thro' two yards and a half of rump steak and oyster sauce ; he was a man of true taste, and died of a parish dinner. " Doctor," says he, " I'm very bad." " What's the matter, Mr. Muggins ? " " My old complaint, a tightness across the chest." " Open your mouth. O, I see plain enough." " What do you see, Doctor ? " " Only the leg of a turkey with a skewer stuck in it. Here, Molly, bring me the tongs, and I'll pull it out while I sing Tolderol, etc."

Before you exclaim " What nonsense ! " have the goodness to read the pantomime songs of last Christmas. The verses you smiled over then are far more puerile ; and the songs you enjoyed in 1890 are far, far worse than anything Grimaldi sang. Nor must what he added be forgotten. He took several days to mellow himself, as he called it, into a song. On most occasions, at Sadler's Wells, it was his practice to bring on the stage a large sheet, and, to use his own phrase to the audience, " Ax their leave to sing it to paper." This quaintness, which told well at Islington, he however never attempted at Covent Garden, though the comic inanity of expression with which he delivered it was inimitably effective. Some of his famous songs were heard at Covent Garden, including

> London now is out of town,
>   Who in England tarries ?
> Who can bear to linger here,
>   When all the world's in Paris ?

J. GRIMALDI

Song in Character – "All the world's in Paris".

GRIMALDI IN "HARLEQUIN WHITTINGTON"

From a print after George Cruikshank in the Author's Collection

which he was singing in " Harlequin Whittington " while Napoleon was planning to escape from Elba.   But the Wells was the place for songs.   Here they were billed as prominently as himself.   There were, besides " Tippetywichet " and " Hot Codlins," his musical description of the clown's bazaar, " Looney's Lamentation for Miss Margery Muggins," " Thinks I to Myself," " Me and My Neddy," and " London cheats ; or there never was such a time," also the famous ballad of the madman who stole the Monument and, when in danger of arrest, swallowed it at a gulp, put Aldgate pump in his hat, Gog and Magog in his pocket, the clock of St. Paul's on his watch-chain, and the cupola on his fob ; then spat out the Monument at the constable and escaped.   Grimaldi also had an astrologer's song :

> " For here you've twins by Gemini."
> " By Jem and you," says she, " Oh fie,
>   I ha'nt got no such thing, sir."

But most famous of all was " Hot Codlins," originally sung by Grimaldi as a Talking Bird.   Its lasting popularity entitles it to be placed among the most famous songs of our country if not of the world.   Considering how persistently the gallery called for it during over half a century of pantomimes, we can but faintly imagine how strong was the enthusiasm in its youth.   Here we have only the words and not the Grimaldi tradition to help us to understand :

> A little old woman her living she got
> By selling hot codlins, hot, hot, hot ;
> And this little woman, who codlins sold,
> Tho' her codlins were hot, she felt herself cold.
> So, to keep herself warm, she thought it no sin,
> To fetch for herself a quartern of——

(Here the gallery shouted " Gin."   Joey exclaimed " Oh, for shame," and went on with the chorus, " Ri tol iddy, iddy, iddy, iddy, Ri tol iddy, iddy, ri rol lay.")

> This little old woman set off in a trot,
> To fetch her a quartern of hot ! hot ! hot !
> She swallow'd one glass, and it was so nice,
> She tipp'd off another in a trice ;
> The glass she fill'd till the bottle shrunk,
> And this little old woman they say got—Ri tol, etc.

This little old woman, while muzzy she got,
Some boys stole her codlins hot ! hot ! hot !
Powder under her pan put, and in it round stones :
Says the little old woman, " These apples have bones ! "
The powder the pan in her face did send,
Which sent the old woman on the latter—Ri tol, etc.

The little old woman then up she got,
All in a fury, hot ! hot ! hot !
Says she, " Such boys, sure, never were known ;
They never will let an old woman alone."
Now here is a moral, round let it buz—
If you mean to sell codlins, never get—Ri tol, etc.

" The strength of Grimaldi, the Garrick of clowns, seems like that of wine, to increase with age ; his absurdities are admirable," wrote Theodore Hook. His performance in " Harlequin Gulliver," when he was thirty-eight, was judged to be his masterpiece by Thoms. Cruikshank gives us an idea of the Brobdingnagians in an illustration to the *Memoirs*. One such was the Princess Glumdulditch, who was wheeled on in a go-cart, with Grimaldi as her doll.

Then, again, there was the gigantic canary, which Grimaldi pronounced, in his unctuous voice, to be a " Casso-wa-ry," and with which he sang the duet beginning,
"Say, little, foolish, fluttering thing,
If you're a cock bird, why not sing ? "
he being all the time quietly seated on a Brobdingnagian quartern loaf, into which he might have eaten his way like a mouse into a cheese.

Then who but Cruikshank could paint the inconvenience poor Joe endured from the bayonets of the Lilliputian soldiery as they marched through the palace gate which he was bestriding ? or show how, when the King of Lilliput's palace was in flames, he plied the Lilliputian engines, and extinguished the fire in a way which would have delighted Swift ?

At forty Grimaldi was ageing. At Covent Garden he was still playing serious parts—such as the slave of a Greek captain in " The Children of Cyprus "—but he would not abandon acrobatics. To the last he struggled to continue to inspire Clown with a dynamic fury of violence. A journal commenting on the number of clowns who were veritable tumblers at this time puts a qualifying " perhaps " before the name of Grimaldi. There is a tragedy in that word. Men waited in the wings to catch him as he staggered from the stage and

110

chafe his limbs. " Every time he came off," state the authors of his *Memoirs*,

> his sinews were gathered up into huge knots by the cramps that followed his exertions, which could only be reduced by violent rubbing, and even that frequently failed to produce the desired effect.

When " Harlequin and Poor Robin ; or, the House that Jack Built " was produced at Covent Garden on the Boxing Day of 1823, J. S. Grimaldi was the Clown, and Joseph sat on the wrong side of the curtain. That was practically the end of the stage career of one who could produce the strongest effects by minute touches of quiet humour, yet could not keep a reserve ounce of mental or physical energy out of the fray. His connection with the stage, however, did not end at once. Being given the post of assistant manager to Thomas Dibdin at Sadler's Wells—now ceasing to be the summer theatre and keeping open all the year round—he was at hand to give a characteristic touch to the Harlequinades. Thus, in " Merlin's Mount ; or, Harlequin Cymraeg and the Living Leek " in 1825, a chest of glass, a bull's head, a barber's cue and a powder puff, with a chair and umbrella, were transformed into an elephant, with Pantaloon seated on his back under a canopy.

His ardent passion for his art had invested clownship with the rites and secrets of a religion. It had practices of its own and a language of its own. It had dignity. If his son had proved worthy of the trust it might still be a great English tradition. But, though Joseph passed on to him the Saturnalian regalia, the boy could only see the sceptre as a red-hot poker, the orb a sheep's heart and the crown a tuft of blue wool. There was " much to approve and nothing to find fault with "—unless it were a " propensity to be coarse and indelicate "—in the performance of one who promised " to be as excellent a clown as his father." He had learned a great deal, but not the love of his art. Being a handsome young man he was a favourite in the melodramas, and like Joseph was renowned in combats such as the fight for the standard in " The Pacha ; or, the Hero of Choumla." But his success was too easily won. He had been carried on his father's shoulders, and the position was comfortable. When his benefit was given in the autumn of 1826 he induced the old man—though now so infirm that if he had any aptitude for tumbling it was " through bodily infirmity, for I am worse on my feet than I used to be on my head "—to appear. Thomas Dibdin introduced a special scene into Planché's " The Caliph and the Cadi ; or, Rambles in Bagdad," and Joseph sang " Hot Codlins " once more. The boy's way was as clear as his father's had been at the time of " Mother Goose." Good clowns were growing old and new clowns were bad. Williams of Sadler's Wells had so little respect for the great traditions of motley that, on receiving an encore for his song, he responded with

> The cat's in the cupboard, the meat's on the shelf,
> If you want any more you may sing it yourself.

Upon which Grimaldi's admirers hissed him, and a critic wrote, " If this Mr. Williams is a lunatic, he had better be locked up—if sane he should be discharged." But instead of seizing his chance, and repaying his father for the glory he had inherited, J. S. Grimaldi drank himself into a state of lunacy. Joseph had to look elsewhere for gratitude. Being sadly in want—his wife had had to look for work in the chorus at Covent Garden—he asked for a farewell benefit at Sadler's Wells. It was arranged for March 17, 1828. A friend who called at his house in Exmouth Street in the afternoon found him in bed in a state of utter weakness. All he could say was " I'll play to-night if it cost me my life," before he burst into tears. He arrived at Sadler's Wells punctually at seven o'clock with his doctor. Thomas Dibdin explained the state of his health to the audience, and their friendliness again made him cry. His weary old legs trod for the last time the boards where his weary infant legs had danced. He acted, in " Sixes, or the Fiend," his famous part of Hock, a German soldier who, being shut up in a prison, finds plenty of consolation in a flask of wine. After the final performance—" the celebrated dance between Mr. J. S. Grimaldi and Mr. Ellar "—Joseph, dressed in black, with white waistcoat and gloves, told his audience, " I have no hope left that I shall ever again be able to appear before you," and thanked the managers, whereupon a voice cried, " They ought to give you a pension for life." He became dangerously ill as soon as he had left them.

112

There is no need to repeat the story of Covent Garden's refusal to grant him a benefit, or of the offer of Price, lessee of Drury Lane, to " oblige so distinguished a veteran." But Hood's account, not in the *Memoirs,* of how Joey asked him to write his farewell speech must be given here :

> Slowly and seriously as my visitor advanced, and with a decided stoop, I could not forget that I had seen the same personage come in with two odd eyebrows, a pair of right-and-left eyes, a wry nose, a crooked mouth, two wrong arms, two left legs, and a free and easy body without a bone in it, or apparently any centre of gravity. I was half prepared to hear that rare voice break forth smart as the smack of a waggoner's whip, or richly thick and chuckling, like the utterance of a boy laughing, talking and eating custard, all at once ; but a short interval sufficed to dispel the pleasant illusion, and convinced me that Grimaldi was a total wreck.
>
> > Alas ! how changed from him
> > The life of humour and the soul of whim.
>
> The lustre of his bright eyes was gone—his eloquent face was passive and looked thrown out of work—and his frame was bowed down by no feigned decrepitude. His melancholy errand related to a Farewell Address, which at the invitation of his staunch friend Miss Kelly—for it did not require a request—I had undertaken to indite. He pleaded earnestly, that it might be brief, being, he said, " a bad study," as well as distrustful of his bodily strength. Of his suffering he spoke with a sad but resigned tone, expressed deep regret at quitting a profession he delighted in, and partly attributed the sudden breaking down of his health to the superior size of one particular stage which required of him a jump extra in getting off. That additional bound, like the bittock at the end of a Scotch mile, had, he thought, over-tasked his strength. His whole deportment and conversation impressed me with the opinion that he was a simple, sensible, warm-hearted being, such indeed as he appears in his Memoirs—a Joseph after Parson Adam's own heart. We shook hands heartily, parted, and I never saw him again.

Of course, Drury Lane was crowded. The programme included a selection of popular scenes from the most approved pantomimes. Grimaldi played in the barber's shop from " Magic Fire," which was introduced as a scene in a pantomime enlargement of Dibdin's skit, " Harlequin Hoax." He was unable to stand for long ; a chair was brought, and he " sang that comic song about blue ruin and hot cod-lins." Then he recited Hood's excellent speech :

> It is four years since I jumped my last jump—filched my last oyster—boiled my last sausage—and set in for retirement. Not quite so well pro-

vided for, I must acknowledge, as in the days of my clownship, for then, I dare say, some of you remember, I used to have a fowl in one pocket and sauce for it in the other. To-night has seen me assume the motley for a short time—it clung to my skin as I took it off, and the old cap and bells rang mournfully as I quitted them for ever.

He wished his audience " that greatest earthly good—health," and they, too, never saw him again.

Sadly he lingered. There was little joy for a man, broken in middle life, watching his son rush to ruin. All the comfort in life was in the sacred grounds of the Wells, the land of The Grimaldi Coach and The Clown's Head tavern. He would wander up and down beside the tall poplars and the narrow river, stopping to mark with vacant eye the luck of anglers who, year by year, paid less attention to the old man. But Clerkenwell was not to him the crowded stacks of bricks and mortar the building fever had turned it into with the quickness of a pantomime trick. His mind lived in the days of the fields where his pigeons flew, the fields where he caught his flies, the fields where he wooed the adorable Miss Hughes.

Rapidly weakness overcame him. Very soon he was unable to carry out his duties as assistant manager, and in 1832 had to leave the delectable land. For the sake of cheapness he took a country cottage far away in Prospect Row, Woolwich, though he still retained his share in the theatre. (He held it to the time of his death, as the licensing papers of Clerkenwell Sessions-house show.) There was now only one thought in his mind. He wanted to save his son. In " Bunn on the Stage " there is a long letter offering that manager " as many models and tricks as would furnish six or seven pantomimes without fee or reward, provided an arrangement can be made for my son." How vain those efforts were we all know, but the story of Grimaldi's tragedy is not yet so old that we can read unmoved :

Your kind offer to me to superintend the forthcoming pantomime (however gratifying to my feelings) I shall never forget, but must decline. I could no more sit in an armchair to instruct a pantomime, than I am capable of jumping out of a garret window without injuring myself—for this reason, should anything go contrary to my wishes, all ailments would for a moment vanish ; for I must exert myself, which in all probability might end in a bed of sickness, and might terminate my existence.

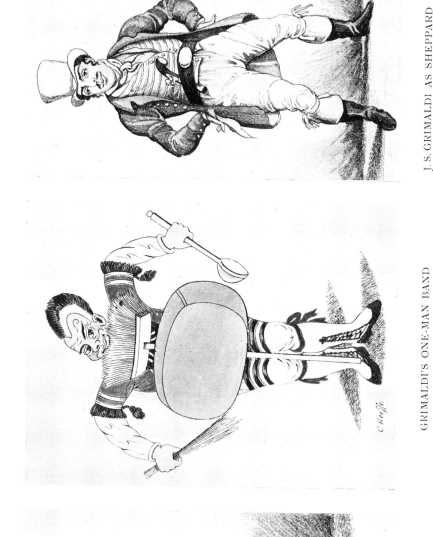

GRIMALDI'S LAST SCENE

*From a drawing by Brown,
member of Sadler's Wells' Orchestra*

GRIMALDI'S ONE-MAN BAND

From a drawing by O'Keefe

J. S. GRIMALDI AS SHEPPARD

*From a drawing by Brown,
member of Sadler's Wells' Orchestra*

J. S. Grimaldi never lacked " another chance " even to the last days of his life which ended on December 11, 1832. His mother died two years later. The old Clown's life seemed to have ended. Yet, unlike the clowns of popular fiction, the dauntless spirit of the motley was the spirit of the man. Instead of giving way to despair he decided to return to Sadler's Wells. The problem of expense he solved by selling his odds and ends, as is plain in this rhymed appeal [1] to Ellar the Harlequin (it was followed eight days later by a rhymed acknowledgment) :

From J. G. to T. Ellar.

My Dr Friend Tom, ansr this I pray
Do you mean to have my Instrument, say Yea or Nay
For if I do not hear from you without more delay
In a short space of time, I shall send it away
So Dr Friend Tom, use no more Ceremony
But come and take the Music and bring me the Money
I have something still left, for your judgement's approval
Which I wish to dispose of, before my removall
A case with Two Fiddles of excellent Sounds
You shall have the Case and Fiddles for the sum of £5.
So Dr Friend Tom, remain yrs till I Die
The once Merry Momus, Poor Joe Grimaldi
I shall quit Woolwich soon, for another situation
And glad enough I shall be, to return from Transportation
Once more enjoy society, the Song the glee and Laugh
Tell odd story's, think of present, but not forget the past
Be Merry and wise for Time approaches fast
For Death will you know have the odd trick at last.

April 20th 1835   J. GRIMALDI.

Back at Sadler's Wells he decided to write " The Life and Adventures of Joseph Grimaldi," which he completed on his fifty-eighth birthday, December 18, 1836. A bibliographer who saw the manuscript thirty-five years later described it as a " genuine and faithful " autobiography, " full, frank, and delightfully clownish, childlike and simple." But the publishers would not accept it in that form.

[1] Another item in Messrs. Maggs' collection of Grimaldi manuscripts.

Joseph was broken-hearted. " I feel truly miserable," he wrote to an unnamed correspondent :

> I am sure my end is approaching. O for the days when I was delighting Audiences at Old Drury and the Wells. I will do all that I can to assiste yr poor Friend, but come and see your old Friend and have an hour's chat with him.

The last time he visited Sadler's Wells was at a benefit in January 1837, so that the performance of " Mother Goose " could be announced as " under the supervision of the veteran Grimaldi." He sat on the back seat of a box. In the pantomime, a duet between the Clown and Jim Crow (the first of the nigger minstrels) included the verse :

> CLOWN.—Prythee tell me, Master Crow,
> Why you look so full of glee ?
>
> JIM CROW.—Why ? coss our old friend Joe
> I'm delighted here to see.

As his finger pointed to the box the audience ignored the stage and tried to catch a sight of the veteran. When the Clown proposed—

> Now he's here, to welcome him,
> With a hearty three-times-three !

there was a shout of approval. With a friend's help Grimaldi reached the front of the box. Amid his tears, he told them

> You may judge the feelings of one who has travelled through the world of pantomime, and reached the declining years of life without losing one jot of his enthusiasm, though shorn of all his strength.—God bless you !—God bless you all !

Again he plucked up courage. In the March of 1837 he contracted with Thomas Egerton Wilks to rewrite his *Life and Adventures*, and agreed to give him half the proceeds. The revised manuscript was to be ready by December 1. Grimaldi was elated. He spent his evenings at the Marquis of Cornwallis in Southampton Street, Pentonville, whose proprietor, George Cook, used to fetch him on his back and take him home in the same manner. On the last evening (May 31) his spirits were high, and he had a full audience in the coffee-room to hear his stories. After he had been carried home he said to his host, " God bless you, my boy, I shall be ready for you to-morrow night." He died in his sleep.

116

He was buried in the ground of St. James's Chapel, Pentonville. Of the Harlequinade only Norman, the old Pantaloon, was present. There were not many people there to see the end of " the big boy, for he was no more " who " was of us, our familiar."

·   ·   ·   ·   ·   ·

What became of his last labour of love no one can tell. Wilks translated the matter from the first to the third person, a process described as " very much like mixing your effervescing powders the night before to drink in the morning."   Dickens, who revised the manuscript of Wilks, had not seen the original.   It stayed in the hands of Grimaldi's executor, and was last heard of in 1873 when it fetched 100 guineas at the sale of a library of a Mr. Percival of Highbury. Henry Stevens, who has left an account of the manuscript, bought most of the lots and presented them to the British Museum, but the *Life and Adventures* is not in the collection.

Cap. Bellauita .   Cap Mala Gamba.

PANTALOON

As he was on the stage, so he was off it, clothes, powder, and all; he was not acting a part in the harlequinade, he was merely being himself. It was undoubtedly this strange discovery that set us writing a play about him.

Of course bitter controversy may come of this, for not every one will agree that we are right. It is well known among the *cognoscenti* that actors in general are not the same off the stage as on; that they dress for their parts, speak words written for them which they do not necessarily believe, and afterwards wash the whole thing off and then go to clubs and cross their legs. I accept this to be so (though I think it is a pity), but Pantaloon was never an actor in that sense; he would have scorned to speak words written for him by any whippersnapper; what he said and did before the footlights were the result of mature conviction and represented his philosophy of life.

SIR JAMES BARRIE.

A VENETIAN PANTALOON

From a print in the British Museum

JAMES BARNES

From a water-colour drawing in the British Museum

OLD age is a lost joke now. To beguile the old Pantaloon, as Shakespeare puts it, has ceased to amuse, though it was one of the world's favourite pastimes from Greek burlesques to Victorian Harlequinades. Not without reason was *Pantalonnisme* or *Pantalonnade* the French term for the performances of clowns. Nor is it without significance that while Arlequin was refused admittance to the Elizabethan stage, " Panteloun " was acting in " Dead Man's Fortune " with antique fairies who danced while " the musique plaies," and evidently had an important part, because the " plotte " of stage directions (all that remains of the play) ends " Enter the panteloun and causeth the cheste or truncke to be brought forth." The explanation of his presence in the cast, however, is simply that his name was given to any ancient man, not necessarily of the Commedia dell' arte.

Pantaloon himself was a Venetian. He was a parody of that city's merchants, wearing their distinctive garb of *culottes*, which continued to the ankle, and a black cloak worn in mourning for her lost colonies. Probably it was this cloak which led Byron to write

> Her very byword sprung from victory,
> The " Planter of the Lion " which through fire
> And blood she bore o'er subject earth and sea,

and to explain his reference in the note, " That is, the Lion of St. Mark, the standard of the republic, which is the origin of the word Pantaloon—Piantaleone, Pantaleon, Pantaloon." As the old man was always known as the *Magnifico*, the theory is extraordinarily plausible. But Professor Skeat dubs it " ridiculous," and proves his point. St. Pantaleone was a saint, associated with Venice, whose name " is certainly Greek, and he is said to be known in the Greek Church as Panteleēmon," which means all-pitying.

In English pantomimes he retained his cloak and his dignity as Columbine's father until the time of Giuseppe Grimaldi. Then he became, for a time, the most important clown in the Harlequinade. Delpini played him in this manner and, being a tall man, added to the humour by submitting to the henpecking of Master Menage, as a short Judy in a great deal of starch. According to some authorities the frozen pigtail and other peculiarities of the modern Pantaloon were invented by Barnes. Certainly, in " Mother Goose " Louis Bologna still wore a cloak and skull cap, but Norman, who was at Covent Garden for several years before and after Barnes' first arrival, is shown by the prints of " Harlequin and the Swans ; or, the Bath of Beauty " to have dressed in this fashion.

Nevertheless, James Barnes is the name that comes first to mind when one thinks of Pantaloons. He was a little man with a spare visage, small piercing black eyes, a red flannel waistcoat and red heeled shoes. That is how he was seen on the stage by others. How he appeared off the stage is described by himself :

> Boots sufficiently large, in case my bitter enemy, the gout, might make his appearance, (as he generally did just about Christmas pantomime time ;) light mixture trousers, striped waistcoat, black surtout coat, and a Brighton beaver great-coat (new) ; black hat, quite easy enough, and tied to the buttonhole for fear of accident ; a full starched collar, and black cravat with red stripes. So much for dress—now for figure : middling size, face red, nose and chin long ; sharp eyes, dark, small ; carroty whiskers—I beg their pardon, patches of hair on each cheek, just peeping over the collar.

Like Barrie's character in the play he was merely being himself when he went on the stage. His journal of a visit to Paris, which was printed in *Bentley's Miscellany* two years after his death, reveals a merry soul whose irascibilities and fears are as funny as his quips. He was born, not to pantomime, but to shoemaking. While still an apprentice he ran away to sea. On his return he joined the army. His stage career began at Bartholomew Fair in old Richardson's booth. " I am," he wrote,

> not ashamed to own it. Many others, who have prospered much more than I have, began there. There were * * * * * * * —No, d—n it !—I am only an old pantomimer, whom anybody may laugh at, and nobody cares for. Some of my contemporaries are now in possession of good homes, and mix in genteel society. Mind, they did not tumble head over heels as I did.

THE MANAGERS LAST KICK, OR A NEW WAY TO PAY OLD DEBTS.

SOME HARLEQINADE FASHIONS OF 1811

From a print in the Author's Collection

His first " good engagement " in London was at the Lyceum Theatre, when the Drury Lane company acted there, after the fire, in February 1809. At Christmas 1810 he was the Pantaloon in the pantomime of the " White Cat." Generally, the night before the Christmas Eve was considered a bad theatrical night. The manager produced the " White Cat " on that evening, and called it " A Night Rehearsal to the Public " :

> This drew an immense second price (and that little dog-hole of a theatre held three hundred pounds), and the pantomime going with perfect success, the manager got the descriptions and critiques of it in all the newspapers of an intervening Sunday, which happened to fall on Christmas day. The success of the " White Cat " (and I suppose they liked their Pantaloon) procured me London engagements until the year 1834. I think the " White Cat " was performed nearly sixty nights in the first season.

After a summer engagement at Sadler's Wells in 1812 Barnes was taken by Grimaldi to Covent Garden, where he " supported " John Kemble as a Roman citizen in " Coriolanus " or a carrier in " Henry IV., Part I." His representation of imbecility was considered unsurpassable, especially in such parts as Lord Sands in " Henry VIII." and forcible Feeble in " Henry IV., Part II." This, naturally, came out in his Pantaloon. " What a hobbling old rascal it is ! " wrote Leigh Hunt of his performance. " How void of any handsome infirmity ! His very gout is owing to his having lived on twopence farthing." He was noted for his way of encountering " bumps and thumps and slaps and bangs," and for his unintelligible chatter. He was also a popular dame, his creations in this genre ranging from the Queen of Golconda in " Harlequin and Mother Bunch ; or, the Yellow Dwarf " in 1821, to Priscilla Puddingsleeves, the cook in " Hop o' My Thumb and his Brothers ; or, Harlequin and the Ogre " in 1831. When practically the first English pantomime was transported to Paris in 1825 Barnes was the Pantaloon, and his close companion, Tom Ellar, the Harlequin. They lodged at the house of Madame Bambayet. This is how Barnes tells the story :

> Good old creature ! we were both in love with her. I believed I pretended more than I really felt, or I should never have got my stockings mended ; but I found out that she liked Ellar the better of the two. She

had seen his neat figure in the patched jacket, and that had tickled her fancy. I was jealous—as most pantaloons are,—and I hit upon an ingenious and diabolical expedient to. disgust Madame Bambayet with Ellar. I succeeded, she looked upon him with horror ever afterwards. The pantomime in which we both played in the theatre had a great run ; it was the first English pantomime that had been carried over there for many years, consequently we had no rehearsals after it was produced, and nothing to occupy our time in the morning ; so sometimes we used to amuse ourselves by going to St. Cloud, and angling in the Seine, where we caught a sort of gudgeon. Our bait was a box of gentles ; and this box was kept with our other tackle in the closet of our double-bedded room. One night it so happened that I came home earlier than usual. I had quarrelled with Ellar about this same Madame Bambayet so, when I got in, out of revenge, I boldly emptied the contents of the gentle-box into Ellar's bed, underneath the sheet ; got into my own bed, and pretended to go to sleep. Ellar soon came home, and retired to rest. I chuckled ; for I knew that Madame Bambayet would come into our room the first thing in the morning, to see whether we wanted anything. Madame did come in ; and, peering about, she saw what she did not quite understand : those gentles that found Mr. Ellar's bed too warm for them had made their way on to the shining tile floor, and there were hundreds of them hopping and rolling in all directions. She exclaimed " Grand Dieu ! ques que c'est ? " Ellar was asleep ; so I quietly pointed to him and said, " He could not help it, *but he was subject to them !* " Oh ! I wish you could have seen the look of horror depicted on the old lady's physiognomy ! " Ah ! les vilaines bêtes ! " Ellar waking, and raising himself up, shook off another hundred, and Madame Bambayet hastened as quickly as possible out of the room.

When I went downstairs the old lady proposed sending for a medical man ; but I told her it was of no use ; that it was all over, and Mr. Ellar was only troubled that way three or four times a year, and that it was a great relief to his constitution.

I settled his business with Madame Bambayet, for she never paid him any attention afterwards, and did not wonder at his always looking so pale ; in fact, she was glad when he was gone !

Five years later Barnes went on a second pantomime expedition to Paris. This is the subject of his journal. It contains, however, very little about the performances. Mainly it is a record of innumerable doses of " my old remedy " brandy, joys and disappointments over meals, acid comments upon the mother of Columbine, nocturnal struggles with what he calls " punaises (dictionary)," wanderings in Paris, and the fighting that dethroned Charles X. Yet, besides 1e-vealing the soul of a Pantaloon and being, in consequence, uncommonly good reading, it does offer a glimpse or two of what the tricks of the English Harlequinade meant to French taste. His departure (on May 23) is told in detail—how he was given fourteen pounds in advance just before he got upon the coach, how he gave to " little Paulo " (then Clown at Covent Garden) seven pounds for "*his* mother and *my* own," how he bought " some oranges and a knife with six blades," and how he shed tears when he left London behind. At every stop he swallowed brandy and more brandy, until " my fellow-passengers began to think I was not quite so dull a companion as they imagined at starting." Then a shower spoilt the oiled curls, the flop Leghorn bonnets and enormous ribbons of the females, who were " making a dash out of London " to astonish the country folk. For the rest, Barnes must be allowed to tell his own tale—minus his protracted accounts of meals and nights with the insects :

[Extracts from the " Journal of Old Barnes, the Pantaloon, on a trip to Paris, in 1830 "; published in vols. vii. and viii. of *Bentley's Miscellany*.]

" We had not long left Dover when a breeze sprung up, to the joy of the captain and crew, but death to all the passengers. Oh ! the heaving of the vessel, and the heaving of the voyagers ! Not the slightest occasion for the stomach pump,—especially for myself. The veterinary gentleman at Dover had provided against that, although I went regularly through every action and attitude, so much so, that the rest, who really were ill, and no mistake, thought I was making fun of them, particularly Columbine and her mother, who sat nearly opposite to me, only to the leeward. I held tight by the arms of the bench, as I used to do in Mother Goose, for fear of being pitched forward : so they had an excellent view of my face whenever they dared to lift their heads up, and see the ' much ado about nothing ' I made. My dreadful faces and noises set them off ten times worse than ever, and they held up their hands, and turned up the whites—no, the yellows of their eyes, as much as to say, ' For pity's sake, Barnes, don't do it again ! ' But Barnes could not help himself.

" We landed, and were surrounded by a swarm of commissioners (fine names for cads !) from the different hotels, none crying ' stinking-fish,' although there was a very prevailing smell of it ; but we soon shook them off. I know well how to get out of a mob ; I have done it in pantomime for the last twenty-five years. I can knock two men's heads together, without myself offending them. Now came the overhauling at the custom-house. My pantaloon's dress was an object of debate and curiosity ; and though I had left our free country, where there is still a powder tax, I was in fear that a duty would be levied on my white wig. But when the searchers came to my little hat, about the size of an extinguisher, I thought they never would have left off laughing. However, they all passed examination. This was *more* than did the cargo of pantomime tricks that had been made in London, and had been sent over the day before in charge of Ronaldson the carpenter, and Seymour the mechanist. They were detained, as the French custom-house authorities could not possibly describe them. There was a sofa that changed to a fire-grate ; a pot of porter with cotton-wool froth, which would transform to a nosegay ; a twelfth-cake that turned into a rat-trap ; and a a long string of sausages, which in an instant became a ' suit of darbies.' There was an infinite variety of these ingenious tricks ; but the Messieurs of the Douane (who would do any one) did not comprehend any tricks but their own ; so our director was obliged to go and argue the topic with them, whilst we made our way to Mrs Symmond's, the Flying Horse Hotel, and arrived just in time for dinner. The roasted turkey looked and smelt nice. But, O Lord ! that cursed chemist at Dover !

" I was told, but I do not know with what truth, that it is contrary to law for one diligence to pass another so long as it continues in motion. As we travelled occasionally at about the rate of four miles an hour, I did not envy the impatience of some Englishmen in the opposition diligence behind us. They had the benefit of all our dust, and we did not kick up a little. They did not know the custom, and execrated the conducteur and postilion to the very best of their ability. I have heard much swearing in my day,— for instance, William Barrymore, on the first night of one of his pantomimes, when the scenery stuck, or a trick failed. Oh, dear ! I am not very parti-cular ; but I never yet discovered that blasphemy relieved a theatrical or any other defect. That Barrymore would swear until the scene-shifters' ears curled up. Well, presently the driver of the hindmost diligence sent the head of one of his fore-horses up to the window where our dear travelling companion, Monsieur Singe, was looking out ; and, of all the droll scenes I ever beheld, I think it beat them, for the poor monkey was actually con-vulsed with fright, and poured forth the most pitiful cries at the sight of the horse's head, which ever and anon snorted in at the window. The gentle-man's want of nerve kept the passengers of both diligences in a roar of laughter. At last he made a bolt off his Italian master's lap, and hid his ugly face in the straw at the bottom. Then Columbine's mamma became alarmed, and lifted up her lower extremities into a position which was exceedingly perplexing to the inmates of the interior.

" If you wish to see the Palais Royal to advantage, enter it at the pas-sage from the Rue Vivienne ; thence the brilliancy is more apparent. Try it on a moonlight night, and the light and shade is new and startling. My kind old friends (God bless them !) the Messrs. Grieve, the scenic artists of Covent Garden and Drury Lane theatres, are precisely the men to catch and depict such an effect. Then the gay shops for everything—the jewellers, clock-makers, the hattery, hosiery, stickery, stockery, perfumery, footery, wiggery,—the print sellers, the cafés, the *estaminets* (N.B. Bad Baccy !) told that the commodity was a Government monopoly. Could immediately understand why the tobacco was of an inferior quality. Then the eatables and drinkables !—Lord ! it did your appetite good only to look at them !—the *dindon aux truffes*, which means turkey cut up, and stuffed with small pieces of Indiarubber. I did not touch it, on account of the latter material. Don't catch me munching catchouch. Have to poke it down, perhaps, with a black lead pencil.

"Then there were the theatres in the Palais Royal, and the puppet-shows. In one of the latter I saw Mr. Punch, three times the size that he is ever exhibited in London, behave infamously to his wife, slapping her in the most indecorous manner ; ay, and fifty females in the *salon* stood by enjoying it, but not one Englishwoman. Mark that, for the honour of my country ! Then you may enter a splendid café, with a half hundred marble tables in it, superb looking glasses on the walls, every appurtenance and impertinence in the most expensive style ; yet the proprietor, civil to his visitors, does not object to two of them playing twenty games of dominoes for the sake of two glasses of 'eau sucré.' Perceiving the interest this beverage excited, and the play and skill depending on it, though I never would encourage gambling, I ordered some 'eau sucré.' When it came, and I tasted it—Lord ! where were their palates ?

"Is not it strange that travelling only 150 miles, there should be such a vast difference in tastes in human beings ? I could not touch their insipid drink, and they had positively endured the trouble of twenty games of dominoes for it.

"Returned to the Hôtel de Lisle, having partaken of some wine and *eau de veau,* as Ronaldson (the old calf !) would still call it. Went to bed, thought of home and Old England, Poor dear Mary, Tom Ellar, Paulo, and of Mr. Bradwell and his mechanical changes. Ruminated,—that is, ' chewed the cud ' of reflection, until I went to sleep.

"Up betimes. I am like the late Mr. Simmons ; I never can lie *long* in bed. Roused the rest of the party, and *out* to breakfast—very un-English. An Englishman likes his breakfast at home—the very paying for it strikes you. Columbine's mamma said the green tea tasted of coppers (why did not she take coffee, the old fool !) ; and when I mentioned that the white sugar was possibly made of beet-root, she avowed that she tasted the salad in it.—Mem. Poor thing's stomach out of order already. I was sure of it, for she left her egg for anyone else to foster like a cuckoo. Harlequin ate it (the Jew Frenchman), and would have swallowed anything. He drove me wild by seeing him devour a nearly-raw beefsteak, cut very thick, which reminded me very forcibly of ' a pound of Antonio's flesh nearest his heart.' I really was compelled to call for a little brandy, and a little more after that, to compose my nerves. How can people be so filthy in their appetites ?

"Noticed a much cheaper and better display of the theatre play-bills than in London. There are certain stations on columns or buildings, in various parts of Paris, on which the bills of all the theatres are posted daily, and where the public regularly look for them. Should there be no performance at night, the word RELACHE is in a large type, conspicuous on the bill. This sometimes appears on two or three play-bills. Seymour remarked to me knowingly, that there must be a very popular piece being acted at the time, for it was performed at three different theatres, and was called RELACHE. He advised me, if it was printed to buy it, and send it over to Mr. Moncrieff to translate for the Coburg theatre.

"Promenaded the streets; Paris all gaiety; the Boulevards crowded with well-dressed ladies; coffee roasting under a wood-fire, in a tin turn-about machine, before almost all the grocers' shops; floor-mattresses ripped up, beaten, and re-made in the open thoroughfares; old women trimming poodles on the bridges; letter-writers in stalls, on any subject; prints exhibited for public sale, which would be torn down in London by any coal-heaver who was a father of a family. Many more theatrical portraits in the print shops than in our metropolis. The public think much more of actors and authors than they do with us; both are encouraged. Monsieur Scribe, a comic dramatic writer, gets above two thousand pounds a-year. The Parisian public respect and uphold him.

"Next day, the Jew Frenchman came to the hotel to procure lodgings for us. Now, Seymour, who, as I stated before, was our machinist, had brought a pantomime trick with him from England, of which he was jealously proud; he could not bear anyone to touch it but himself. I forget what the transformation was, but something changed to a windmill; and, as we hunted through the streets of Paris for lodgings for our fellow adventurers, Seymour, who was a little punchy figure, carried this trick, which was large and heavy, on his shoulder: while Ronaldson followed, with a large basket-work and papier-machée swan under each arm. The wind happened this day to be very boisterous, with sudden gusts round the corners of the streets; and it was fun to me to observe Seymour blown about, with his windmill on his back; and old frosty-faced Ronaldson behind him with his property birds. Every where, when we stopped at '*appartement garni à louer*,' these monstrous things were put down in the street to the admiration of the populace; and they really, in some instances, prevented the lodging-house keepers from taking us in on any terms.

"At nine '*appartements à louer garni*' out of ten they refused to take us and our tricks in; so I told Seymour to carry his windmill back to the hotel, and Ronaldson to follow him with the property swans; and presently I had the satisfaction to see Seymour blown round the corner, windmill and all.

"Soon our pantomime was ready at the theatre, and with great note of preparation out it came, 'Rôle de Pantaloon, par Monsieur Barnes, premiere artist des Theatres Royales de Londres'; and I am proud to say that we were attractive; for the manager was not a bankrupt until after we had returned to England. The audience received us with profound attention; none of that noise and whistling, and 'Hey-ho! Billy Burroughs,'—'Throw him over,'—and ' Order, order,' that salute your ears from the gentlefolks who visit our upper galleries, where the person who calls out ' Silence ! ' makes more noise than all the rest, and empty ginger-beer bottles are flung at bald heads in the pit. No ; the people are better behaved to both actors and authors ; and if a person happens to be pertinaciously troublesome in any way, he is *invited* out of the theatre by a gensd'arme, in a uniform somewhat like that worn by the Oxford Blues, in Dighton's time.

" Tuesday, 27th July.—The National and the Temps, two principal newspapers, appeared as usual, without any license, and they had printed about five times as many as was usual. People reading them mounted on chairs in all directions. Canon fired at Vincennes to alarm the populace early in the morning,—some said they were shooting the *reporters*. Soldiers were marching into Paris all day. The tradesmen began to shut their shops ; and if Polignac and Peyronnet had shut up theirs then, much bloodshed would have been spared. Columbine's mamma asked me my opinion, whether we should be kept prisoners of war ? I told her I did not think it likely that any one would keep her. There must have been between four and five thousand people in the Palais Royal. These were cleared out by the troops. Saw Mr. W—— W——, a London gentleman I used to know at the Sans Pareil theatre, a friend of old Scott. He had a speculation with the diligences in Paris. He was in a terrible stew. The mob had taken three of his coaches to barricade the street. He had no resource ; and when the soldiers and populace began to fight in earnest, he had the pleasure to see the balls whizzing through the panels and glasses of each of his dillys. But, Lord ! they took sofas, tables, rolling-stones, wheelbarrows, anything to block up the way ; they unpaved the Rue St. Honoré; they put the lamps out. The soldiers fired on the people and killed several. Police officers went to the two newspaper offices, broke the doors open, and brought away the types and presses—several devils (printers') seized. Much firing of guns in the night. Put my bed on the floor, or I should not have had a wink of sleep. Heard a monstrous noise, peeped out of the window, and saw labourers carrying about the dead bodies of the men that had been shot. Turned sick, and wished myself at the Crown and Cushion, Little Russel Street, Covent Garden. Theatres closed. Brought home a bottle of brandy from Wood's, thank God ! or I don't really know what would have become of me."

After he had to leave the stage through ill-health in 1834 Barnes had no other support than the sovereigns he borrowed from his staunch friend Ellar. Though a few years before his popularity had been great enough for special proclamations to be issued whenever the two visited Sadler's Wells, he was utterly destitute four years after his retirement, partly because the Drury Lane Fund refused to acknowledge him as an actor. Just as he was about to enter the workhouse the news came to the ears of Wieland, Clown at Drury Lane, who caused a benefit to be given at the English Opera in the Strand. The performance included a tableau of Shakespeare's " Seven Ages of Man," with Barnes to represent the lean and slippered Pantaloon. As a large sum was raised a happy old age was predicted for him. But he died two weeks later. Until that moment he had no friends except Ellar, who he desired should receive the funds of the benefit. Afterwards, practically all he left was claimed by relatives—until then not heard of. His place was taken in the mid-Victorian Harlequinade by W. A. Barnes, apparently not a relative, but the best Pantaloon of his day all the same. Afterwards Paul Herring, at Astley's in the 'fifties, at Covent Garden in the 'sixties, and at Drury Lane in the 'seventies before his death in 1878, won this distinction.

Pernoualla   Cucorongna

DEBURAU

Ci-dessoulx git et loge en terre
Le très gentil fallot Jehan Serre
Qui tout plaisir allait suyvant
Et grand joueur en son vivant
Non pas joueur de dez ni quilles
Mais de belles farces gentilles.
Or bref, grand il entroit en salle
Avec une chemise sale,
Le front, la joue et la narine
Toute couverte de farine

Et coiffé d'un béguin d'enfant
Et d'un hault bonnet triumphant
Guarny de plumes de chappons,
Avec tout cela je repons
Qu'en voyant sa grâce nyaise
On n'estoit pas moins gay ni ayse
Qu'on est aux Champs Elyséens.

CLÉMENT MAROT (1497-1544).

DEBURAU.

Tabarin

3

PARISIANS' laughter yielded so long to the sway of London and Rome that the French fools begat no original type. Yet in the Italian guise of Arlequin, Punch or Pierrot, or the English guise of Clown or Auguste, there is distinguishable a Gallic soul unlike the types whose costumes he wears. His character may be either " *très gentil* " or grotesquely callous. Nevertheless, he is the same at heart, and often wears the same face—" *toute couverte de farine.*"

Was it altogether by accident that the famous fools of Molière's youth were bakers? The temptation is to say that why they left their ovens to act in the faubourg St. Laurent was because they had been inspired to clown by the flour on their faces. Gros-Guillaume, whose enormous belly was girdled with two belts so that he resembled a hogshead, could by the motion of his lips throw the flour on his face over those he spoke to. His companions were Gaultier-Garguille, who played the schoolmaster, and had a nose which suggested the handle of a pump, and Turlupin, a demure valet or scheming cut-purse. Their performances were unlicensed. The theatres asked for their suppression. Richelieu consented. He ordered the companies, however, to admit the *bateleurs* into their ranks. This partly explains how the sack-beating joke of the clown Tabarin came to be included in *Les Fourberies de Scapin.* Moreover, Molière served his apprenticeship to the theatre as an author of knockabout pieces after the Italian manner.

Gros-Guillaume, Gaultier-Garguille and Turlupin died within one week. They were replaced by Guillot-Gorju, Jaquemen-Jadot and Jodelet—French fools with a strain of the Commedia dell' arte. Before the end of the seventeenth century, the Hôtel de Bourgogne and the fairs of Paris were occupied by Arlequin, blatant, mischievous, constantly alert. But when Thomassin played the part, he became

133

as *très gentil* as Jehan Serre.   That was at the beginning of the eighteenth century when custom ordained he should speak in Italian—fashionable ladies were attended in their boxes by interpreters—though critics were crying out for French.   When *Arlequin Bouffon de Cour* was performed in 1716, Thomassin concluded the piece by saying, in a jargon half French and half Italian, he would tell them La Fontaine's fable of " The Miller, his Son and his Ass."   He alighted like the miller, mounted like the son and trotted like the ass.   " I am the miller, I am the boy, nay, I am the ass," he said, and that was his answer to those who quarrelled over what language he should speak. French conquered, for Thomassin became the hero of the plays of Marivaux, " *ce grand anatomiste du cœur humain.*"   In these his Arlequin is shown to be equally composed of tears and laughter, quite unlike the Italian rogue.   Marmontel describes him thus :

> His character is a mixture of ignorance, simplicity, cleverness, stupidity, and grace ; he is a kind of sketch of a man, a tall child, yet with gleams of reason and wit, whose mistakes and follies have something arch about them. The true way to present him is to give him suppleness, agility, the playfulness of a kitten, with a certain grossness of appearance, which renders his conduct more absurd ; his part is that of a patient, faithful valet, always in love, always in hot water, either on his master's or his own account, troubled and consoled as easily as a child, his grief as entertaining as his joy.

The last of the great Arlequins of Paris was Carlo Bertinazzi, known as Carlin, who restored the *cannevas italiens*.   He wore the motley from 1741 almost to his death, at the age of 70, in 1783.   Even increasing *embonpoint* did not lessen his popularity.   Among his admirers was Garrick who, noting his posture after receiving punishment—rubbing the place with one hand while threatening his master with the other—said that Carlin's back wore the expression his face would show did not the mask cover it.   He could express emotion merely by the way he cocked the corners of his hat or made the sides droop.   His manner was so natural that if he made a glissade across the stage the spectators trembled with concern for his safety ; did he seem in danger of striking his head against a wall, they would cry out " Take care."   Children in the stage boxes often talked to him. Playgoers, coming a second time, would ask for " the scene of

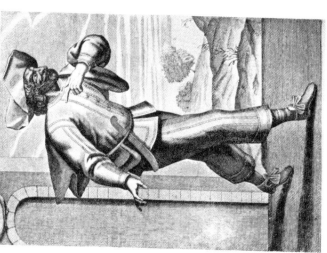

TURLUPIN

From a print in the British Museum

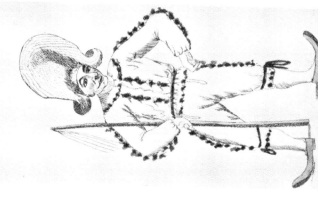

LAURENT

From the frontispiece to "Furibond; or, Harlequin Negro", 1806

GROS-GUILLAUME

From a print in the British Museum

Arlequin and the children " to be repeated, as if it were part of the performance.

After Carlin, Arlequin was again gallicized. Florian's plays, said Goldoni, even imparted sentiment, passion, and morality to this "amphibious character." The statement is fully borne out by Florian's own words. He desired to change the *Arlequinade* into a picture of familiar virtues. Since a man is rarely called upon to sacrifice his life for duty, country or honour, the theatre was now to show him how to be a good son, a good husband and a good father. Consequently Florian set out not to copy either the philosophy of Delisle's Arlequin or the pastoral delicacy of Marivaux's but to paint one who was good, sweet, ingenuous, simple without being stupid, guileless of speech ; who naïvely expressed the sentiments of a very tender heart. This he managed in *Le Bon Ménage* (1782), *Le Bon Père* (1783) and *Le Bon Mère* (1785) ; but when writing *Le Bon Fils* he decided the situation of the good son, obliged to choose between his mother and his mistress and forced to sacrifice the one for the other, was " *trop vif, trop grand pour admettre le moindre comique.*" Arlequin's costume was flung aside—practically for ever, since such modern plays as Maurice Magre's *Arlequin* are resurrections rather than revivals.

Yet the same character reappeared as Pierrot. Here again an Italian figure was transformed to express the French ideal. Throughout the eighteenth century, Pierrot had been a lout. He was a character of minor importance until played by Delpini who, however, kept strictly to the idea of a creature so stupid as to think that if he raised his leg level with his shoulder he could use it as a gun. Deburau changed all that. In his acting, Pierrot's stupidity became feigned. Like the French Arlequin, he mingled laughter with tears. But like the English Clown, he was mischievous and moved by base desires such as gluttony, and the fear of punishment. These characteristics, however, were dominated by the inexhaustible sarcasm he expressed without words and " almost without a face." Under the persecution of Arlequin and Colombine, he was revealed as Molière's misanthrope. Yet he was, in France, as much everybody's familiar as Clown was in

England. He was not, says Janin, " so-and-so " with a proper name and a certain social position. Gilles, as Watteau named Pierrot, is nobody—and, in France, everybody :

> Gilles c'est le peuple. Gilles, tour à tour joyeux, triste, malade, bien portant, battant, battu, musicien, poète, niais, toujours pauvre, comme est le peuple ; c'est le peuple que Deburau représente dans tous ses drames.

Jean Gaspard Deburau was born in 1796 in Bohemia. He was the fifth son of a soldier turned acrobat, who performed with his children in many parts of Europe. In Paris they all won success, except Jean Gaspard. Even when he left them to try his luck at the house of the performing dogs, he failed. But at length his fortunes changed, as Mr. S. R. Littlewood, in " The Story of Pierrot," tells :

> Now, as it happened, and as it always happens in cases like these, the little Tight-rope Theatre was just at that time exactly ripe for Deburau's decision. It had become almost by chance the nursery of the re-born art of pantomime. . . . But it was demanded by law that if anything like a drama or pantomime were performed at the Funambules, a certain compromise must be observed to protect " legitimate " theatres from unsanctioned rivalry. According to this compromise, each actor at the Funambules had to make his entrance upon the tight rope itself, or in some acrobatic posture. Lemaître himself had to leave the show, largely because he was unable to comply with this condition. Deburau, to whom all such exercises were familiar from his cradle, found it almost as natural to walk in upon his hands, as to continue his performance the other way up. Gradually, the little dumb-shows grew in length and importance.

They even aspired to reproduce the splendour of the English pantomime first seen in Paris when Barnes and Ellar crossed the Channel. This visit, however, may not be the explanation of the English pantomime at the Funambules. Probably the true cause was Laurent, one of the Clowns set up by Drury Lane in a vain attempt to rival the genius of Covent Garden. Unlike the other French and Italian pantomime people who became popular in London, he did not settle in this country and never adopted the national type of schoolboy humour. Laurent's Clown, who seemed inspired by mischievous malice, was said to be " ingenious, not humorous." He was more agile and less characteristic than Grimaldi, but was well above the common run in his mastery and finished skill. At first he was an apprentice of Philip

WATTEAU'S ARLEQUIN

From "L'Oeuvre d'Antoine Watteau gravé par les soins de M. de Jullienne",
folio (undated) in the British Museum

Astley but ran away. His old master found him performing at a puppet show on the boulevards near Pont Neuf, brought him back and was well repaid for his trouble, because Laurent became the foremost circus clown of his day. He was a richer man than Grimaldi. Old Astley raised his salary to ten pounds per week, which was doubled by his " benefits." In a few years he saved £3,000 and purchased the Lyceum Theatre in the Strand (afterwards the English Opera House), which he called " Laurent's Theatre of Mirth." Here he presented the spectacle of " Florenza, or the Castle of Toledo," a pantomime called " The Clown Emperor of China," besides " Neptune, or Woodcutter Harlequin," wherein he played nine chaıacters. When Astley's was burned down in 1803 he gave his profits to the sufferers. But his ambition to be a manager cost all his hard earned savings, and in 1807 he accepted the part of Clown at Drury Lane in " Furibond ; or Harlequin Negro." One of the scenes was in a haunted castle where he was terrified by a spectre who, after his head had been cut off, walked away with it under his arm. In another scene he was married to a black servant who produced six little ragged children which danced round Clown and called him father " until he ran off in a passion." The next Christmas he played Friday in " Robinson Crusoe." But Drury Lane was too large for the " little, frisking " pantomimes of those days. His efforts were more profitable when he played in " Harlequin in Egypt, or the Siege of Jean D'Acre " at the New Royal Circus, when a critic wrote :

> To say the clown of Laurent is inimitable is no more than doing justice to one whose name may be ranked with that of Grimaldi, without offence to the warmest admirers of that grand master of mimicry, throughout its most whimsical gesticulations. His *serious* action, in *Rolla*, etc., entitles him to the same degree of praise as was so generally bestowed on Grimaldi's Robinson Crusoe.

Laurent's costume was peculiar, consisting of a high straw hat of an exaggerated Napoleonic shape, flapping shoes and white breeches and blouse with coloured trimmings. Returning, after a series of setbacks, to Paris, he exhibited *Ombres Chinoises* (shadow pantomime), tumbling and other performances, with his children after the fashion of the Deburau troupe. Perhaps he joined the Cirque Olym-

137

pique of Franconi whither Lemaître, after he had failed to " *monter sur la corde*" at the Funambles, went to "*monter à cheval*." Or perhaps he joined Deburau. There is no certainty, for the name of Laurent is too common ; nevertheless, the probability is that the Laurent who was Deburau's lieutenant was the youngster who made his début at Drury Lane with his father at the age of seven and gained words of encouragement from London critics. When Deburau staged *Ma Mère l'Oie, ou Arlequin et l'Œuf d'Or* in 1830, Laurent was Colin. It was described as *Pantomime—Arlequinade—Féerie*, a grand spectacle *dans le genre anglais, avec changements à vue, travestissements, métamorphoses*, etc. There is no reason for Colin to be named in the dramatis personae for he is Arlequin throughout. As the show opens he has eloped with Colombine, and *Cassandre, le comique et Pierrot* are in pursuit. The inn scene from " Mother Goose " is recognisable, especially when Arlequin jumps through a map which immediately changes into a picture entitled " Adieu." Most of the jokes, however, have more violence than their English counterparts. The innkeeper, for instance, is killed with a blow of a sabre aimed at Arlequin by Pierrot. Then Cassandre is shot. With pincers Pierrot extracts from his body a bullet which explodes. Cassandre comes to life and asks what the noise is. Finally Mother Goose rescues Colin and Colinette.

The resemblance between the French pantomime and the English became more remote. Take the example quoted by Maurice Sand in *Masques et Buffons—Les Épreuves*, by Deburau and his son Charles. It is the love story of Arlequin and Isabella whom Pandolphe, her father, desires should wed Leandre. That, however, is kept as far in the background as Grimaldi kept his plots. The centre of interest is Pierrot, Pandolphe's servant. After sniffing at a pastry-cook's, he enters—but it has become a milliner's and he goes out. Again he sniffs outside the pastrycook's window, and again the shops change places. It happens a third time. He vents his anger upon passers-by until they unite against him and there is a " mill." He escapes by hiding under the gown of a mountebank. He joins a fair, beats the big drum too loudly and has to take refuge in a tavern. His

138

Sous vn habit de Mezetin.
Ce gros brun au riant Visage.
Sur la guitarre avec sa main
Fait vn aimable badinage.

Par les doux accents de sa voix.
Enfants d'vne bouche vermeille
Du beau sexe tout a la fois
Il charme les yeux et L'oreille.

WATTEAU'S MEZZETIN

From "Œuvres des Estampes Gravées d'après les Tableaux et Desseins
de feu Antoine Watteau", folio (undated) in the British Museum

head is cut off. Arlequin, disguised as a doctor, glues it on and demands a fee, but Pierrot complains that his head is not properly attached. Pierrot turns laundress. When a whiskered Englishman brings him some soiled linen, Pierrot throws him into a tub. Later on he wants to wash himself, puts on a bonnet and petticoat and enters a bathing establishment for women. It changes into a roasting house and he finds himself on a grill. He comes through this ordeal with the loss of his clothes. So he enlists. A quarrel with the corporal leads to a duel. His pistol is loaded with a candle. It hits the corporal full in the face. For this exploit he is raised to the rank of drum major.

These unrelated escapades still betray the French pantomime's origin. In " The Old Clo' Man," however, Deburau's fantasy was coherent. Gautier's account of the performance has been used by Sacha Guitry in " Deburau " and Mr. Granville Barker prints a translation in the book of his English version. The old clo' man, acted by Laurent, passes with a sword under his arm. Pierrot clutches the hilt and sheathes the blade, which seems to have drawn itself, into the old man's body. He takes the smartest clothes he can find from the pack, flings the corpse into a cellar, goes home and prepares himself for a ball. Suddenly the cellar flap is pushed up and his victim's ghost arises calling " Old Clo' ! Old Clo' ! " Pierrot snatches a billet from a stack of wood. The ghost dodges and parries, but at last is knocked into the cellar by a blow on the head. Pierrot piles all the wood on the cellar flap ; then mockingly calls out " Old Clo' ! Old Clo' ! " and goes to the ball. So does the ghost of the Old Clo' Man, who forces him to be his partner in a dance. Pierrot is pressed against the ghost until spitted on the sword protruding from its breast.

At this time a real tragedy was being acted behind the scenes. The theatre was an unhealthy place. Mushrooms grew in the dressing-rooms. Deburau suffered for years from asthma. But he did not leave the stage. His last appearance was in *Les Noces de Pierrot*, in 1846. He was received rapturously. There was a call for his usual dance, but most of the audience, seeing his strength was failing, silenced the demand. Deburau died a few days later.

139

Before his death Pierrot was no longer a clown.   He was, to quote Baudelaire, " pale as the moon, mysterious as silence, supple and mute as the serpent, lean and long as a pole."   There was no longer a resemblance to the English Pierrot :

> Where Deburau thrust in the point of a finger that he might afterwards lick it, the clown thrusts in both hands and both feet, and this may express all he does ; his is the vertigo of hyperbole.   This Pierrot passes by a woman who is washing her door-step ; after emptying her pockets, he seeks to cram into his own the sponge, the broom, the soap and even the water.

The French Pierrot was shorter lived than the Clown.   Legrand, who was Deburau's successor, carried the character still farther from mirth.   At the time of his master's death he was acting Pierrot before the London public at the Adelphi.   He had little success.   In 1849 he returned to the Funambules where he acted with Charles Deburau in *Les Deux Pierrots*.   At length he had a Pierrot theatre of his own.   But the vogue passed until *Le Cercle Funambulesque* was formed.   Their Pierrot was purely sentimental.   As the hero of the play in dumb-show, *L'Enfant Prodigue*, he acted the world over. But that has nothing to do with clownship beyond its possible influence in popularising the costume until from the masquerades it passed to the entertainments on the beach.   And the seaside Pierrots—if the " concert parties " of a derivative type be included—have supplied the town with several good clowns, including W. H. Berry, whose concise mimicry, especially that of an excessively versatile circus performer, is only too often lost in vapid " musical comedies." He would be well advised to become a Pierrot once more.   That the motley is still potent has been proved by Pélissier's " Follies " and the " Co-Optimists."

THE GRIMALDI TRADITION

I once knew that Clown, they called him Joe ;
But he died long ago, long ago !
He had a tuft of wool on the top of his head,
In the place where the clown's wool ought to grow.
His fun made the world cry out oh, oh, oh !
As he danced to the fiddle and the bow ;
     But though he is dead
     His spirit is not fled,
As we'll make all the town quickly know-ow-ow !
As we'll make all the town quickly know.

    "Harlequin King Alfred the Great ; or the Magic Banjo and
the Mystic Raven." Royal Marylebone Theatre, 1850.

GRIMALDI SHOPS.

From the Illustration by George Cruikshank in the "Memoirs of Grimaldi."

SIGNOR PAULO

From a Scrap-Book in the British Museum

TOM MATTHEWS

SAD stories of the deaths of clowns form the last chapter in the history of Regency pantomimes. Being an acknowledged actor, Grimaldi received the Drury Lane Fund's bounty. The rest of the aristocracy of the Harlequinade, when broken in health, were left to starve. Yet their traditions enabled Clowns and Pantaloons, bearing their names but not of their blood, to make fortunes in the next fifty years. After their time motley was a shrivelled relic, and its tricks old customs observed almost religiously like the singing of " Hot Codlins " and " Tippetywichet " which continued to the 'sixties. Yet the Harlequinade became a deflated wineskin when Grimaldi retired. The strength of his new vintage had stretched it to the uttermost. Once emptied, it could not be completely refilled. The old story of eloping lovers, then the basis of every Harlequinade, had been deranged by the swollen size of this minor character. Most of his antics bore no relation whatever to the plot. British audiences had grown used to that. Tradition, which covers a multitude of absurdities, enabled the disjointed performance to remain in a slowly dwindling vogue. But in a country where Grimaldi's fame was unknown, such incoherence was intolerable. When " Mother Goose " was taken to America in 1831 the Clown broke his heart. He was E. J. Parsloe who had played the part of a cat, Pierrot and wolf to J. S. Grimaldi's Clown at Covent Garden. On the voyage over he had injured his spine by a fall down the companion way. All the same he was capable of exertions that would have been sufficient to win applause in London. In New York the silence of the audience was broken only by the cracking of pea-nuts. On the fourth night of such treatment, Parsloe broke down while he was changing from Squire to Clown and burst into tears.

At first the gaps in London's Harlequinades were filled passably well. When J. S. Grimaldi left Covent Garden, his place was taken by Signor Paulo, son of Paulo Redigé, Le Petit Diable. Once at Sadler's Wells he had been put forward as a substitute for Grimaldi, but without success. As " clown to the rope "—the comparatively humble task of supplying comic relief to equilibrists—his popularity was sure. At that time the French performers on the slack wire wore tights and triple-tufted wigs. Paulo adopted the costume and originated the conventional rig of the Clown whose clothes were then of any shape or pattern from Laurent's straw hat and yellow one-piece garment to Kirby's towering mass of yellow curls and fleshings, or Grimaldi's crest of blue wool, like the plume on the helmets of Wellington's gunners, and tightly fitting breeches. In 1826 Paulo was the Clown at the Adelphi in " Harlequin and the Eagle ; or, the Man in the Moon and his Wife," a mixture of Celtic folk-lore and tripe shops. He went to Drury Lane under Elliston, who took a keen interest in pantomimes. While rehearsing the Christmas after-piece, this manager happened to be tricked into buying a handkerchief twice over in Field-lane at the bottom of Holborn-hill, celebrated—according to Moncrieff who told the story—for " translated understandings, that is, second-hand shoes, orphan fogles (stolen handkerchiefs), and lost property of every description retailed under the especial superintendence of a select tribe of the chosen people." The result was an old clothes-shop scene. Paulo and T. Blanchard (Pantaloon)

> purchased the same handkerchiefs at least half a dozen times over, the said handkerchiefs each time, at a wave of the harlequin's wand, flying from their pockets to the place whence they had been taken, in front of the clothes shop, and when the motley worthies, subsequently in a rage, drag out the Hebrew to wreak their vengeance on him for his double dealing, they find him to their horror come to pieces in the scuffle, literally turning out to be a bundle of old clothes.

Paulo played at Covent Garden in 1831 as the Clown of " Hop o' my Thumb and his Brothers ; or, Harlequin and the Ogre." He died four years later at the age of 48. His name was kept alive 'n pantomime by James Paulo, the Pantaloon, who died in 1883 ; also by T. W. Paulo and his son—Harry Paulo, a mellow Clown who is with us still.

Ere their deaths, the old Clowns were supplanted by one of the next generation. Covent Garden's choice in 1832 fell on

Tom Matthews, who had a reasonable claim to be considered Grimaldi's pupil, and had the natural advantages of a jolly round face, a rich semi-hoarse roaring voice and a mouth, according to H. J. Byron, " like Piccadilly Circus."   He was born in 1805 (a year later than his life-long rival, W. H. Payne) and at an early age worked in the offices of the *Independent Whig*.   Here he spent four years ; then went on the stage.   Probably he was not the T. Matthews who " supported " Miss O'Neill at Covent Garden in 1818, but he was at Sadler's Wells in the early 'twenties just when that theatre's character underwent a radical change. From the spring of 1822, when the phenomenally successful " Tom and Jerry " was performed with the added attraction of pony races " passing into and round the pit," pantomime ceased to be given in the summer.   As the theatre's venture in keeping open all the year round was not checked, the management decided to confine Clown to Christmas as at the patent theatres.   Therefore, until the time of Phelps, the usual attractions were such spectacles as " Pictorial Illustrations to Shakespeare," Ducrow's equestrian review of the arts and sciences, and the aquatic drama [1] of " Black Rover ; or, the Shark and the Bloodhound," with a monster ship on the Wells' Atlantic to " tackle half the pit with its bowsprit and ponderous figurehead."   Clowns were no longer able to practise their art all the year round.

At first Tom Matthews was in the chorus.   In 1828, at the time of Grimaldi's farewell, he was the barber in " Harlequin Hoax "—it was in the barber's scene from this pantomime that Joseph appeared. Another promotion came during the run of " Fairy Red and Fairy Blue " that year.   When J. S. Grimaldi's part was given to W. H. Payne who had been playing dames, Tom became the Lover.   At Christmas he was Schambumthumptakit, the clown of " The Hag of the Forest Raven ; or Harlequin and the Persian Rose."   In 1830,

---

[1] On the stage or in the arena " real water " excites wonder.   This was not remarkable in ancient Rome when mimic sea-fights or nude nymphs bathing were part of the show.   To-day, however, water is dragged on the stage by the scruff of the tank.   Why a generation that remembers the aquatic spectacles at the Hippodrome should take pleasure in pools or streamlets at Drury Lane can only be explained by the instinctive joy felt by animals at the sight of water.

the announcement was made in big type that " Mr. T. Matthews will, in the character of Clown (and for the first time) sing Tippety-wichet." The next summer he was " * * * (afterwards Clown) " in " The Devil at Dunmow ; or, Harlequin and the Flitch of Bacon," sang the " Favourite song of ' Thump'em the Drummer ' " and re-vived the popular Grimaldi-Barnes duet of " Ran, Tan, Tan." Two of his pupils (not destined to be heard of) took part as a miniature Clown and Pantaloon. Furthermore, when a ball was given on the stage he was the master of ceremonies. He was both dame and Clown in " The Ocean Queen ; or, Harlequin and the Enchanted Aloe " at Christmas, 1831. Then he was engaged at Covent Garden. There was some trouble at the Wells next Christmas. They an-nounced " Humpty Dumpty ; or, Harlequin and the Fairy of the En-chanted Egg," with the intention of introducing a French clown named Anzelo. The scheme had to be dropped in favour of " Sea Devil ! or, the Freebooter's Boy Harlequin and Old Father Æsop or Little Cock Robin and the Children in the Wood " with Montgomery, Gram-mani, and Charles Stilt (a clever tumbler who remained at the Wells until his death in 1851) to make up for the loss of Tom. Yet, appar-ently, the management did not feel safe. On the bills appeared this notice :

> It having been customary during this season of Pantomime, for some few persons to call for an obsolete song called " Hot Codlins," much to the annoyance of the generality of the Audience, and the great interruption of the Performance, the Manager takes the present opportunity of respectfully announcing to the visitors of this establishment, that no Song, or Performance of any description, will be allowed to be introduced, but such as is announced in the Bills of the Day.

Doubtless they were thankful to get Tom back in the spring of 1833. He took precedence, in the bills of " Harlequin and the Fair One with the Golden Locks ; or, the Giant's Isle," over Grammani and Jefferini. When Bunn installed Ducrow and his horses at Covent Garden the next Christmas, the Wells kept its Clown again in a revival of " Goody Two Shoes." But that was his last performance there for many a day. The next year, in " Harlequin Guy Fawkes, or the Fifth of November," and the year after in the revival of " Mother Goose " that Grimaldi witnessed—it was announced as under the veteran's superintendence—the Clown was Jefferini. " The gods at this house," it was reported, " invariably call for Hot Codlins, however incapable the clown may be of singing it, and in the instance of Jefferini, we pronounce it the least humorous we have ever heard." His real name was Jeffreys. He was very tall, and the length of his legs made " drives " through shop windows dangerous. Once he injured himself internally. In consequence he had to cultivate a ludicrous grimace of pain in order to conceal his real suffering. This fixed the type of his humour. Thus, borrowing an idea from an actual thief sentenced at the Mansion House, he would appear as under arrest for stealing a lobster. To the policeman he would say, rubbing the place where he had hidden the lobster, " Haven't I been punished enough already ? " His career began at the little Panharmonium at King's Cross as Desperetta in " The Dumb Maid of Genoa," in the same year that he first went to Sadler's Wells. In spite of the critic's unfavourable opinion, he was so popular at Clerkenwell that he sat for the sign of the Clown Tavern (named after Grimaldi) in St. John-street. He kept a tobacconist's shop called " The Little Snuff Box " in Garnault-place, Camberwell, which was also a gambling house.

Occasionally Wieland[1] visited Sadler's Wells. His career began when he was fifteen as a Drury Lane monkey during the craze for stage monkeys of 1825. At the time of Barnes' death, he was famous for burlesque dancing, especially in " The Mountain Sylph ; or, the Flight of Taglioni " in which he gave an imitation of the ballerina. His Clown was described by Dickens as having " grotesque humour of no ordinary kind," like that of Payne who was installed at Covent Garden at the end of the 'thirties, when clowns were so plentiful that Tom Matthews was overlooked by Boz.

Yet whatever merits the new generation possessed, they were unable to prevent the decay of the Harlequinade. Though the new pantomime, written by the rhyming punsters of Fleet-street and painted by Royal Academicians, was a longer and more elaborate

---

[1] There was a " Little Wieland " in Drury Lane pantomimes of the 'eighties. There is a clown-like juggler on the music-halls to-day billed as " The Great Wieland."

" after-piece " than the brief show Grimaldi and Barnes performed, Clown dwindled. The " opening scenes " told a complete story, so that there was no need to continue the hero and heroine's adventures when they became Harlequin and Columbine. Bereft of the duty of pursuing them, Clown had merely to exhibit a number of tricks just before the curtain fell. Likewise Pantaloon, no longer the angry father of Columbine, survived in the uncertain state of being either Clown's parent or jackal. Without a master to exercise his wits upon, Clown vented his mischievous instincts upon all and sundry. There was no point or sequence in his exploits beyond the crescendo of his Saturnalian desires. The danger was that his performance would grow tedious for lack of drama. But the necessary sense of conflict was soon forthcoming. To create lively opposition, the representative of law and order was hatched just at the time he was needed.

Jokes are supposed to be birthless. Pantomime policemen, however, were practically a new character in clownship. The officer of the law who supplied comic relief in the Elizabethan and Jacobean plays was quite a different type. Instead of being outwitted or roughly treated to supply a diversion, he was a person having authority. It is true that the prologue to Middleton's " Roaring Girl " mentions the type of tavern lady " That beats the watch and constables controls," and in the play itself the sergeant is eluded, but such an event is not usual. Even Dogberry's men " comprehended two auspicious persons," in spite of his instructions that if a suspect would not stand, " why, then, take no note of him, but let him go—and thank God you are rid of a knave," whilst the preposterous Elbow in " Measure for Measure " has only to threaten " mine action of battery " to assert his authority. Likewise, in " Endymion " the pages sing to the constables, " Soberly let us be led." Even the merry Dekker shows no contempt for the constable. To his imaginary " gull," he suggests, " Marry, if the sentinel and his court of guard stand strictly upon his martial law and cry ' Stand ' . . . do it in some jest : for that will show you have a desperate wit, and perhaps make him and his halberdiers afraid to lay foul hands upon you," and the sarcasm is obviously at the expense of the gull. The watch of Old London was too strictly kept,

148

it seems, to be represented as ineffectual even in the broadest of comedies, and so it remained until the Restoration.   In the Plague year, however, so many recruits were enrolled to guard tainted houses and so many of the original constables died, that the tradition of the force was lost.   In a prologue to a play performed in 1667 Dryden speaks of the gallant's valour " which with the watch began," and *The Spectator* (1712) mentions " a gentleman that has several wounds on the head by watchpoles . . . to carry on a good jest."   Poles were not a good substitute for the old bill or halberd.   Consequently, the watch became more and more incapable.

But, as far as the stage was concerned, indignation had not yet turned to derision, except for the trifling instance of the outwitted constable in " The Emperor of the Moon," and even in pantomime the law's representative was obeyed.   The Harlequinade tradition was that he should be a personage to be feared.   Maurice Sand in his *Masques et Bouffons* describes *Il Sbirro*—the policeman of the Commedia dell' arte—as "ever a type greatly in vogue."   His hat, cloak, boots, sword, moustache, and nose hung together on a nail so that the Arlequin could sometimes disguise himself in authority.   But the real *Sbirro* lurked in waiting, and, " being strong of hand and tight of grip," he was feared by all.   That was the kind of constable who appeared in eighteenth-century pantomimes.   As a rule, the usual pursuit of the lovers was carried out without the help of the law, but in " Harlequin Sorcerer," the most popular show of the time, he was seen at Lincoln's Inn-fields early in the century and during several Covent Garden seasons later on.   On being appealed to by Pantaloon, he soon tracked the eloping pair.   Harlequin changed himself into an ostrich, but Columbine was taken into custody and conducted to her father's house.

Exactly when the tradition changed it might be rash to say, but there is reason to believe this occurred in the time of George IV., when the " Charleys " were mocked by all.   They were, says Leigh Hunt, " staid, heavy, indifferent, more coat than man, pondering, yet not pondering, old but not reverend, immensely useless."   In Thomas Dibdin's " Harlequin in his Element ; or, Fire, Water, Earth, and

Air," performed at Covent Garden in 1807, Grimaldi shut a watchman in his box, stole his lantern, and aroused the street with his rattle. But uncontrolled delight in baiting constables was first expressed by Pierce Egan in " Life in London." In " Tom and Jerry," the stage version, the comic possibilities of the watchman were eagerly seized. To teach his country cousin " how to box a Charley," Corinthian Tom upsets the constable's box, and after a fight the scene " closes on two watchmen cuffing one another by mistake." Here we have the first of the " mills," or scrimmages, popular in pantomimes of a later date.

What installed the policeman in pantomime was the unpopularity of the force when Peel instituted it in 1829. From the very beginning the Bobbies—also known as Peelers, Blue Bottles, Raw Lobsters, Blue Devils, and " Royal Blues or the Cook's Own "—were held in even less respect than the Charleys, especially when, a fortnight after they had commenced their duties, Constable John Jones stole a scrag of mutton from a butcher's shop in Somer's Town. His excuse that he took the joint to show his wife added to the public's merriment. " Who stole the mutton ? " became a street cry, and the chorus of " The New Policeman " song was known all over the town :

> Hullo, New Police,
>   Who in blue coats strut on,
> Your fame you won't increase
>   By stealing joints of mutton.

Pantomime soon developed the joke. That Christmas at Sadler's Wells the last scene but one of " The Hag of the Forest Raven ; or, Harlequin and the Persian Rose " was a " Preparatory School for the New Police," and the year after there were four policemen in the cast. Tom Matthews was the clown in these performances. And that he was responsible for making the novelty into a tradition seems proven by this letter from Macready :

> Mr. Thomas Matthews.—I was never so diverted in my life as at your admirable entertainment last evening. There is, however, one little suggestion which I would wish to offer you. I have been thinking of it all night. You may remember that a gentleman is coming out of a shop with a brown paper parcel in his hand. As he advances across the stage the parcel is abstracted from his possession by the pantaloon, who is, in his turn, deprived of it by a policeman, apparently in the discharge of his legitimate duties.

150

The policeman, upon that, makes a vulgar sign at the pantaloon, whom he has robbed. You then, Mr. Matthews, with admirable dexterity, pilfer the same parcel from the policeman, at which the pantaloon makes the same sign to you. Now, it occurred to me that, inasmuch as the pantaloon, when he has robbed the gentleman, makes that sign to the policeman, and the policeman when he has robbed the pantaloon repeats it, you, when your turn comes for larcenous dexterity, should accompany the same act by the same gesture. This was my idea as it occurred to me after witnessing the performance, and I merely put it to you, Mr. Matthews, as the suggestion of a person wholly without experience in such matters.

Provoked by the possibilities of the butt in Constable X, Clown became demoniac and eschewed quiet humour. A clown who, like Tom Matthews, indulged in subtleties, was promptly branded an " acting clown." Even knavery was subservient to the joke of falls and blows. Clownship was synonymous with horseplay. If the Harlequinade stage-directions of this date were decipherable, there would probably be little trace of Grimaldi's constant care not to stray too far from reality. Investigation, however, is baffled by the punning language of the clown's scenario. Here is an example (from " Harlequin Sinbad the Sailor ; or, the Great Roc of the Diamond Valley and the Seven Wonders of the World " at Drury Lane in 1864) which is typical :

> A great bustle in our street (not a crinoline) ... an unexpected present of jam which causes an upset in the police system. .... Clown tries to be one of the party, but the part he plays don't suit ... a door and a-dored ... above and below which makes Clown bellow ... he takes great *panes*, and gets a few more pains than he wanted. .... A nice buss and a Blunder-buss. ... Turn-ips and Turn-ups, and a dirty turn-out.... Giant Rhubarb, forced well up, and so are Clown and Pantaloon.

This code originated in the jokes of those who invented the pantomime tricks, such as the case of the changing of a pot of beer into a woman without a head which was billed as " the comparison between a pot of beer without a head and a good woman." When the practice was combined with Regency slang, the inscriptions became unintelligible. Thus the manager in Thomas Dibdin's " Harlequin Hoax " explains that " Pantomime authors have a dialect of their own." Liston wishes to know what " come the sly, queer the old one, take Miss Kelly out of a cupboard, cut a mug at the Clown, and brush off P. S.

with a roley poley " may mean. The manager is told to represent Pantaloon, and Liston is asked for " a Grimaldi grin " in order to pass muster as Clown. Then Harlequin runs round the stage, makes faces at Liston, gives him a hard slap, pulls away the manager's chair just as he is about to sit down, and when they strike at him dodges so that they strike each other. But though the pantomime " book of words " yields no information, there is a press-cutting in a scrap-book at the British Museum which gives this account of the Harlequinade just after Grimaldi's day :

> If Clown receives a slap of the face, he pays himself instanter, by knocking down the offerer of the insult. If Pantaloon in turning a corner, by accident runs against his brother motley, and is struck down by the collision, he bears no ill blood, but lays his hand to the leg of his fellow, and pulls him down after him, with the amiable desire of " making all straight between them." Clown is not offended at the kind solicitude of Pantaloon, as some of dully-framed beings might be ;—not he ! he throws a somersault, springs to his feet, gives a horse-laugh, which would frighten the best behaved animal in christendom, to show that he thinks nothing of the affair—he takes a prodigious leap, that seats him comfortably on Pantaloon's shoulders, and whirling over with his adopted hobby, tumbles into a baker's truck which is just entering. The vivacity of these gentlemen is as truly surprising as their surpassing honesty. Other folks would limp off after such untoward accident, or seek the nearest doctor to ascertain if all their bones were sound. On the contrary these ever-merry and never-daunted rogues, take the matter with the greatest sang-froid : tripping up the baker, whitening him with his own flour, and making him revolve like the earth upon its axis, with his own " rolls," they both set to work to empty his baskets, and fling the loaves in each other's faces, laying flat a brace of noses in the " doughty " operation. . . . Nothing can stop them in their ardent pursuit of knowledge. They will search for wisdom in a barrel of herrings, smash a barber's block to see if there isn't something in it, and dust his periwig of the powder, if it's for nothing but to get a little out of him. Another amiable trait in the character of Clown and Pantaloon is their good fellowship. Under all circumstances they pull together. Though they baste one another—a proof, merely, as in an Irish scrimmage, of their partiality for each other—they allow no one else
>
> " To step between them and their fighting souls."
>
> Like Beatrice and Benedict, they wage a merry war with one another, and all the world ; and another proof of their popularity, as well as extensive acquaintance, is that their droll appearance excited no wonder in the streets. As " Charter'd Libertines," they have full liberty of pranking it in Regent Street, as any other less populous and respectable situation. No one stops to look at them, though they stop to look at (how very kind of them !) and

play a trick upon everybody. No gentleman can carry an umbrella without an uncivil interference ; trade is at a standstill because they are all alive ; journeymen of all crafts are knocked down, and eased of their moveables by the most open and barefaced ill-doers. Redress is out of the question ; a shopman aims at them with the broom that sweeps the store, and smashes —his own window. They slip through the fingers of the policemen, constables, and watchmen, like unskinned eels ; every cranny is a refuge ; they bolt through doors, dart through glass, climb walls, and slip down chimneys with a celerity that sets pursuit at defiance.

Violence, however, does not suffice for clownship. The Harlequinade was decaying. Nothing revealed this as plainly as " the trick." The metamorphoses which Grimaldi had imbued with natural, everyday humour, changed to mechanical contraptions. At first there was some regard for amusement. Take, for instance, those in " Harlequin and Poor Richard ; or Old Father Time and the Almanack Maker " at Sadler's Wells in January 1841. A pawnbroker, given a child as " a pledge of love," agrees to put it " up the spout " (slang for " in pawn ") and pushes it up the water pipe. Besides the transformations of the public house sign of " Old Tom " into a cat and of a Cheshire cheese that Clown is cutting into a mouse-trap which imprisons him, a cheese presented to the Queen becomes first a Royal Cradle and then a dozen children. The idea of a sham mirror— a piece of gauze with figures imitating each other on either side—was also introduced. Contrast these notions with the chief trick of " Harlequin and Cinderella ; or, the Little Fairy and the Large Glass Slipper," staged the next year. At first there was a board bearing the notice, " An active Controller of the Exchequer wanted." Clown, who obtains the situation, is seen asleep at his desk in a room above a smith's anvil where Pantaloon forges Exchequer bills. There is an explosion which rouses the chancellor and causes Pantaloon's arrest. Then a large masked head appears with the inscription, " A great nob behind the curtains." Political allusion gave place to mechanical puns such as those recorded in the " penny plain, twopence coloured " pantomime sheets still sold in the toy theatre shop in Hoxton. A tub of bear's grease changes into a bear, a door into a draught of physic, an organ grinder into a knife grinder, a public house into a tea-pot, a dish of gooseberry fool into a grinning idiot, a shooting gallery into a potting shed, a box of bulls' eyes into policemen with lanterns, an alarm clock into a baby, a book bound in calf to a calf, a chest of pledges into a gin-soaked teetotaller, a case for pantaloons into Pantaloon, a jar of capers into Harlequin, and a bell (marked " Belle ") into Columbine. These miniature pantomimes which contain topical allusions to the erection of the Nelson Column and the Crystal Palace, belong to the period described by Mr. Percy Fitzgerald who states :

> Part of the stock-in-trade of the old clown was a number of tricks or mechanical contrivances. A clown was supposed to have a genius for inventing such things. They were expected from him. How well I see them now. Nothing more clumsy, or less delusive, could be conceived. You heard a rattle, and an immense chest came rolling in on wheels—the cord very palpable. Harlequin then slapped the ground, and there came a sudden flapping of doors, pulling of cords, etc. A legend was shown—" England's Hope "—and a little boy dressed as a Cupid walked out. Often the cords would not work, and the flap stuck fast, and then the thing was wheeled off contemptuously out of the way. It is astonishing how these clumsy make-shifts were accepted, even at first-class theatres. There was no attempt at deception or illusion ; the attempt was enough. How we loved also the spirited jumping, flying rather, through the trap in the wall, or the face of the clock, a dashing business, Harlequin leading the way, Pantaloon after him, and Clown rather reluctantly, but still coming up to the scratch, and how delightful the rolling out on the floor through another trap below. This seemed never to pall. We saw it year after year. There was usually some inscription, attended by the usual " flapping," such as " BOOKED THROUGH." All this was meagre enough, but managers relied on their Clowns putting in plenty of " business."

Another change for the worse was the reliance placed upon words. Though dumbness had been forced upon the clowns of pantomime in the eighteenth century by Acts of Parliament, the measure had made for the perfection of their art. During the rigid enforcements of the law brought about by the jealousy of the patentees just before the Act of 1788, Delpini had drawn legal fire by shouting " Roast Beef " without music. Therefore the only commentary they might use was apt grimace. Clowns could chant the patter of their songs and indulge in duets of back-chat such as the one in " Fairlop Fair " when Barnes sang :

> " Was there ever such a fool ? "

and Grimaldi responded more or less musically :

> " Old Daddy, except yourself."

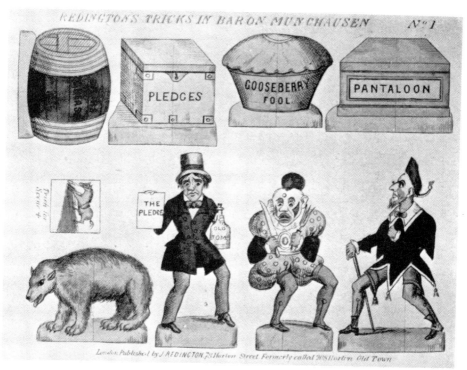

PANTOMIME TRICKS

but each action had to express itself.   As the law fell into abeyance, Barnes indulged in unintelligible chatter and Grimaldi in quips, such as his conversation with the oysters.   His talking, however," was so rare and seasonable that it only proved the rule by the exception." After his time, Leigh Hunt considered that clowns spoke too much :

> To keep on saying at every turn, " Hullo ! " or " Don't " or " What do you mean ? " only makes one think that the piece is partly written and not written well.

Clowns had to hold communication with the audience, even if it were only to shout " Here we are again " at the beginning or " See you to-morrow night " at the close.   But when they muttered to characters on the stage, the effect was rather like the ill-trained dancers in a ballet who frame unsounded words with their lips.   Yet between the spells of violence, a bout of repartee came not amiss.   Dickens, according to Mr. Fitzgerald, treasured the memory of one classic jest.   Clown had, as usual, stowed a stolen leg of mutton in his capacious pocket where it was detected by the Old 'Un :

> " I ain't got no leg of mutton," swore Clown.
> " Oh, Joey, Joey, why, I see you take it with my own eye."
> " I didn't."
> " Oh, but I saw you, Joey."
> " Well, then, it comes to this : *I'm a liar.*"
> " Oh, no, no, Joey, I don't say that."
> " Yes, you do.   *I'm a liar.*"

Jests of this kind become traditional and gather humour like a snow-ball.   Yet a stock of them will not make a clown.   There were no shoulders capable of bearing Grimaldi's " mantle " (to use a word much favoured before *Punch* pointed out he wore no such garment). However well Tom Matthews remembered his master's methods, he was unable to preserve the Harlequinade in spite of a prestige in his life such as even Grimaldi had not known.   From Covent Garden he went to Drury Lane, where he performed, on and off, for thirty years. He can be traced in 1847 at the Surrey in E. L. Blanchard's " Harle-quin Lord Lovel ; or, Lady Nancy Bell and the Fairies of the Silver Oak," and in 1850 he was engaged at the Royal Marylebone where J. A. Cave, celebrating his skill in stealing the secret of the nigger minstrel's musical instrument, caused the pantomime to be entitled " Harlequin Alfred the Great ; or, the Magic Banjo and the Mystic Raven." In accordance with the tradition of theatre clowns Tom was no mean dancer, and took part in opera and ballet, but his talent in pantomimes was such that he was engaged to stage one in Paris. He was always known as " the Inimitable." His popularity was so great that two pickpockets, it is said, returned his watch when they recognised him. Balfe composed " The Life of a Clown " in his honour. The Queen and the Prince Consort more than once invited him to their box. But, because of the growing importance of " the opening," he relinquished the motley (except when he came back from his retirement for Cave's revival of " Mother Goose" at Sadler's Wells). Likewise at Covent Garden, W H. Payne ceased to take part in the Harlequinade.

Again new clowns were needed. Richard Flexmore, who imitated Taglioni and other ballerine with grace and a little burlesque, was the most popular. He was born in 1822, and at an early age worked to support his mother as a warehouseman by day and a call-boy by night. While engaged at Whale's Tea Gardens, Bayswater, he was given the part of the lout in a comic ballet called " The Sailor and the Lout," though he could not dance. After a couple of steps he seized a broom, struck an attitude, shouted " Richard's himself again " and ran off the stage. Yet he learned to dance " quite perfectly." In addition, his extraordinary agility, hoarse voice and humour made him " decidedly the funniest, most original and most clownish of clowns since the days of the truly inimitable Grimaldi," in the eyes of *The Times.* Incidentally, he was the victim of the migratory instinct of theatrical biography. Anecdotes told of one clown often stray into the lives of others. Next to the story of the visit to the doctor that has both Carlin and Grimaldi for its hero, there is the episode of a private performance given in a sultan's palace which occurs in the biographies of Gustave Fratellini, Jean Gaspard Deburau and others. Though the details of the exploit may be changed from " pyramids " to trapeze, the point is always that the acrobat looks down upon the ladies of the harem who are peeping through eyeholes

156

in a screen. In the case of Flexmore, the anecdote strayed not into the biography but into his life—he found himself credited with a scapegrace son after the pattern of J. S. Grimaldi. In consequence, he wrote this letter to *The Times* :

> A short time since a lad between 18 and 19 years of age was charged by Mr. E. T. Smith, the worthy manager of the Theatre Royal, Drury-lane, with attempting to defraud him of the sum of 10*l*. by representing himself as the son of Mr. Flexmore, the clown. . . . Being myself under 28 years of age, I was certainly a bachelor at the early period of 10. I undoubtedly have had many sons presented to me during the performance of the various pantomimes in which I have been engaged, all of whom have been christened with the kind encouragement of the public ; but this unlooked for offspring having by the conduct alluded to evinced symptoms of rather a disreputable tendency, I must respectfully decline to father it.

Flexmore was at Covent Garden for several years. With W. A. Barnes, he appeared there under the management of the foolish " Wizard of the North," but even " the best Clown and the best Pantaloon in London " were unable, according to Henry Morley, to compensate for tricks which worked badly and were so pointless as not to be worth working at all. Flexmore died in the August of 1860. The Christmas before his death he joined Boleno, " one of the dryest and therefore one of the best of clowns," at Drury Lane. Boleno drilled the " Household Brigade and Marine Parade Volunteers," consisting of maids-of-all-work with mops and led them in a charge against an army of French cooks.

In these hands the Harlequinade still remained boisterous though its peculiar charm had vanished. What its conventions were like may be gathered from a contributor to *Chambers' Journal* in 1864 who took Clowns to task for not obeying the conventions of the 'fifties :

> Do you ever reflect upon the painful fact that English boys are now growing up wholly ignorant of the nature and efficacy of the Buttered Slide ? But how should they do otherwise when pantomime after pantomime ignores its existence, or else allusion to it is so brief and faint, that all, save expectant well trained eyes, fail to detect it ? Yet what wholesome food for mirth is here ! What statical and dynamical lessons—the laws of gravitation, of bodies in motion, of falling bodies, of impact ! Remember the bold colouring and breadth of detail of which a Buttered Slide in its integrity admits : the confidence of Pantaloon invited ; his ready acquiescence gained ; the prompt

appropriation of a goodly roll of freshest Dorset. (Mouths water sympa-thetically as you portray the intensity of pleasure derived from the licking of the unctuous morsel). "Now," in husky dulcet tones, you whisper Panta-loon—"now we'll have a lark!" and forthwith amply grease the path. Supers enter, fret their brief hour on the stage, and form a prelude to the approach of—"Student!" whose hapless lot it is ever to fall in evil panto-mimic places; he slips, trips, scrambles, falls and ever rises, Antæus like. Still you, ecstatic, ply the butter; he never for a moment halts, or falls upon his back, or moves his eyes from close perusal of his book; until at last, commiserating, you point and grin, and cry aloud: "Poor gentleman."

Again the Spill and Pelt [1]; to what has that degenerated? Why, once in an evening a knot of long striding youths and screaming maidens, all in sad-coloured attire, hurry pell-mell from wing to wing, pursued by a police-man or two, and a mere handful of high-flying carrots. What a falling off is here! We have now no longer the organised mob—imagemen, fishwomen, greengrocers, crockery sellers, bakers, police—running in Indian file across the stage, out at one wing, round at back of flat, and in again at the other, for you and Pantaloon to spill and pelt, and bring every scene to a conclusion amid a protracted eruption of vegetables, crockery, images and fish.

Melancholy changes for the worst, these; but they almost vanish in comparison with the next cause of complaint to be preferred against you. What has become of the red-hot poker? On behalf of the entire community, I repeat, with becoming warmth of expression, WHAT HAS BECOME OF THE RED-HOT POKER? Down on your marrow-bones, every mother's son of you —for I don't believe there is a living Clown who can give his heart the slap and say honestly: "I never rob the people of this famous usage"—down on your knees, and ask pardon of the injured British public.

Every clown can be practically funny. Be the enemy of mankind, and you become the audience's dearest friend. Be cruel—brutally, increasingly, perpetually cruel, and lo! you are intensely funny. In a spill and pelt, take care that people really are hit. Never mind hurting the supers—supers have no more right to feel pain than eels have. Check the growing activity of Pantaloon. Some of these old boys have actually taking to turning glib somersaults! Prefer the Lover to Sprites; he takes ill-usage so debonnairly, while you can't hit a sprite. Look to your legs! Why they're getting straight; you aren't knock-knee'd nowadays; neither do your calves grow at the side of your shins! Shew us your tongue oftener. And you don't eat enough of the right sort of food—sausages, raw fish, vegetables, and the like—nor do you sufficiently signify by gesture whether or not what you eat delights the palate. As for sausages, it is years since a legitimate chain of them has been seen at a West End theatre. (Let us hope that the authorities

[1] Otherwise known as the "rally." In 1872 one of the supers at Astley's hit the clown, either with a large fish on the head or with a carrot in the eye (the evidence was conflicting). After the show, Clown struck the super till he "bled like a pig." The case was heard in court and Clown fined £2.

of the university of Cambridge are not growing lax in the discharge of one of their chief duties, and neglect to supply the original article from which to model.) Remember Corporal Nym's dictum : " The good-humour is to steal at a moment's rest." Lastly, and above everything, let us have plenty of red-hot pokers.

The Christmas following the death of Flexmore decided the fate of Clown. His place at Covent Garden early in 1859 had been filled in an emergency. Flexmore, whose early privations led to atrophy, was taken ill while playing the Wolf (afterwards Clown) in " Little Red Riding Hood." His skin was stripped from him and given to Henry Payne. Though a son of W. H. Payne, who was the Wicked Baron, he was a serious dancer, and as such had been originally cast for Harlequin. He retained Flexmore's place, however, though two other Clowns were brought to Covent Garden for " Blue Beard ; or, Harlequin and Freedom in Her Island Home," in the season of 1860-1. One was Boleno, lured from Drury Lane. The other was Wattie Hildyard, who began in Astley's circus, but took kindly to pantomime until he received a bequest from an aunt of three pounds a week on condition that he should renounce both the ring and the stage. Then he went to live at Deptford with an aged female relative to guard against backsliding. When Mr. H. G. Hibbert, who told this tale, visited the old fellow, the female constable was strategically sent on errands while the old Clown's costume was pulled out of a drawer, laid on a bed and gloated over.

Other theatres adopted Covent Garden's plan of trying to conceal by the multiplication of Clowns their loss of the secrets of the Harlequinade. At Drury Lane, in Blanchard's " Peter Wilkins ; or, Harlequin and the Flying Women of the Loadstone Rock " (1860-1), Huline of Hengler's circus and Little Huline formed a trio with Power. This increased demand, aided by the call for pantomime troupes from the Continent, brought into existence the cult of the pantomime family. Thus, at the Haymarket in 1858, in " Undine ; or, Harlequin and the Spirit of the Waters," Clown was Charles Leclercq, Harlequin Arthur Leclercq, and the Water-Spirit Louise Leclercq (Carlotta Leclercq was the Columbine at the Princess's) ; and at his Majesty's in 1860, in Blanchard's " Tom Thumb ; or, Merlin the

159

Magician and the Good Fairies," Charles Lauri was the Clown, J. Lauri Harlequin, Jenny Lauri Columbine and H. Lauri Pantaloon. But numbers would not ensure success. Sala in the 'seventies declared :

> Modern clowns are, as a rule (Mr. Harry Boleno, who is one of the old school, may be admitted as an exception), desperately dull ; and many are mere contortionists or acrobats, who have no admissible claim to be called clowns at all, and endeavour to compensate for their normal dreariness by tying up their limbs in abnormal knots or exhibiting dancing dogs or educated pigs. Some of the modern clowns dance nimbly enough, but not one of their number merits to be named in the same breath with the incomparably droll and graceful Flexmore—now, alas, deceased.

Yet how could Clown, though author as well as performer, save a performance that had been robbed of all design ? Even after the story of the elopement had vanished from the Harlequinade, the practice had persisted awhile of changing all the characters in the preliminary story into the motley worthies to give some sort of coherence to the two parts of pantomine. At the end of the fairy tale the hero and heroine were addressed by the Fairy Queen who spoke a couplet such as :

> And that you may not further fear,
> As Harlequin and Columbine appear,

and condemned the Baron and his varlet to be those proclaimed rogues—as if motley were akin to broad arrows—Clown and Pantaloon. Children had the pleasure of detecting Harlequin by the chance display of particolour and spangles, Clown by a glimpse of coral lips through the ample mouth of a mask, and other characters by furtive attempts to ease buttons and loosen tapes. Such delights were lost when two separate sets of performers were employed, the Clown coming up one trap as the Baron descended another, a convention which led to the strange result that (so Mr. H. G. Hibbert used to tell) Wattie Hildyard and J. L. Toole never met though they acted in the same pantomime. At length, to simplify matters still further, the Harlequinade was entirely disconnected. In Grimaldi's day it had been an afterpiece. Now it was an afterthought. Sentimental regard for bygone laughter was all that kept it alive. Yet Augustus Harris was not unmindful of this appeal. In the early 'eighties he

HARRY PAYNE IN 1890 — BY PHIL MAY

From a drawing in the Author's Collection

drew Harry Payne from Covent Garden and installed him as Drury Lane's standing Clown. He also attracted Charles Lauri to play, in addition to animals such as a poodle, cat and donkey, the part of second Clown, before he went to the Lyceum, where in 1893 he "made up" in exact imitation of Grimaldi. The new generation of stage Clowns, however, was refusing office. What was the use of qualifying for a profession engaged for three months in the year, at most, to perform tricks at so late an hour each night that the house had begun to empty itself? Bert Coote, who was a Clown at Drury Lane with Frederick Evans and the Great Little Rowella in 1880, turned aside from the motley. Frederick Evans initiated his son into the ways of the Harlequinade the next year, but Will, though his stage face always reveals the born Clown, also declined the honour when he grew up. Fred Kitchen, son of another noted Clown, was similarly bred, but gave the benefit of his training to music-hall sketches. In consequence, the red-hot poker passed into the hands of those who lacked knowledge. Harry Payne, however remote from Grimaldi, saw what was wrong. He deplored that those entrusted with what was " really an art " could not act. He said :

> You know very well what Grimaldi was : he had all that sort of thing about him. When he stole sausages he had an expression on his face and figure. He was not a mere knockabout; no man can be a clown proper who is that. I never knock a man down unless there's a reason for it. The only time I ever knock a man down without a reason for it is when I have missed one man and knocked the other down, for which I have always been very sorry.

To this he added a story of an accident during a " drive," the term to denote Harlequin's plunge through a window and return over a grating. Payne pulled at his leg and, growing annoyed because the man failed to come through, pulled harder—but the leg was broken. That story is typical of the altered character of the Clown. Persons of less importance were now called upon to carry out the acrobatic tasks. Consequently, whereas Grimaldi ended broken in health and fortune in middle life, Harry Payne died (in 1895) still on the active list though sixty-five years of age, and left £5,858. " I consider,"

said J. A. Cave, " that clowns are very long-lived strong old men."
Of Tom Matthews, then eighty years of age, he said :

> He's not very strong now, but he attributes that to a life of laziness in
> later years and thinks that if he had kept on working a little longer—he was
> only about sixty-three when he retired—he would have better health now.
> Occasionally Pantaloons retire because the work is too hard for them ; the
> Clown, especially if he be spiteful, having it in his power to make things very
> unpleasant for the Pantaloon ; but the Clown can keep on to almost any age,
> especially if he's steady.   I quite think Tom Matthews was wrong to retire.

Since the death of Harry Payne, there is little to record.   At
Drury Lane Whimsical Walker kept some semblance of life in the
Clown, in spite of the scene shifters' constant prayer to " cut it short."
During the season of 1901-2 he staged a joke which has been repeated
in nearly every Harlequinade since.   The scene was Clown's coffee-
stall at the seaside ; because of the annoyance caused by a string of
dishonest customers, he took a stick to a singer of " Queen of my
Heart " ; but, though soundly beaten, the minstrel continued right to
the fall of the curtain.   Whimsical Walker has returned to the circus
of late years, spending his leisure in Dan Pegotty's upturned boat at
Gorleston-on-Sea.   Being at this distance from town he was unable to
join the clowns brought together by Grock at his lunch on April 17,
1924.   Bluff, hearty Harry Paulo was there, offering to play Pantaloon, at seventy-seven years of age, whenever his host liked.   Will
Simpson, blinking the wisdom of his seventy-six years through glasses,
disputed with the aggressively cheerful Fred Delaney, who is no more
than sixty-eight, concerning things that happened in the arenas of
the Continent many years ago.   " The managers," says Will Simpson,
who was at Drury Lane in 1879,

> have killed the old play by engaging people who knew nothing about it.
> They brought in a couple of knockabouts from the music-halls to play the
> Robbers in " Babes of the Wood " or the Policemen in " Aladdin " and for
> cheapness made them do the Harlequinade at the end as well.   It was such
> poor stuff that people wouldn't stay to look at it.

Another clown at the luncheon was J. M. Jones, who, at the age of
seventy-four, conducts a dancing academy in person.   When the conversation turned to the good old custom whereby advertisement revenue

derived from the Harlequinade was the Clown's perquisite—not forgetting the plentiful supplies of edible sausages that the company
lived on when Harry Payne was Clown at the Lane—Mr. Jones
recalled the times when he arranged the Harlequinades at the Grand,
Islington.   A shopkeeper wanted to be advertised by a pig.   It was
kept in a basket.   When released during the performance it ran
amok, chased the " dandizette " across the stage, made the Clown rush
for safety, charged across the footlights and scattered the orchestra.
Finally it landed in the "real water" tank below the stage, where it was
caught, replaced in its basket, and carried for safety to the " flies."
During the night it broke loose and made a noise like a dozen burglars.
When a cordon of police had discovered the real cause of the uproar
it was returned to the shop.   Clown received a leg of pork.

Tradesmen's advertisements, which now provide the management
with revenue, are practically all that is left of the Harlequinade, apart
from one or two well-intended but desultory revivals during the
Christmas holidays of 1922 and 1923.   Very seldom is the man in
the motley the genuine Clown.   The veterans of the Harlequinade,
whatever their circumstances, properly resent the terms offered them
to stage these advertisements of fish-shops and furniture dealers.
Wealth is not their portion now.   Their end is symbolised in the
Clown who died not so many years ago in hospital.   As the light
failed his mind went back to the darkened scene in the old pantomines
just before the " transformation."   His last words referred to this.
" Now," he said, " it's the cat scene, doctor."   Clown is as dead
as Harlequin and Pierrot.   Like them he has suffered a change from
laughter to fantasy.

THE MUSIC-HALL COMEDIAN

To the majority of Londoners Mr. Leno's personality must be much better known than Lord Salisbury's or Mr. Balfour's. That, to be sure, is partly because he can be personally inspected any evening for a shilling, while they cannot. But then he has an influence which they have not. What he says ("with song and dance") comes home to (Cockney) men's business and bosoms. Instead of high politics, which nobody understands, not even the politicians, he discusses latch-keys, mothers-in-law, "our court," the lodger, chuckers-out, and "booze" —themes which knock at the heart, stir the inmost fibres of being, are, in short, in Maeterlinckian phrase, at once the Treasure of the Humble and the symbols of Wisdom and Destiny . . . He takes the meanest little subjects, the follies and weaknesses of the unsophisticated vulgar to be met in all the tramcars and in most of Mr. George Gissing's novels—and by a touch of fantasy he gives them freshness, distinction, "style." But his fantasy, at its wildest, always has direct reference to life.

A. B. WALKLEY.

Stg: Lauinia. · Cap· Cerimonia ·

WHAT excites curiosity, according to the author of "Social Psychology," is an object "similar to, yet perceptibly different from" the very familiar. That seems to explain the popularity of exhibitions of household management on the stage. Pantomime kitchens transform the humdrum tasks of humble homes —not in the nightmare fashion of Mr. Sime's charwoman who scrubs huge steps made of soap—into operations separated from the necessity of getting things done. Democracy is all but the inventor of this type of clownship. Peoples whose welfare depends on the conquests made by their lords and masters are less likely to feel the importance of domestic trifles than those whose lives are bounded by the business of making both ends meet. Consequently there are only faint traces of jokes with this flavour in the entertainments of long ago.

Aptly enough, the first hint comes from the medieval convent where Hroswitha wrote plays to edify the nuns. She causes a persecutor of Christians to be stricken with madness in a kitchen. Consequently, instead of wronging the virgins, he embraces kitchen utensils, blackens himself, and in this disguise is beaten by his own soldiers. Another hint—nothing more—occurs in " The Supposes," Gascoigne's translation of Ariosto which was acted at Gray's Inn in 1566. Here the cook, cursing the lackey who carries his basket for tarrying to beat bears on the way home, complains, " By that time we come to the house, I trust that of these twenty eggs in the basket, we shall find but very few whole." The French farces of Molière's youth, market-place performances designed to amuse not the King but the crowd, referred to domestic worries. One of their famous jokes was the retort to Gaultier-Garguille's complaint that the maids combed their hair in the porridge pots and frying pans, whereupon Turlupin cried, " I've found you a model servant. She always combs her head in the wine vat."

The resourceful Italian troupe in Paris only trifled with such ideas. Their shopping episodes were nearest the mark, for their kitchens were meant to burlesque, not domesticity, but the ways of the opera. One of the first English pantomimes of the early eighteenth century contained a shop where Harlequin, Scaramouche, Punch and Pierrot were caught pilfering, and flew off on spirits in the shapes of a cat, a hog, a goat and an owl. More akin to music-hall usage was a popular scene, revived many times, in " Harlequin Sorcerer." When pursued into a laundry, Harlequin changed into an old washerwoman, who soaped the linen, washed the clothes and hung them out to dry ; then dabbed soap suds in the faces of Clown and Pantaloon. This, however, was an isolated instance. Even at Sadler's Wells the humour of the home was exploited very occasionally. In " Harlequin Neptune " (1776) Harlequin hid Columbine in a rotiffeur which, when turned round by Clown, contained only a large pig roasting ; and Clown in a fruit shop made " the laughable mistake " of turning a cut melon the wrong way up. Like these examples, the shopping jokes or homely songs of Grimaldi were not a conscious mimicry of everyday life. Yet the increasing popularity of food shops in the scenes of the early nineteenth century Harlequinades reveals the new tendency in humour. While clowns wore motley, however, household matters did not lend themselves to the stage. The time was ripe for a return to nature. Another " clod, clot, lump " was hatched. To avoid confusion with Clown he was termed " the music-hall comedian " (now inaptly shortened to " the comedian ").

Traces of his origin may be found in the burlesques that Planché instituted. He definitely took shape in the burlesque pantomimes which ridiculed romance in a more boisterous fashion. The more civil fun of the burlesques produced the fashion of the principal boy. The horseplay of the pantomimes demanded the hero, and heroine as well, should be knockabout creatures wearing grotesque masks. Even the daintiest ladies of legend were played by men. In " Harlequin Good Kynge Arthure " at Sadler's Wells in 1841, Guinevere was a " dame," who, when a herald thundered at the castle, lifted up the latch unwarily and was knocked down with the final blow meant for

168

the gate. This change of spirit favoured knockabout humour in the home, an idea first exploited in "Harlequin Cherry and Fair Star; or, the Green Bird, the Dancing Waters and the Singing Tree," written by George Ellis and staged at the Royal Princess's Theatre in December, 1852. The curtain rises on the Royal Nursery of Cyprus in an uproar. Some of the children are trying to duck each other in a large portable bath; others are playing at smothering each other in a large cradle; others are fighting with pillows, quarrelling over a cat, playing leap frog, sailing boats in a wash-tub, trundling hoops or whipping tops. A maid is dragging an unruly boy (in a bathing costume) to a shower bath, and another maid attempts to use a large comb, brush and pot of pomatum on a howling youth. Meanwhile Cherry (F. Cooke) is imitating a popular juggler by lying on his back and balancing a baby on his feet. He is chased by a maid who falls into the bath. A second maid is pushed into the shower bath, and a third into the cradle, until the King of Cyprus appears with a birch. Princess Fair Star (Mr. Daly) then arrives from boarding school with music case, crotchet box, large slate, blotted copy book and a letter from her head mistress. When the Court retires to rest the boys fight for the pleasure of peeping into Fair Star's bedroom—and after other such " business " the plot at length begins just before the end of the act. There is no resemblance here to the burlesque extravaganza presented by Rebecca Isaacs at the Strand three years later with herself as Cherry and Fanny Beaumont as Fair Star.

Fashion firmly established the new vogue of clownship. In Blanchard's " Harlequin Hudibras ; or, Old Dame Durden and the Droll Days of the Merry Monarch," at Drury Lane in 1852, Deulin as Charles II. rushed in with a small carpet bag and a large umbrella. Tom Matthews played Hudibras, afterwards Clown. Entering Dame Durden's kitchen, furnished with " utensils of the usual grotesque pantomime size," he sat down before a huge joint. Because the servants had spilt hot gravy over him and handed him the wrong end of the carver, he flung the vinegar they had poured into his wine glass at them, but hit Dame Durden full in the face. He dried her with the table cloth. Charles entered and knocked him down. Dame Durden fetched sticking plaster and covered Hudibras' face in an excess of zeal.

To all intents and purposes Clown was deposed. " The Inimitable Tom " soon doffed the motley for good and appeared only in the " openings." W. H. Payne, and Frederick Payne his foil, did likewise at Covent Garden. The natural ambition of the born clown was to be a comedian. There was an article in the *Temple Bar* of 1861 by a writer who, having to confess that he had never seen Grimaldi, asked,

> What right have I, therefore, to complain, and make odious comparisons, and throw a wet blanket on those who are inclined to enjoy themselves with the sport of our Deulins and Leclercqs and Bolenos—poor Flexmore, also, has danced the inevitable dance of death—and Paynes? Pray is not Mr. W. H. Payne as great a pantomimist as ever lived? Have you seen him, as the Earl of Mercia, receive the petition of his overtaxed vassals in Lady Godiva; and after superciliously glancing at it through an enormous eye-glass, contemptuously wipe his feet upon it? Have you seen him retire to rest in the Great Bed of Ware, or rise in the morning and go through the ordinary operations of the toilet? You say you have, and the force of pantomimic humour can go no further.

Though the spirit of burlesque grew less boisterous, the fairy tales continued to be domesticated for pantomime use. In A'Beckett's " Ali-Baba and the Forty Thieves; or, Harlequin and the Genii of the Arabian Nights," at Covent Garden in 1866, the robbers' cavern was a club-room, containing inner caverns furnished as card-room, billiard-room, dining-room, kitchen and lounge. The poverty of Ali-Baba's home was expressed in terms of a tax-gatherer with a large notice, " Water Rate, 17 Quarters due last Michaelmas," a butcher with a bill, " Not received a Halfpenny for 14 years—Terms Cash," and a milkman with "Your last ha'porth—out of chalk." Frederick Payne as Ganem serenaded—in competition with the traditional cat —Morgiana with a trombone, and threw a stone which broke Ali-Baba's window. W. H. Payne entered with a ladder and, in the dark, placed it against the ladder brought in by Ganem. They met at the top, struggled and fell. Morgiana discovered the robbers in jars marked " Cod's liver oil." They were arrested by an Inspector and a body of police with bull's eye lanterns.

There was a touch in the incongruity of this everyday humour blended with far away romance, of Shakespeare's showmanship. It was too effective to vanish with other Victorian ideas of entertainment. Nevertheless, it had to be modified. The retirement of Matthews and Payne enabled the Vokes to establish a type of pantomime that made broad mirth a minor consideration. Their "Cinderella" in 1878-9, however, was a financial failure, and Drury Lane came into the hands of Augustus Harris. After his first pantomime, "Bluebeard," a quarrel sent the Vokes to Covent Garden, where they failed again, but "Mother Goose and the Enchanted Beauty" at the Lane was a success. The new company had been brought from several quarters. The principal recruit was Arthur Roberts, "father of music-hall comedians." He started life in a solicitor's office. At the age of nineteen he took to singing in the tavern entertainments. When Harris asked him to play Dr. Syntax, ten years later, his fame was measured by a salary likely to startle managers. In "A Playgoer's Memories," Mr. Hibbert described him thus :

> He had a rare knack of comic "make up," a clear staccato style of singing, a most expressive eye and an incomparable eloquence of pantomime —without a word of introduction or explanation he would suggest, for instance, that a woman looking in her mirror noticed a little untidiness of coiffure. Minutely he would dissect and elaborately reconstruct the panoply of fashion. With such antics the actor would engage his audience for the space of minutes—a marvel of observation, of mischievousness, of super-simian mimicry.

The next year Arthur Roberts played Mrs. Crusoe in "Robinson Crusoe," and the year after Ali Mi in "Sinbad." Then some trouble with the licensing authorities caused him to leave music-halls and pantomimes for *opera bouffe*. But the fervent worship he inspired made Harris look to the music-halls to find people for his pantomime. "The invasion" it has been called. Yet pantomime was invented by *forains*, and always drew its players from the music-houses, booths and even the boxing-ring. That had long been a sore point with critics and actors who thought the stage debased by tumblers and mountebanks' men. In the season of 1749-50 Quin and Peg Woffington refused to undergo the degradation of acting on the same stage as the famous Turk who " exhibited on the wire," though performers of this type were always encouraged by Rich. At the same theatre, in the " Aladdin " of 1788, Mendoza and Humphreys sparred. In 1822 Theodore Hook described this " national theatre " as the only place " where there is real tumbling, and where a fellow walks with his feet on the ceiling and performs innumerable monkey tricks." Bunn, referring to " the humbug of the professors of the marvellous," related how in his day, " Rope-dancers, posture-masters, patent skaters, tumblers, strong men, flies, and fools of every description," tendered their services for " the celebration of the year's most momen-tous event." Speculating on the chance of a pig, or a donkey, or live poultry being required in the pantomime, and knowing that a shilling a night was paid for the use of such properties, rogues would turn dealers in such articles, " and rear them in the hope of realizing a nightly profit by them." So it continued to 1852, when Devani, the great contortionist, carried out his " wonderful evolutions " in " Harlequin Hubidras " at Drury Lane ; to the next year when a family named Ethair gave a display of posturing, and to the year after when " the Italian Brothers " performed feats of strength. Yet Leopold Wagner's pamphlet on " The Pantomimes," published in 1881, bewails the time when " knockabout niggers, clog dancers, gymnasts, contortionists, Whitechapel songsters and other music-hall ' novelties ' were not considered indispensable for success." There never was such a time. For the first century of its existence panto-mime was the staple amusement. It offered employment for tumblers, singers and dancers at all seasons—at the patent theatres throughout the winter and at the music-houses and circuses throughout the summer. When this custom passed they found employment in tea gardens or taverns, except when Christmas brought them together. Therefore, as the music-halls were supplied with performers from the theatres' Christmas shows, the " invasion " was merely an annual migration.

The noteworthy pantomime families prove this. The Lupinos, for instance, are descended from a puppet-showman who came to England from Bologna early in the eighteenth century. After travelling from fair to fair he settled at the Bumper, in Bow Street, kept by Dick Eastcourt (the comedian of whom Steele, curiously enough, wrote, " This pleasant fellow gives one some idea of the ancient pantomime"), and married his host's illegitimate daughter, who inherited the tavern. Here Georgius Richard Eastcourt Luppino was born in 1713. The son, apprenticed to Rich, followed Woodward to Dublin and married a daughter of Madame Violante, the rope-dancer. Later, he acted in Richardson's travelling booths, and appeared as Harlequin to the elder Grimaldi. He had two children, George and Rosina. As a child-dancer Miss Lupino was highly praised for charmingly portraying " the manners of the American savages " in " The Black Festival ; or, Love in America " at Sadler's Wells in 1800. She became the principal dancer at Vauxhall Gardens and the Adelphi Theatre, and had a numerous family by James Hook, a theatre musician. From this time onwards the name of Lupino often appears on playbills. Astley and Richardson employed a dress designer of that name. There was also a Harlequin and a Pantaloon belonging to the family. George Lupino was a circus clown, one of the Six Lupinos, high and low tumblers. His son, George, was *inter alia* the demon spider in " The Spider and the Fly ; or King Jokose of Go-for-'em Castle " at the Britannia in 1890. To-day, Stanley Lupino, Barry Lupino and Lupino Lane are among the most accomplished, in tumbling, dancing and mimicry, of pantomime performers. They have been beholden to the music-halls for part of their training.

The fame of the Conquests is also based on a tavern. They are the descendants of Benjamin Oliver (1805-72), who adopted the name. In the 'thirties he was a member of the Sadler's Wells company, and Mrs. Conquest danced at Astley's. In 1851 he bought the Eagle Tavern and Grecian saloon in the City Road. Their seven children went on the stage. His son, George, also married a ballet mistress and gave three sons to pantomime. For over twenty years Benjamin and George managed the Grecian Theatre, which became noted for remarkable pantomime monsters and " fight scenes," through traps, slides, flying machines, and other mechanical contrivances. George Conquest then took over the Surrey. When he died in 1901 his son

Fred ran the theatre, but handed over its cares to his brother George, who stayed there for three years, and in 1910 became manager of the Britannia, where he acted that Christmas in " The Forty Thieves." Arthur Conquest, the third son, was the Old Man of the Sea in " Sinbad the Sailor " at Drury Lane in 1906, and played in the next six pantomimes there. George Conquest, great-grandson of Benjamin Oliver, played " Amelia Jane, the Goose " in " Mother Goose " at the Surrey on Boxing Night in 1921.

Yet, in spite of the rise of the music-hall, the pantomime still marked the milestones in the road of the clown. Not only did it provide wider scope for the comedians' humour of the humble home, and opportunities for the interplay of personalities kept in watertight compartments as " turns " for the rest of the year, but it was their nursery. Joe Elvin began in " Hop o' My Thumb " at Brighton in 1872, Bert Coote in " The Babes in the Wood " at Sadler's Wells in 1873, Charles Coborn in " The Forty Thieves " at Sandgate in 1875, Fred Kitchen in his father's pantomimes in the 'seventies, Will Evans in " Robinson Crusoe " at Drury Lane in 1881, T. E. Dunville in " Cinderella " on tour in 1887, and George Graves in " Aladdin " at Manchester in 1900. A hurried examination of Mr. John Parker's " Who's Who in the Theatre " shows that to name all who developed their youthful talent in this manner would be too lengthy a task.

Whatever his failings as a showman, Augustus Harris knew how to pick his people. Nearly all the most popular comedians of his age appeared for a season or longer at Drury Lane. Even if he had wished to do more, to perfect his company until he had formed a band of Saturnalians to shake respectability's throne, circumstances other than the question of finance would have prevented him. There was, to begin with, the legend that pantomime was solely designed for children, a legend belied by the very nature of the entertainment and shattered by the first successes of children's plays. There was also the peculiar but profitable modesty of newspapers to contend with. Consequently, Marie Lloyd only remained for three pantomimes, playing a Princess Allfair in 1891, Red Riding Hood in 1892, and Crusoe's sweetheart in 1893. In the last one she came to grief with

174

a song called " A Saucy Bit of Cracklin'." She was, quite unconsciously, a woman with a mission in life. She represented the extraordinarily belated reaction against the eighteenth century vogue of respectability. In France it was killed by the Reign of Terror, in England by Marie Lloyd. In her contemplative moments off the stage she might grow sentimental and approve edifying quotations from Ella Wheeler Wilcox, but on the stage she blasted false sentiment. Prudishness wilted before her. She would not leave unsaid those little harmless details about everybody's everyday life that the Victorians considered sins unnamed among Christians (and the Georgians the essentials of literature). Except to inveterate Puritans and newspapers, Marie Lloyd's happy unconcern was irresistible. Hygiene, sexual commerce, underclothes and drink, were all natural matters for comment. " These," she seemed to say, " are topics any lady might say to another lady over the garden fence while hanging out the washing, so where's the harm ? " That argument was unanswerable. Her humour lay in imparting heart to heart confidences not to a bosom friend but to a thousand strangers. Intimacy across the footlights was a jest the public was very fond of. When Marie Lloyd " modestly disrobed and retired to rest " in " Robinson Crusoe," Mr. William Archer heard a gasp of satisfaction at every string she untied. He had no wish to assist at her toilet. But he was " in a minority of one." She was a social reformer, in her way, as courageous as Ibsen. Our delight in her was generally because we realised that the spasm of shame felt at hearing the unmentionable mentioned or the unrevealable revealed has no justification in reason.

In the Drury Lane pantomimes that boasted Marie Lloyd, Little Tich played Humpty Dumpty, Hop o' my Thumb and Man Friday. Then he was, to quote Mr. Archer, " thrown to the wolves of criticism." Yet, not only were his jests inoffensive, but his humour had the direct bearing on life that made the Christmas pantomime of that age beloved. Even now, when he no longer dances in boots as long as he is high, his appearance suggests a head pushed through a curtain with a marvellously animate doll's body hung under the chin. At the same time he is determined to impose a sense of his importance upon us.   Little Billy Robinson's claim to celebrity cannot altogether be laughed at.   When he protests that we must have heard of Billy Robinson, his pathetic, yet proud, earnestness almost compels an involuntary " Of course."   That grocer, too, is so real that smells of his shop have come with him.   His inane amiability seeks to compel a response just as it does when employed by the real salesman.   His disclosures concerning the fingering customer who steals his soap and scrubbing brushes strike us as indiscreet.   Before he dances into the wings the rapt onlooker is under the impression that he is in the grocer's shop wondering what on earth he came in to buy.   Whatever the manikin he represents—the débutante at Court ; the affable, but omnisciently offensive waiter ; the meticulously courteous Frenchman ; the sailor with troublesome trousers—it only escapes reality by being too true.

There was also Dan Leno.   He was an acrobat at the age of three and a champion clog-dancer in his teens.   While he was performing at provincial music-halls, George Conquest heard him sing " Milk for the Twins " in the character of " a distressed female."   In consequence, Dan Leno played in two pantomimes at the Surrey, until Augustus Harris called him to Drury Lane in 1888 to be the Baroness in " The Babes in the Wood and Robin Hood and His Merry Men and Harlequin who Killed Cock Robin."   The next year, as the widow in " Jack and the Beanstalk," he omitted the clog-dance in order to give all his attention to the humour of the humble home.   One of his first ideas, however, was nothing more than Grimaldi's idea of a love song interrupted by a chorus of cats.   But the description of Hickory Wood shows what made his dames remarkable.   When he acted a queen, she was " quite a possible queen," even though she lived in such conditions that a pair of braces was the natural thing for her to buy the king on his birthday, and the mistake of handing him the wrong parcel (containing lingerie) to be opened in full view of the court, the not unnatural outcome of her ways of life.   In his studies of women in a humble walk of life :

His gait, his manner, his expression were altered, and all his dignity had vanished.   He was homely, discursive, and confidential, not to say occa-

176

Yours Truly, Dan Leno

From a photograph lent by Mr. Dan Leno, Junior

sionally aggressive. His own personality was, of course, ever present; but when I saw him playing these kind of parts, the impression he left on my mind was not so much a picture of Dan Leno playing the part of a woman in a particular walk of life as the picture of what Dan Leno would have been if he had actually been that particular woman.

Wash tubs filled with tattered underwear and kitchen tables laden with a mass of uncooked, adhesive pastry, were not necessary to Dan Leno. All that is raw and primitive in womankind he could burlesque as wildly as his perpetually startled eyes, strained mouth and disconcerting legs burlesqued the appearance of withered femininity. As a designing Sister Anne, who wonders does she "push" herself too much, but tries all the same to capture the heart of Bluebeard with " When the Heart is Young," until her hair gets caught in the strings of her harp; as Widow Twankey, making fatuous observations upon the tricks of the Slave of the Lamp ; as Cinderella's step-mother, mocking the flunkey who has tried to prevent her coming to the ball, his humour had so much " direct reference to life " that those who looked on pantomime as a childish toy protested against his satirical powers. Yet after his last appearance at Drury Lane in the " Humpty Dumpty " of 1903, no other comedian could take his place. Red-nosed mirth was out of fashion, and the new style, humour mixed with sentiment either in the Cockneys of Albert Chevalier or the Scots of Harry Lauder, was too complete in itself to merge into pantomime. Comedians no longer dealt in what Mr. W. R. Titterton described as

> the true bread-and-butter stuff, the divine surprises of every day—the fun of getting drunk, of going on the spree, of backing a winner, of meeting a fairy ; the dangers of falling in love, of getting married, of coming home late, of having a mother-in-law, of meeting the broker's man ; the fun of fires, fights, christenings and funerals ; the fun of being a policeman, a porter, a plasterer, or a publican ; the fun of losing one's job, the grotesque folly of being an exceptional person.

To replace this, Drury Lane's first experiment was to engage two actors—the volatile James Welch and the stolid Fred Eastman—to play a pair of princes in " The White Cat." The next was to introduce Harry Fragson, not a clown but a jester, whose piano was perhaps the most powerfully disintegrating force pantomime has ever known. Then came Neil Kenyon, a bold venture because Scottish comedians seldom lend themselves, so to speak, to extravagance. Comedy distils naturally from their national character. Generosity in a man so mean that he omits to wash on reading " Please tip the basin " is incongruous; humour in a man who refrains from laughter until he retails the joke, is incongruous; tippling in a race temperamentally addicted to alcoholic prohibition, is incongruous; and so forth. For these reasons Will Fyffe can make us laugh (and cry) over a village clown who is true to life, and Neil Kenyon can keep laughter crackling though acting a Hielan' bargee who seems to be actually on the towing path. Fanciful costumes are a hindrance to this style. Let him appear as serious as possible so our amusement can be excited by the violent conflict between the quality of what we see and the quality of what we hear. As a poet Neil Kenyon's brow is serene, and his eye rolls in fine frenzy while he recites the story of Miss Perkins who ate gherkins till they " upset her workin's." That is his pantomime style. He only acted once, however, at Drury Lane. Wilkie Bard, who joined the company the year after, restores the clown's face, a mask of white, a nose tipped with crimson and a black streak across each eye; his words make sibilant nonsense, but he delivers them with the expansive, sententious air of a Cabinet Minister of the old school. The next year he became Twankey in " Aladdin," and George Graves arrived to play Abanazar. He is Pantaloon revived, both in appearance (false nose and red, tufted wig), and in his reiterated cry of " God bless my so-ul," but this " Old 'Un " is far more spirited than of yore —he represents the joke of decrepitude simulating youth. When he was joined by Will Evans, who shows that he was born a Clown in his joyous face and cheerful delight in causing confusion, the old partnership of the Harlequinade was resumed in spirit though not in motley. It was popular, and lasted from " Hop o' My Thumb " in 1911 to " Puss in Boots " in 1915. When Pantaloon, after appearing as a grand duchess, left the Lane, he was replaced by Robert Hale, whose keen sense of satirical mimicry distinguishes his dames from all others. While escaping the meticulous imitation of womankind that makes the female impersonator objectionable, he draws a portrait so like reality that his divergences into masculinity are surprisingly comic. By

178

degrees, however, Drury Lane's humorous resources gave out. When its last pantomime was removed to Covent Garden the store had sadly decreased. Yet there was enough left to enable Mr. Walkley to write :

> The only important item that we missed in the new Cinderella from last year was the business of laying the tablecloth—the tablecloth that so obstinately refused to be laid—in the Baron's House. But then the Brothers Egbert (the new Baroness and Walter) show us how to beat carpets, and so perhaps the course of instruction in household management (that invaluable feature of the Drury Lane pantomime curriculum) is as rich as ever.

Apart from Nellie Wallace's fidelity to the pantomime washtub, the humour of the comedian is taking a different turn. With the alarming spread of the sentimental infections of the film, mirth has become purposely anti-romantic. This is the spirit of Little Tich as the Spanish dancer. The aquiline contour of her nose is capable of arresting laughter whenever it turns upon us quickly in resentful disdain ; the piled jet-black hair and carelessly-worn shawl have glamour ; so has the swinging skirt—except when it swings too high and shows a ridiculous pair of white pants up to the waist. Similarly, Billy Merson has used his lack of inches to mock at the awfulness of pirates and such like, even to burlesquing Hamlet with the aid of a typewriter, a telephone for soliloquies and a cinematograph version of " The Murder of Gonzago." Following the general trend, George Robey also has neglected the humour of humble life in order to travesty kings and queens. The most inveterate mocker, however, is Harry Weldon. No hero's glory is safe from his tarnishing. The worshipped pugilist challenges all-comers with a phrase borrowed from the conjurer, " Will any lady . . . ? " The American millionaire sings of the admiration of his fellow men with a somnolent fervour of satisfaction that reveals its depravity. The Toreador, tired of the moral obligation of swaggering, boasts how he caused the bull to kiss him by making a noise like a cow.

But though the joke of household management suffers from neglect, every-day life is not yet ignored by the music-hall comedian. George Formby was the apotheosis of the ordinary, presenting himself to an audience used to every kind of extraordinary performance as a

Lancashire simpleton trying vainly to acquire some sort of stage accomplishment. Alfred Lester, as hairdresser, shop-assistant or hotel porter, expresses the incongruously tense emotion of life's minor joys and triumphs, by means of howls of anger, moans of despair, shouts of triumph, mumbles of shame, screams of baffled revenge and growls of annoyance, while maintaining throughout a mood of unutterable depression. Leslie Henson takes little note of every-day states of mind but revels in every-day things. Any common or garden object is to him a possible joke. He takes instinctively to " The wit of goods and chattels." He can change a settee into a barrel-organ by turning the tassel of a cushion round and round, or into a rock on the seashore by hiding in its seclusion while rubbing his back briskly with a handkerchief held towel-fashion. But his byplay with properties is exceeded by Harry Tate, who has inherited Grimaldi's love of construction. In " Motoring " and " Flying," his muddled mechanisms tickle our delight in the petrol engine. In " Broadcasting," the public's passion for wireless apparatus is expressed in terms of ironmongery. An umbrella, a pail, a tea-pot, a tinker's barrow and stock of pans are solemnly attached to a " four-and-six-penny listening-in set," while the jargon of radio-telephony is discussed. One of the experimenters is arrested and another loses his life in an explosion, but their purpose is accomplished for a voice has issued from the " loud-speaker," saying " If you hold on for five minutes, I'll tell you the time." On the other hand, in " Fishing " marvels are produced with the slightest effort. All the immemorial lies of anglers here come true. Before Harry Tate can adjust his rod there is a veritable hail of fish. A trout as large as a barrel wrestles with its captor. An eel yards long flies through the air. The village idiot casts snuff upon the waters and stuns the fish as they " come up to sneeze."

As soon as it was discarded by the music-halls household management was adopted by the films. When Charlie Chaplin left London for America, as a member of a troupe called the " Wow Wows" that included Whimsical Walker, he took with him the lessons of Dan Leno. In Los Angeles he used his knowledge. He produced fantasy from the meanest little subjects. But his embodiment of poverty revealed a fundamental difference. The scarecrows of the music-hall wore discarded clothes as the livery of squalor. Charlie Chaplin recognises that discarded clothes may once have been worn by the rich. They are to him a masquerade. The worn-out gloves picked out of a dust-bin, the cigarette case filled with odds and ends of tobacco scraped from gutters, the bulging boots, the small bowler and the carefully buttoned cast-off morning coat, express a confident joy that he deceives the world. Unlike the comedians who are all, in one way or another, anti-sentimental in the effect they produce, he is wistfully romantic both in his outlook and in his appeal. Chaplin, seeing his part differently, may say :

> I am not a clown. My clowning may have esoteric meanings. I prefer to think of myself as a mimetic satirist, for I have aimed in all my comedies at burlesquing, satirising, the human race—or, at least, those human beings whose very existence is a satire on this world.

But our laughter is not satirical. The joke lies in the mingling of the real and the unreal. At times we are carried away by his humanity, but, while our eyes are still filling with water, he will galumph down the streets with boots pointing east and west to reassure us that he is a clown. His misfortunes would be tragic without this reminder. Take a scene in " A Dog's Life " for instance. He is seated on a form with other applicants for work. The first man is called. Chaplin, who is second, goes with him, is turned away, comes back to the form, finds his place filled and has to take the end seat. Each time his turn comes his eagerness betrays him in like fashion until all the vacancies are filled. In itself the incident is saddening, but there is so much running about that we are in no danger of forgetting his unreality. His triumphs are not so noticeably clownlike. One can almost believe in this self-possessed tramp who, while resting behind a fence, sees a sausage-cooker's can on the other side, puts his hand through a hole, takes a sausage and, as he eats it, helps himself several times to mustard.

In " A Dog's Life " the traces of his origin in knockabout films that employed photographic tricks to make impossibilities happen in the story, were disappearing. In " The Kid " he becomes credible. There is just a glimpse of the clown at the beginning when the baby is thrust by fate into his hands ; but the story of his struggles to keep the child, despite the interference of officials and the lack of means, has the illusion of reality. The household management is comic because unlike, in its crudity, anything that happens in a normal kitchen; it is, all the same, credible as the makeshifts of a tramp trying to adapt himself into a nurse and his garret into a nursery. The joke belongs not to clownship but to life.

Now Mr. Charles Spencer Chaplin has shed his " derby," tightly-buttoned coat, moustache and cane, household management jokes seem definitely out-of-date. Since 1912 a style of humour not in touch with reality has been increasingly popular. The public's amusements are at present dominated by the Saturnalian mood of the negro. While Marie Lloyd was still supplying in " Every Little Movement has a Meaning of its Own," or " A Little of What You Fancy Does You Good," the touches of nature that made all classes kin, the appeal of the aberrations of jazz evidenced itself in an almost universal attempt to play, sing or whistle " Alexander's Rag-Time Band." After the outbreak of war the rage developed into a frenzy. From the time Ethel Levey made stentorian noises and stiff sema-phoric movements to the brazen outbursts of the band in " Hullo ! Ragtime " at the Hippodrome, syncopation has ousted sense. Real negroes on the music-halls to-day rarely wield negro influences. It is the white performer who finds inspiration in the spirit of the black labourers in certain of the Southern States where financial conditions amount to slavery. Subjection leads to a state of misery that the un-formed mind reacts against in fits of gibbering joy. This is what the composers of jazz have tried to copy. Inspired by the negro's mes-meric sense of rhythm [1] and nostalgic obsessions, their songs have spread the world over. In addition, we are being taught crazy speech and frenzied gestures similarly derived. Negro influences hold the

---

[1] Of the African negroes' music, Mr. Norman Douglas says : " Vaguely perturbing, these negro melodies and thrummings ; their reiteration of mono-tony awakens tremulous echoes on the human diaphragm, and stirs up hazy, primeval mischiefs."

182

public in a spell. Take note of the amazing enthusiasm aroused by Nora Bayes. All the triumphs of Marie Lloyd—or of actress, prima donna, ballerina and virtuoso—are scanty compared with the storms of applause she arouses, not at special performances but night after night. Her fantastic gestures, sudden changes of voice, her restlessness and wild abandon, belong not to our traditions but to a people whose reason has been arrested. Yet her appearance is strictly conventional. She has grey hair, a matronly figure, a certain dignity when in repose, and the general air of a woman with an assured position. When she sings to an imaginary boy with " dirty hands, dirty face," her gestures and tones are expressive, but when she sings her characteristic jumbles about " sweeties " or yearnings for Kentucky, her outcries and swayings are only to be described as Saturnalian. What is at the back of this strange vogue ? Has the war produced in Europe the negro's mood ? Are we turning in sympathy to an oppressed race because the times we live in are burdensome ? Are we reduced to take delight in gibbering joy, in pleasures divorced from direct connection with everyday life, because reality will not bear thinking about ? But the vogue began before the war. There may be no particular meaning in what the people choose when they desire some new thing.

.   .   .   .   .   .

Though their rewards were handsome, the comedians of the music-halls have suffered as the clowns of the Harlequinade before them. Dan Leno's success was his undoing ; he became mad, gave away bank notes to stage-door idlers, changed his audiences' laughter to jeers, and died in an asylum. Marie Lloyd, after three unhappy marriages, had to come back to the halls for her livelihood to sing " I'm the ruin that Cromwell knocked abaht a bit " while her life ebbed. George Formby, dying of consumption, made a jest of the cough in order to provide for his wife and children before it killed him. T. E. Dunville and Mark Sheridan committed suicide in despair.

Compared with these tragedies, the fate of Arthur Roberts is not pitiable. Yet it was sad to hear that the Captain Coddington who was once the glass of fashion for young men-about-town, should need to take his " benefit " now that he had passed three-score and ten. Though he sang " Good—Damned Good " in a manner lively and alert, this celebration of the jubilee of his career made one think of Grimaldi's farewell. When he gazed from the stage of the Alhambra and saw the tense, eager crowd that seemed to be bursting a space too small to hold all his admirers, the lump in his throat became swollen. " I don't know whether to stand on my head and let it fall out of my mouth or wait till it drops to my feet and then kick it away." But his clown's instinct was not overcome. When a bouquet was handed to him, how thoroughly he pulled our legs ! " These," he said wistfully, " are very beautiful flowers, but I miss the blossom that would remind me most of my youth. It was a flower I was very fond of, then." In a voice as smart as the crack of a whip, he added, " Hops ! " But the pathos in his voice was not merely make-believe. When he said, " I have mustered my courage or couraged my mustard," he was making a jest of a tense emotional ordeal. If he had had a thousand tongues, he declared —and we believed him—he would yet not have been able to express all his thanks. His eyes filled with tears as he asked us to think of him whenever his name was out of the bill, and filled again as quickly as he brushed them away. But his voice soon regained its strength, and with the erect bearing that has always been his and that made his jest now sound as a true word, he shouted, " And if anybody wants a juvenile lead in 1925—here I am ! "

CIRCUS CLOWNS

Ça a été comme une rénovation de la farce italienne, où le clown, ce niais de campagne, ce gymnaste-acteur faisait revivre en lui à la fois Pierrot et Arlequin, projetant l'ironie de ces deux types entre ciel et terre ;—la grimace du blanc enfariné, comme étendue et projetée sur toute la musculature de sa gaillarde academie.

EDMOND DE GONCOURT.

Collo Francisco.   Cicho Sgarra.

L'holandois.

12

PIERROT, said Hugues le Roux in his book on the circus, was " dispelled by the cloud of powder which the clown, launched from the other side of the Channel, scattered in the air as he tumbled on the French stage." But the clown of the ring (however strongly held may be the opinion to the contrary) is derived not from the Grimaldi tradition but the Pierrots who tumbled on horseback at Astley's Paris establishment. Dismounted Pierrots were also employed in his arena. This was objected to as a breach of the law by rivals at the theatres. Astley made a platform to be supported by horses, and on this his tumblers performed with the agreement of the police. When Napoleon made war against Great Britain, Laurent's mother ran the circus until it was transformed into a barracks. On the signing of peace Astley claimed compensation—and got it. Out of the ashes of his enterprise grew Franconi's Cirque Olympique, first and greatest of Continental rings.

Besides Laurent, Astley brought to London the equestrian clown Fortinelly, a Punch who performed daring feats of horsemanship. At the beginning of the nineteenth century, however, the comic relief was supplied by pantomime folk. With Laurent in " The Pirate ; or, Harlequin Victor " in 1800, were Bradbury as Pantaloon, Johannot as Ali and Decastro as an attendant. Vacancies were filled in the following years by equally notable clowns. One was old Dicky Usher, who set out in a washing tub drawn by eight geese from Westminster, landed at Waterloo Bridge, entered a car with eight cats in the traces, and was carried with his cats to the Coburg on the shoulders of the Thames watermen. Another was Sloman, known chiefly on account of the attack of a spiteful journalist who likened him to a spurned football, a crushed frog, and a dog with a tin can tied to his tail. Another was Southby, Laurent's pupil, who became fireworks

187

manager at Vauxhall. These clowns were distinct from those of pantomime. As soon as the strictness of the law forbidding speech was relaxed, they were instructed to utter jests. In *Bentley's Miscellany* for 1838, W. J. Thoms gives this account of their training :

> The equestrian clown at Astley's, as the Mister Merryman who attends the horsemanship at that theatre is professionally designated, has, as the reader has before now no doubt painfully experienced, a certain series of standard jokes, which have remained unchanged any time these twenty years. It is, perhaps, not generally known that these jokes were for the most part coined originally by the Westminster scholars. The fact is so, however. The jokes were made by the Westminsters, and brought out at Astley's, where the Clown, having been fee'd and properly instructed how to perpetrate them, used to fire them ; the rival makers listening with the greatest anxiety to ascertain which told best. Those which were most successful became of course stock jokes.

Incidentally the clown's cry of " Here we are " comes from Astley's. During the first part of the performance, which took place on the stage, the arena was filled by what " Boz " called " the half price." When these were ejected and their orange peel cleared away, saw-dust was dexterously shaken in a complete circle and a hoop of gas jets let down. The clown was the first to enter, and the riding master next.

After the visit in 1838 of Gontard, " First French Grotesque and Celebrated Buffoon," there were other types of clown at Astley's but the jester came first. Dewhurst was billed as the " principal elocutionist " of the " Grotesque and Buffoons known by the appropriate sobriquet of ' clowns ' " a few years later. He was succeeded by the " Celebrated Hibernian Jokist," Tom Barry, who had the support of Twist as the buffoon and Signor Felix Carlo (a contortionist) as the grotesque. When " Harlequin Tam O'Shanter and His Steed Meg; or, the Fairy Thistledown and Witches of Alloway Kirk," marking a revival of the equestrian pantomimes after the lapse of a score of years, was performed in 1843, a special clown had to be engaged for this part of the programme. In the melodramas, Barry always supplied the comic relief in parts such as an Irish farrier in " Murat." He also played in farces after the pattern of a popular example written around the characters of Button the tailor and his man Snip. This clue suggests that Dickens drew Signor Jupe who

188

PIERROT IN ASTLEY'S CIRCUS AT PARIS

From a wood-engraving in the "Memoirs of John Decastro"

earns a brief mention in "Hard Times," at Astley's. His white nightcap, "embellished with two peacock's feathers and a pigtail bolt upright," is the only part of his costume described, but we learn that he was assisted by his performing dog Merrylegs and how his performance was described in the bills. He threw "seventy-five hundred-weight in rapid succession back-handed over his head, thus forming a fountain of solid iron in mid air," and enlivened the "varied performances at frequent intervals with his chaste Shakespearean quips and retorts," besides appearing in his favourite character of Mr. William Button, of Tooley Street, in "the highly novel and laughable hippo-comedietta of The Tailor's Journey to Brentford." But his career ended before the story began because he had "missed his tip at the banners and was loose in his ponging," which is to say, he was short in his leaps and bad in his tumbling.

Barry left Astley's in a huff in 1853 and went to Drury Lane, but died four years later. A sketch of the ring—contained in a scrap book of Astley's in the library of Mr. C. B. Cochran—shows him without make-up but with the triple-tufted wig, and wearing a graceful, close-fitting costume, elaborately ornamented. It is of some importance to note details of appearance because these supply evidence in tracing the development of the redoubtable circus clowns of the present. Little Croueste who, with J. Lupino as Pantaloon, was the Clown of "Harlequin Sancho Panza; or Don Quixote and his Rosinante" at Astley's in 1858, also adopted the tight-fitting trousers. He, too, was a jester, advertising his "Budgets of Bon-mots, Jests, Joy, Mirth, Merriment, Music, Fun, Folly, Frolic, Fancy, Freaks, Strange Stories, Hints at the Times, Pleasing Puns, Play on Words." But the most remarkable of this type was William Frederick Wallet, a pompous gentleman with a large moustache, whose engagement at Astley's caused Barry to leave. Wallet's career lasted from 1828 to 1868. He styled himself "the Queen's Jester," uttered Shakespearean jests, and wore a costume consisting of tights, Hessian boots, tasselled cap and brocaded tunic, which, he announced, was according to designs in a medieval missal. Because the newspapers repudiated him as a clown, he gave a lecture on the fools of olden time to show he knew more than they did.   He was still more high-handed with audiences and managers.   When a spectator annoyed him by demanding " variety," he said to the rest, " He has a wife and children at home, but comes here with two of the commonest sort of women.   That's what he calls variety."   When engaged at the Brooklyn Circus, New York, he was called upon, without rehearsal, to appear in " Jack the Giant Killer," an after-piece elaborately set out with a " splendidly modelled castle, single headed and double headed giants, male giants and female giants that swallowed live children."   Wallet was given a huge wooden sword and left to his own resources.   He took this revenge for the slight :

> On the entrance of a ponderous giant with his massive club I stood upon my defence like a man and a hero.   With the first blow I scalped him ; my sword then went through his eye and out at the back of his head.   The next severed the head from his shoulders, and sent his trunk rolling in the saw-dust.   I then belaboured his body with my sword till the basket work flew in a thousand pieces, and then in great terror appeared " Snug the Joiner," a canvas man called Long Jem, who crept from the interior of the giant to the extreme delight of the audience and made rapid tracks towards the dressing-rooms.   The other giants shared the same fate one by one, without the slightest assistance from my friend Jack the Giant Killer.   Having despatched the giant horde, I next took a flying leap on to the top of the mimic castle.   My weight crushed it to atoms, and I fell buried in the ruins.

When the manager, trembling with passion, asked, " Is that the way to fight giants ? " Wallet replied, " The proper mode is to dig a large pit, then cover it over with light boughs and twigs hidden with sods and grass, and when pursued, your light form passes over this in safety, but the giant's weight breaks all beneath him and he is buried in the pit "—at least, that is how he told the story.

Elaborate spectacles were common in the circuses of those days. When Sanger's took over Astley's, it was noted for such pantomimes as " Harlequin and O'Donoghue ;   or, the White Horse of Killarney " in 1850 and " Aladdin and the Wonderful Lamp ; Ali Baba and the Forty Thieves ;   or, Harlequin the Spirit of Mystery and the Magic Cave " in 1885.   The show of 1863 was remarkably ingenious.   The title was " Harlequin and Friar Bacon ;   or, Great Grim John of Gaunt and the Enchanted Lance of Robin Goodfellow," and

190

"THE HALF PRICE" AT A ROYAL CIRCUS PANTOMIME

From Pyne's "Microcosm of London"

Chaucer, played by Miss Craven from Covent Garden, was the principal boy. When the Pilgrims have passed by in procession, he is left
to make love to Rose, barmaid of the Tabard, angering the landlord
who is keeping her for John of Gaunt. The rivals settle their claims
at the barriers, Chaucer is victorious, is crowned by Rose, ordered to
the dungeons by John and changed into Harlequin by Robin Goodfellow. There were fireworks to finish. Astley's establishment for
the season of 1878-9 consisted of

> 1,100 persons, 180 horses, 60 ponies, 8 camels and dromedaries, zebras, the
> horned horse, Polar bears, 4 giraffes, and 12 ponderous performing elephants ;
> also 18 splendid performing lions that have been playing at the Porte St.
> Martin Theatre, Paris, during the Exhibition, and those that have been
> travelling with Mr. George Sanger's Company in Belgium and Germany.

Special attention was drawn to the *Monstre* lion, the son of Nero, the
largest in England, which had " been christened Lord Beaconsfield,
in honour to the noble Lord on his reception at Verviers ! " In the
pantomime, " Harlequin Cinderella and the Little Glass Slipper,"
" Lord Beaconsfield " was led triumphantly in advance of the British
troops on their march to Cabul, a spectacle which introduced " incidents of the Afghanistan War and the freeing of the Kyber Pass."
This was followed by the " grand spectacular portion of Shakespeare's
Richard III." which, as mounted by Astley, had run for a record
number of performances. " Dear, dear," as Dickens said,

> what a place it looked, that Astley's ; with all the paint, gilding, and looking-
> glass ; the vague smell of horses suggestive of coming wonders ; the curtain
> that hid such gorgeous mysteries ; the clean white sawdust down in the
> circus ; the company coming in and taking their places . . . the pony who
> reared up on his hind legs when he saw the murderer, and wouldn't hear of
> walking on all fours again until he was taken into custody—the clown who
> ventured on such familiarities with the military man in boots—the lady [1]
> who jumped over nine-and-twenty ribbons and came down safe upon the
> horse's back, everything was delightful, splendid and surprising !

Hengler, who built his first circus at Liverpool in 1857 and then
added others in Dublin, Hull, Glasgow and London (Oxford Circus),

[1] Ella, the most famous of Astley's horsewomen, aroused hopeless passions
in the breasts of all the young bloods. Her triumphs ended, however, when
the secret was out that she had a *wife* and family.

employed Continental clowns though he, too, had a jester of the type of Wallet and Signor Jupe.   Hengler's Shakespearean clown, said Hugues le Roux, who may be referring to Charles Watson, the " Hibernian Clown and Lyrical Jester,"

> appears in white tights ornamented with blue or red patches indiscriminately arranged with a short drapery round the hips and a fool's cap on the head. He does not caper and joke, but declaims passages from Shakespeare and sings Irish songs.

Le Roux's theory is that the modern circus clown is a hybrid of this personage and the nigger minstrel.   But there is no trace of the black-amoor in the white-faced wearer of the one-pieced garment.   The nigger is no more absorbed on the stage than ethnologically.   According to Sir Walter Scott, he first appeared as a court jester.   He is also discernible in eighteenth century plays.   But the real craze started directly London saw Jim Crow.   He was a white man named T. D. Rice, with a face of burnt-cork, dressed like a veritable scarecrow in a nondescript costume and a white hat.   His most popular song was " Bone Squash Diablo."   Its refrain, sung all over the town, was :

> Turn about and wheel about,
> And do jest so ;
> Every time you turn about you jump Jim Crow.

Sadler's Wells put forward John Dunn as " The English Jim Crow." Then other imitators arose.   The craze might have subsided, but in 1843 Sand's " Great American Circus " was installed at the English Opera House, and Joseph Sweeney, the " Negro vocalist and Banjo player," made nigger minstrels more popular than ever.   He wore wide trousers striped white and red, a large fancifully coloured waistcoat, no jacket, a huge white collar and a straw sombrero.   What with his new style of dancing and the novelty of his banjo, he was an innovation to be admired—and imitated.   The Bohee Brothers copied his dress and Joe Cave, obtaining the secret of the banjo from a spy in Sand's camp, set up as " The White Faced Nigger."   Then there were the Christy Minstrels.   Next Chirgwin, the " White-Eyed Kaffir."   Since his time Scott and Whaley, one a black-faced butt and the other a knavish negro lawyer, have become the chief coloured-

192

comedians in Great Britain. In America, however, burnt cork is used by the leading clowns of to-day. Albert Jolson, who graduated in circus companies and minstrel troupes, has a " whirlwind style." Frank Tinney has a quiet method ; in fact, he seems to rely mainly on a smile that in itself expresses the crafty simpleton who has supplied the world with laughter since jokes were first invented. In him the fool and the knave meet as they did in Clown, Falstaff and Dicaeopolis. This you sense the moment he appears, wearing a bandsman's scarlet, gold-laced tunic with a pair of baggy black trousers, and carrying bagpipes. He has no tricks, and no songs unless you count the one he begins but regretfully relinquishes because Ernest, who sits in the conductor's chair as the representative of uninspired common sense, objects to its notion of strolling along the promenade on horseback. All Tinney needs to offer for our amusement is a mind that is artless and artful by turns. This is revealed in disputes.

" Hullo, Frank," says Ernest.
" Hullo, Oinest," says Frank.
" How are you, Frank ? " asks Ernest.
" Very well, howse you ? " asks Frank.

Directly Ernest attempts to reply, Frank tells him the audience has not come to hear how *Oinest* is. Before he will play the bagpipes, he wants to be pressed to do so. Ernest asks him to play ; Frank says he would much rather play the violin, piano or almost any other instrument. A musician stands up to offer his violin. In an agonised stage-whisper Frank calls, " Get him down. Get him down." All Frank's conundrums gang agley, but his stories are effective. In the days before " prohibition," he says, it was not always possible to tell when a man had had too much. He remembered that it was necessary for his mother to explain when his father was drunk —the children thought he was dead. " Do you know how to cook starlings, Oinest ? " Ernest has never heard of cooked starlings. Frank with gusto describes the process in detail—the plucking, the crisp bread-crumbs, the boiling butter—" Then throw dem in the dust-bin and open a tin of sardines." What a rich, gloating, self-congratulating smile he has ! When he gives an academic address and succeeds in pronouncing " vis-u-alise," how unrestrainedly he mocks Ernest. " That's got you outer your class, you big Swede." Even the entire audience has to be subdued in this fashion. After informing us that he has been lecturing on " the gender of the cantaloup," he adds, " That's over the heads of youse guys." His quiet subtleties take us a long way from the noisy ring.

.   .   .   .

In *L'Acrobatie et Les Acrobats*, G. Strehly gives a description of two musical clowns of the 'fifties who are certainly concerned in the circus clown's parentage. They were the brothers John and William Price, engaged at Paris except in the spring when they travelled the country. M. Strehly saw them many times between the years 1858-1867 at Strasbourg. They were equilibrists, tumblers and musicians. While balancing on top of unsupported ladders, or performing feats of tumbling and contortion, they played flute and violin duets. But instead of the *affreux sac bouffant*, then usually worn by circus clowns, they had a *maillot* costume to display their athletic figures similar to Barry's, whom they also resembled in using no other make-up than *farine* and in their fidelity to the *perruque tricuspide*. The costume of the brothers Price was passed, with their tricks, to the French clowns. Auriol, who played a French horn while balancing head downwards on a bottle, wore a costume not unlike the Shakespearean jester's. He last appeared in 1873 in the circus scene of a revue. His successors returned to the *sac*.

There is one certain link between Pierrot and the circus clown. Agoust, a juggler who became manager of the Nouveau Cirque, passed on the lessons he had learned at the Funambules to the Hanlon-Lees whom he met in America. They were a troupe named Hanlon, trained by a Professor Lees, who made their London début in 1847. When they came to Paris with a show compounded of Deburau, the circus and the English pantomime—the influence of Grimaldi's steam-coach is discernible—the real vogue of the circus began in Paris. Mr. D. L. Murray has given an admirable survey of the situation that arose when Paris, " then in the throes of the Naturalist novel," satisfied its desire for the macabre in their pantomimes :

194

LAURENT'S "SAC" AT ASTLEY'S AMPHITHEATRE

From Pyne's "Microcosm of London"

In 1872 the Hanlon-Lees appeared at Paris, to be, as the quality of their talent disclosed itself, loudly acclaimed by Zola. If the business of their scenes was conventional, burlesque duels, tipsy misadventures, crazy juggling with household furniture, upsets in stage coaches and collisions of railway-trains, the savage intensity of their silent acting was, to those who could pierce a little beneath the surface, Mephistophelean. Zola saw the personages of their pantomimes in vision, " revelling in broken limbs and riddled trunks, triumphing in the apotheosis of vice and crime in the teeth of outraged morality." There would be a pretty outcry, he said, if he dared to make his novels as brutal as their buffooneries. These ironists of genius were not only the quintessence of the " Realistic " epoch ; they were also the embodiment of the age of mechanical invention. Next to the cruelty of their caricature, what was most remarkable was the precision of their movements. They were human marionettes. The coach in which they made their entry might fall to pieces, but they would roll out of the debris and the confusion into a faultless line sitting parallel to the footlights. The sleeping car of which they were the demon conductors might take fire and explode with a crash : above the wreckage when the smoke grew thinner they would be seen perched safely on the trees by the line. They were the cynic philosophers of the *fin-de-siècle*, the unconscious prophets of the crash of its civilisation.

Because of the Hanlon-Lees, and other troupes such as the Majilton family of dancers, there was a great demand for English performers. That was how the violent horseplay of the Harlequinade came to be introduced into the ring, for Clown[1] and Pantaloon went to the Continent each summer. There was also a type of old English clown who became naturalised on French sawdust and tan. One such was Billy Hayden, a nigger minstrel who changed his face from black to white. He made his *entrée*—could the word be a link with the "entries" of the seventeenth century masques ?—on a donkey, and chattered in this manner :

> I, too, was once a pretty young lady. A witch came by with an ugly little boy. She took me, the pretty little girl, out of the perambulator, and she put in my place the ugly little boy. And ever since then I've been an ugly little boy.

The Pinauds (Pinards?) are also mentioned by Le Roux. They were musical clowns. One would try to play a guitar, only to be interrupted by a musical pig and a musical cannon which was fired at his back. In one of their pantomimes a peasant is attacked by a bull which he

[1] In some of the pantomimes of the Continental circuses, however, these rôles were named Pierrot and Cassandre after the fashion of Deburau.

drives off with his umbrella. While he revels in the sensation of victory, his partner sets fire to his hat. It explodes. In despair he lifts his hands to heaven. Down comes a rain of hats and caps, all crushed and shabby. None will fit. Again he lifts his hands in despair. That is the end.

These have left their imprint on contemporary circus performers such as the Fratellini, but the most important clown of the 'seventies was the inventor of the French Auguste (in Italy called Toni). His costume, according to Strehly, consists of a coat with tails too large, a white waistcoat which is too long, and black trousers which are too short, besides a staved-in top hat, white spats, and a lock of hair, carefully oiled, which forms " a lightning conductor on his almost completely bald head." There are variations, of course, Grock wearing instead of the lock a bright blue fringe on the nape of his neck, and Frank Pichel a great shock of vertical hair. Strehly believes that the first to play the part was the " Vrai Gugusse, a certain James Guyon of English origin whose partner was the enormous but agile Gougou Loyal." The biographer of the Fratellini, however, states that before Guyon the nickname of Auguste was borne by a ringmaster named Tom Belling. He invented the new type of clown at Berlin in 1864, by accident. Once while leaving the ring he stumbled and fell. He smiled at the public drunkenly. Because of his stupid gaze and red nose the wags gaily called out, " Auguste, idiot." The next day, in place of his livery, he wore the suit of a colleague which was too large for him, daubed his nose vermilion and deliberately stumbled. " The Auguste was born." Belling joined Franconi in 1874, but was too phlegmatic for Paris. James Guyon adopted the idea in 1878 and in consequence " made " the Hippodrome on the Avenue de l'Alma. While dying in the British hospital of Levallois-Perret he dodged his nurse, put on his clothes and went to see Footit and Chocolat at the Nouveau Cirque. This led to a heart attack. He died content because of that performance.

Footit and his negro companion Chocolat were better known in England even than Cyrillo et Busby or Boum-Boum. Footit appeared in London in 1885 when the Grand International Cirque was the

196

Christmas attraction at Covent Garden ; there were several clowns, including Daniels le Drole, and also that best of jugglers, Cinquevalli. Footit, like the mounted Pierrot of the Franconi, would sit in the saddle with his face the wrong way and complain, " This horse hasn't got a head." The ringmaster would answer, " It's on the other side," to which Footit would retort, " Turn it round then." In *Au Music-Hall* M. Frejaville quotes the snatch of song he was constantly singing :

> A la maison, nous allons plus !
> A la maison, nous irons jamais pas !

When his circus days were over he appeared at a theatre as a profoundly solemn cocktail shaker. He died 1921. Tommy Footit is his son.

Another noted English clown of Paris was Conrad, who specialised in a rôle, compounded of jester and Auguste, named the *Auguste parleur*. During the Boer War the manager of the Cirque d'Hiver gave a pantomime called " English and Boers " in order to exploit the public's *anglophobie*. In a patriotic rage Conrad refused his office of *parleur*, but agreed to play a soldier of the Queen. Believing the destinies of Empire depended on his efforts he fought furiously. At the end of each performance he was taken prisoner and subjected to grotesque reprisals.

Many details of the recent history of the French clowns are available because of the enthusiasm for their art of the Fratellini. In the *Histoire de Trois Clowns*, Pierre Mariel has gathered the fruit of conversations with them all. Here is the remarkable record of Gustave Fratellini, founder of the family of clowns whose third generation is now appearing in the ring. He was born in 1842. At an early age a passion for acrobatics developed in him, and at ten he ran away from home to join a travelling troupe, only to be restored to his parents, who decided he must study medicine. He served as a surgeon under Garibaldi, but, when captured, practised his circus tricks to amuse his fellow prisoners. In the meantime his family had become impoverished, so that at the end of the war he had no choice but to join a circus until recalled to the army as a gymnastic instructor to the Bersaglieri. Again he returned to the ring and, apart from spells of soldiering under Garibaldi against Austria and for France in 1870, followed this profession henceforth in all parts of the world. Paul Fratellini was born in Sicily in 1877, François in Paris in 1879, and Albert in Moscow in 1886. Their baptism of sawdust was in panto-mime—two of them in the undignified rôles of girls, and the third as a chick in an egg (but he went to sleep instead of hatching out). As soon as their babyhood was over they had to go into training as acrobats, dancers, riders, musicians and conjurers. They, too, travelled the endless road round the world before they came to stay at the Medrano. Then, so rapid was the increase in their popularity, they paid an indemnity to end their contract, and left the *piste* for cabaret and stage, but are now at the Cirque d'Hiver.

If the Fratellini have aroused only a limited amount of enthusiasm in English music-halls, it is because they are characteristically circus clowns. They are less funny in themselves than in what they do, which is the result of acting in the ring, where performances have to be such that they can be appreciated in the round. Take their finale, for instance. François bursts into song while wearing a top hat. Albert sets fire to it. Paul rushes to the rescue with a toy fire-engine, rests a ladder against François and mounts it, hatchet in hand. He drives the hatchet into Albert's head and leaves it there. Albert turns on a hose. François, who has never left off singing, opens his umbrella and marches off with the fire brigade in attendance and the hose pouring its ineffectual drip on the umbrella. There has been no attempt on their part to make themselves known to the audience, no confidences, no signals, no expression of emotions, no facial play, not even as much as a wink. Away from the footlights—in the arena, or the wards of children's hospitals where they often perform—these negative qualities pass unnoticed in a delight in their fertile ingenuity.

Unhappily London no longer possesses a theatre with an arena. The Hippodrome was the last. Here Marceline used to excel in displays of blundering assistance when carpets were to be laid or apparatus prepared for the acrobats. But there are still plenty of circus clowns. When rings are installed for the Christmas holidays at the Agricultural Hall, Olympia, or the Crystal Palace, the " clusters of clowns " number from a dozen to a score. Pimpo and Doodles are

COMICAL WALKER OF THE CIRCUS

From a painting by Harold Knight

TITTI, ONCE OF PARIS

From a painting by C.R.W.Nevinson

among the children's best beloved.   Poodle, whom the films have attracted, is the best equestrian clown.   There is also Winkle, who is represented on the posters in the act of being born, like Botticelli's Venus, from a shell.   The circus clown of to-day plays many parts and wears many costumes.   What his conventional *entrée* consists of is happily described in a sonnet from John Ferguson's " Thyrea " :

> With whitened scalp and nose bedaubed with red,
>   He bounds into the ring and cracks his wheeze ;
>   Bursting with wit, he mounts a high trapeze,
> Then falls into the net dispirited :
> He mimics feats pyramidal, and dread
>   Contortions of some " Modern Hercules,"
>   While at his shins they throw a wooden cheese,
> Or a soft turnip hits him on the head.
>
> When tenting days are done, and nevermore
>   He smells the sawdust, sees the laughing eyes,
> I somehow think that on a daisied floor
>   He'll turn a somersault in Paradise
>   To give some angel-child a glad surprise
> Who never saw a circus clown before.

Such antics he has performed the world over.   In America the circus travels to wheat belts too remote even for the cinema.   French circuses advance to the Sahara.   In " The Edge of the Desert " Ianthe Dunbar describes a clown with a red face, tufts of yellow hair, short black jacket, turned-down collar, flowing red tie and wide checked trousers, whose blundering horsemanship, ending in a feat far more difficult than those he had failed to do, drew laughter from the Arabs at Gabes.   Obviously the subject is vast.   And now the spell of the circus is bringing together authors and acrobats, artists and Augustes, millionaires and showmen, while mellow veterans lay their ringcraft at the disposal of us all, it is difficult to keep account of the knowledge that is willingly proffered.   Day by day letters from brother enthusiasts or fresh friendships made through the freemasonry of the circus's spell, besides new books, new pictures and new plays, bring to light stories of the clown of the ring.   Here, for instance, is M. Régis Gignoux's tribute to Lucien Godard, *le clown autoritaire* of the Medrano, who died in 1924 on the eve of the reopening: "*discrètement, comme la plupart des hommes qui laissant un grand exemple.*" He was no ordinary clown. He had established that to be comic nowadays one must command, because the lord no longer laughs at the jokes of his servant but the servant at the jokes of his lordship. He also demonstrated that one must no longer look for the world's friendship, but for the world's hate:

> Ecœuré d'une époque où le plus médiocre a la prétention de se faire admirer, aimer et applaudir, M. Lucien Godard se faisait conspuer, haïr et siffler.
>
> Il était en habit noir. Il semblait tenir, sur la piste, le rôle de M. Loyal dont M. Hassan, doyen de Medrano, fut longtemps le titulaire, le chef d'emploi, comme on dit à la Comédie-Française. C'est à lui que s'adressaient les clowns qui entraient pour " travailler." Il les recevait, de son haut, comme un fonctionnaire, avec ou sans augmentation, nous reçoit à son guichet. Il les dominait. Il mettait un monocle pour les mieux examiner. Et la scène commençait, celle que nous jouons chaque jour sans amuser personne : " Qu'est-ce que vous voulez ? C'est impossible . . . Ah ! vous avez l'autorisation ? Vos papiers ? . . . Bien . . . Parfait . . . Passez par ici . . . Non, par là . . . Défendu de vous asseoir . . . Dépêchez-vous. Vous voulez des coups de pied au derrière ? Payez, mon ami, payez ! "
>
> D'un geste sec, en coup de faux, M. Lucien Godard ordonnait à l'amphithéâtre de se tenir tranquille, d'obéir. C'était suffisant comme appât. Un coup de sifflet lui répondait, du côté de l'orchestre ou de la claque. Sait-on jamais où se tiennent les agents provocateurs ? M. Lucien Godard, aussitôt, se redressait, comme flagellé et il cherchait d'un regard furieux le téméraire, l'insolent, qui *avait osé* siffler. Il recevait une bordée nouvelle accompagnée de " hou ! hou ! " Alors, l'homme de la loi et des règlements semblait perdre son sang-froid. Il se retournait à droite, à gauche ; il menaçait d'expulsion, d'exil ; il invitait ses adversaires à descendre, à se mesurer avec lui. Un défi collectif au parterre, comme Cyrano.
>
> C'était la révolution. L'amphithéâtre soulevé ripostait par des clameurs féroces. Les galeries se mêlaient au charivari, puis les fauteuils de toutes les séries et enfin les loges. Tout le cirque sifflait M. Lucien Godard.

Other writers and other painters have praised other clowns. But the spell of the circus is stronger when one sits at the feet of the veterans. At the offices of the Voltas, formerly of the troupe of aerial acrobats known as the Hanlon-Voltas, the fruits of sixty years in many parts of the world are to be gathered. Once when Mr. R. E. Wilson, a Continental agent of long experience, was there, the talk was of Volkerson, the most famous Danish clown. At Copenhagen he played a comic Pierrot in the pantomimes of the ring until he was eighty. The public never tired of him. He became too old to tumble. When he was supposed to be knocked down, he had to be assisted —gradually and gently—to fall. The audience laughed and cheered for encouragement. Was there ever a story of clownship that warmed the heart more ?

Although theatre clowns have frequently found employment in the ring and circus clowns on the stage, the types have remained distinct. Their training has been of two entirely different schools. While the theatre clown was reared as a dancer, actor and dumb-show performer, the apprenticeship of the circus clown is served to an acrobat, juggler, musician, rider or animal trainer if not to all four. As a rule the funny man under the " Big Tops " gives an exhibition of his skill in these departments—Pimpo's horsemanship, for instance, is unequalled even by Sanger's other expert riders—but otherwise his humour is of the kind that any clown can be entrusted with at short notice. There is a very clear account of his standardised jokes in a proprietor's mock Act of Parliament, quoted by Thomas Frost in *Circus Life and Circus Celebrities*, which commands

> *And be it further enacted*, that when the scenes in the circus commence, the Merriman, Grotesque, or Clown shall not, after the first equestrian feat, exclaim, " Now I'll have a turn to myself," previous to his toppling like a coach-wheel round the ring, nor shall he fall flat on his face, and then collecting some saw-dust in his hands drop it down from the level of his head, and say his nose bleeds ; nor shall he attempt to make the rope-dancer's balance-pole stand on its end by propping it up with the said saw-dust ; nor shall he, after chalking the performer's shoes, conclude by chalking his own nose, to prevent his foot from slipping when he treads on it ; nor shall he take long pieces of striped cloth for Mr. Stickney to jump over, while his horse goes under ; previous to which he shall not pull the groom off the stool, who holds the other end of the same cloth, neither shall he find any difficulty in holding it at the proper level ; nor, after having held it higher and lower, shall he ask, " Will that do ? " and on being answered in the affirmative, he shall not jump down, and put his hands in his pockets, saying, " I'm glad of it " ; nor shall he pick up a small piece of straw, for fear he should fall over it, and afterwards balance the said straw on his chin as he runs about. Neither shall the Master of the Ring say to the Merriman, Grotesque, or Clown, when they are leaving the circus, " I never follow the fool, sir " ; nor shall the fool reply, " Then I do," and walk out after him ; nor, moreover,

shall the Clown say that " the horses are as clever as the barber who shaved bald magpies at twopence a dozen " ; nor tell the groom in the red-jacket and top boots, when he takes the said horses away, to " rub them well down with cabbage-puddings, for fear they should get collywobbleums in their pandenoodles " ; such speeches being manifestly very absurd and incomprehensible.

Saving always, that the divers ladies and gentlemen, young ladies and young gentlemen, maidservants, apprentices, and little boys, who patronise the theatre, should see no reason why the above alterations should be made ; under which circumstances, they had better remain as they are.

The clown of the circus is not secure from the fate that has overcome his brother of the stage. Just as the over-elaboration of the pantomime destroyed the Grimaldi tradition so the vogue, instituted by Phineas Barnum, of the mammoth circus, threatens to oust this primitive fun from the ring. Those clusters of clowns at Olympia only get in each other's way. Even at the more unsophisticated Agricultural Hall Comical Walker (not to be confused with Whimsical Walker) has to curtail his *entrée* with the geese. In the ring the cry also is " cut it short." Therefore the clown is emigrating to the music-hall where, at present, Joe Jackson is the greatest of our race. Instead of red-hot poker or concertina, he has for his instrument a derelict bicycle which he steals with a great show of alarm lest the laughter of the audience should arouse its rightful owner. But, like all great clowns, his skill in wheeling is nothing compared with his skill in starting the secret mechanisms of our hearts.

GROCK

I sought in mine heart . . . to lay hold on folly, till I might see what was that good for the sons of men, which they should do under heaven all the days of their life.

SOLOMON.

Maramao.   *Cap: Cardoni.*

P'holandois.

18

TRADITION has had little to do with the making of Grock. His is the " clod, clot, lump " freshly hatched. Go to the circus where Adrien Wettach was trained and you will not find his like. Bring circus clowns upon a stage littered like his with musical instruments, yet you will not see any likeness. Performances in the arena depend for laughter on what is done. Performances before the footlights depend on how it is done. The Fratellini reveal a fanciful extravagance in their tricks, but their faces under the make-up are of everyday. Theirs is the clownship of externals. Grock, like Grimaldi, is the funnier the deeper one pries into his soul. He also stands among commonplace materials and his wonder makes them like the sun and stars. His piano is enlarged into man's eternal struggle with fate. His fiddle and bow express all the hopes, trials, despairs, and joys that have ever been encountered and overcome. His chair is raised to the importance of Cassiopeia's. His fall through the seat of it shakes our belief in the security of the universe. Life is full of pitfalls, is his philosophy. Life, he implies, would be very dull if it were not. Yes, undoubtedly, he is profound. To know what humour is one must know what life is. Therefore, the richest laughter can only be created by clowns of the mellowest experience of reality. Grock's tricks cannot be explained in terms of the stage. Why he does this or that can only be understood by referring to the details of his life. He yodels. That is because his parents were Tyrolean singers. He dismantles a piano. That is a joke born of rebellion against the toil of repairing instruments. He enters as an earnest seeker for work. None knows better what the actual search is like. His humour is of the constant struggle against mishaps which, though they cause heartaches, are not worth a moment's worry. That is the leitmotif of his biography. His eloquence consists of three

205

noises : groans, plaintive expostulation and gurgles of joy. Those, for him, are the three notes of fate.

. . . . . .

There lived in the village of Loveresse, near Reconvillier, Switzerland, a young watchmaker named Wettach. He belonged to the usual athletic society that every village boasted, and was a gymnast of exceptional skill. With an Italian named Ricono who worked in the same watch factory he would give displays whenever funds were being raised for widows and orphans. Liking this occupation better than watchmaking, Ricono hired himself out to the Cirque Martinetti and induced his partner to go with him. For Wettach, however, this new life lasted no more than six months. One day a gendarme called at the tent, asked for the young runaway of eighteen years and took him back to his parents. Wettach made watches once more. In due season he married. Gymnastics were still his hobby, but he also spent his leisure in singing Tyrolean duets with his wife or playing the piccolo to her accompaniment on the piano.

Not many months later, in the summer of 1880, Ricono called. He had stayed with the circus and married one of Martinetti's daughters. When the owner died the estate had been divided between his two sons-in-law. Ricono had brought his caravan back to the canton of Berne in order to see Wettach. Would he care, for old times sake, to join him two or three nights a week in a gymnastic display ? The watchmaker agreed. Without a word to his wife he set out that evening to the town where the bills proclaimed that Ricono and Wettach were to perform. Once more he felt the furtive delight of donning fleshings. Once more he knew the thrill of performing in the light of the flares and amid the smell of the horses. But when he returned to the tiring room Madame Wettach was there. Since his first-born was to arrive in a few weeks he was taken aback at first to find she had run all the way from Loveresse on hearing the news. But he would not confess to any shame at his exploit of appearing " almost naked " (to use her term) before the gaze of the public. The wife's indignation rose still higher. She made her last and

206

strongest remonstrance : " Supposing the son we are expecting were to grow up a circus performer ? " Wettach was unmoved.

" Why not ? " he asked. Two months later Adrien Wettach. was born.

Ambitions alter. The gymnast's sole desire now was to own a restaurant. With his savings he purchased one in another canton. When Adrien was six years old a caravan pulled up outside because the proprietor wanted a drink. He entered and was recognised as the clown Franz Wetzel, Martinetti's other son-in-law. Wettach was overjoyed. At his request the mayor of the town overcame his usual prejudices and granted Franz a licence to perform. Now the old clown had several children. They were overjoyed at the comforts of the restaurant. Adrien was overjoyed at the excitement of the circus. He yearned to wear tights. He pleaded to be allowed to sleep in the caravan. He played truant from school to see them perform their tricks every day.

This blissful existence lasted a month. Then the caravan moved on. Adrien moped. He tried to console himself by practising their tricks constantly. But he could neither eat nor sleep for thinking of the circus. He wasted away. Happily there was an understanding priest, a man of medical skill, who had regularly visited the family ever since he cured Wettach of injuries received in a wrestling bout. This doctor discovered the cause of the child's melancholia. He prompted a letter to Wetzel, who at once agreed to take Adrien for three or four months. On the news the little Wettach shook off his illness. He went joyfully to rejoin the clown's children, who welcomed him just as joyfully, each wanting him to share his or her bed. Every morning he was first up, and if the breakfast coffee were late he was in the ring without it. Very soon he was allowed to join the entrée of clowns because he could perform the *flip-flap* and *saut périlleux*. The four months ended. But he found a chance to refuse to go home. An apprentice had sunstroke. The little Wettach, almost the same height, offered to take his place. " What can you do ? " asked Papa Franz.

" I am an acrobat," said Adrien. Though nobody suspected

207

his powers, he had learned secretly how to perform many of the leaps, springs and somersaults that are standardised and named like the movements of the ballerina. Franz was sceptical, but he gave permission; then, in amazement, saw Adrien perform an entrée that was entirely professional in its skill and finish. Wettach received a letter saying that there had never been a boy to show so much talent for the arena as his son. Adrien became a member of the company.

Each October the circus closed down for the winter. Adrien returned home and was sent to school, where he had to learn in less than six months—lessons under canvas were not of a rigorous kind—what the other boys took a year to study, for he must pass his examinations or the education authorities might insist he should leave the circus. Playtime for him consisted of hard training, preparing a new entrée for the summer season. He had a " wire " stretched across the garden and a trapeze hung from the lintel of a doorway. Moreover, he strummed at his mother's piano and blew into his father's piccolo until he could play. Each spring he rejoined the circus with fresh accomplishments and an unabated enthusiasm which made him think little of the hardships of his life when business was bad. Papa Franz was, to give Grock's own illustration, much in the position of the parent who asked his children which they would sooner have—their dinner or a penny. All the little hands were held out for pennies. All the little feet went scurrying out of doors towards the shop. But the father called them from the window. " Don't spend your pennies or there'll be nothing for supper."

On the tramp from town to town, the performers, children as well, had to go barefoot to save bootleather. They poached in the woods and stole cabbages and carrots from the fields. Adrien was an acknowledged master in the gentle art of filching. He had method. He would go to market wrapped in a long cloak, with bags underneath at his waist and the rib of an umbrella sharpened at one end in his hand. As he passed the stalls he would jab this weapon into the baskets and withdraw it with an apple or a turnip on the point. With the help of Charles Wetzel, who was of the same age, he could carry out more involved tactics. Adrien would ask to buy apples and hold out his

208

hat to be filled.   When loaded, it had to be gripped between his knees while his hand dived into his pockets for money.   At this point Charles always happened to arrive and stand behind Adrien as if overcome by curiosity; suddenly he would seize the hatful of apples and rush off with it.   Here Adrien's mouth opened in sheer surprise. Then with a shout he would set off in pursuit of Charles until both were out of the farmer's sight.

Seven years passed.   Madame Wetzel fell from her horse and hurt her knee.   Like most circus injuries the swelling was not properly attended to.   At length her leg had to be amputated. During this operation she died.   Without her head for management Franz was helpless.   He disbanded his company and sent his children to Ricono.   But Adrien stayed with him in order to help him build a shooting gallery (where the old clown still lives to this day).   Then Adrien returned to his home, taking with him all the apparatus he used in twelve different entrées, besides his fiddle, his costumes and his employer's parting gift of a xylophone.   He found his parents in a sad state.   The restaurant had been closed and watchmaking was at a standstill, so that there was no work at all for his father, and his mother was only able to earn two or three francs a day at polishing cog-wheels.   Then his sister came home from boarding school.

" I have a plan," said Adrien.   If she would act as his pianist he could give an entertainment at the big café in the town.   His sister was ashamed.   What would her school friends say?   But there was no choice.   The manager of the café had seen the " Little Adrien " of the circus and agreed.   The customers also knew Little Adrien; when he brought the plate to them they dropped in coins until he had a hundred francs.   The entertainment was given for three nights. The family's debts were paid, clothes were bought for the sister and Adrien had a pair of boots.   The next week they went to another town, the week after to another, and so on for a year until they felt the need of providing novelty.   Adrien suggested that as his parents were Tyrolean singers of no ordinary merit they should join them.   Once again the fear of what the neighbours would say had to be overcome. But they consented, and for a time were willing to bear with being called gipsies because their prosperity had returned. There came a day, however, when no more money was to be made in this manner. It was high time thought Adrien. He was tired of going round with the hat.

Madame Wettach went to an employment agency. There were openings in Hungary where wealthy families required Swiss youngsters to speak French with their children. The sister was to go to a house in Budapest and Adrien to Count Bethlen. They were to start on the Monday. In the meantime Adrien was asked to give three performances in a circus on the nights of Friday, Saturday and Sunday, for which he was to receive twenty-four francs. By Monday morning, however, the manager had disappeared, taking Adrien's fiddle with him, and the youth of sixteen was stranded without a sou. He borrowed the fare home, received the tickets from his weeping parents, and without money for food set off on the long journey. At Budapest the tired youngsters were confronted by a big bearded man whose formidable manner frightened them. They were terrified still more when he said they were to part, since Count Bethlen's estate was in Transylvania. Another depressing train journey. At last the station. Outside his heart leaped for joy. The carriage sent for him had four beautiful horses. So glad he was that when they pulled up before Count Bethlen and his servants at the door of the house, Adrien could not wait to alight, but sprang into the air, turned a somersault and landed neatly in front of his new employer with a bow. " So you are an acrobat ? " they said. No, it would not do to confess he was of the circus. Instead, he answered, " All the children in Switzerland are acrobats."

That was the best time of his life—"the food was so damn good," as he says now, " and it was good for me to eat as much as I wanted while I was growing." Besides the twenty francs a month agreed upon he had everything he wanted, including a horse. They made much of him. He was the joy of the house. He also went to the school to amuse the boys. A Swiss professor there grew proud of his compatriot, especially as he could point to him as an example of what the national passion for athletics produced ! The professor taught him fencing and boxing, and, in addition, found him an appointment as gymnastic instructor at a salary of forty francs a month. In his spare time he gave French lessons privately and repaired musical instruments, a task he had learnt in Wetzel's caravan.

Before the eighteen months of his stay with Count Bethlen had ended, all the rest of the Wettach family had come to Hungary, the father as a watchmaker, the mother as a French teacher, and the daughters, even the youngest who was eight, as companions for Hungarian children because of their knowledge of two languages. Adrien went to visit his relatives in turn. From his father he received all the apparatus, costumes and instruments of his circus life. At Budapest he was made welcome at the house where his mother was staying, and endeavoured to earn his living by knocking at doors and asking people if they wanted to buy oil. In a very short time he was disgusted with " commercial travelling," but nothing else offered until, while he was buying new strings for his violin, he heard a man complaining that he had a business letter he could not read because it was in French.

" I am a translator," said Adrien. Afterwards the shop owner offered him the job of teaching his three sons. Adrien agreed to be their tutor on condition that he should be taught the business of making and repairing musical instruments. But it was not a good bargain. He was given so little food that he had to get up in the middle of the night to raid the larder. After six months of this, an accordion player came to the shop to ask if they knew a pianist willing to join a trio to play in the beer gardens. " I am a pianist," said Adrien. He brought out his clown costume and xylophone, and the same night the three made a big success. That he considers now to be the start of his career—he was nineteen years of age.

Three or four months later Adrien was called upon by Alfredo, a circus clown of some note. He wanted a partner. " Have you ever worked in a circus ? " he asked. " I have been in a circus seven years," said Adrien. That was Thursday evening. In spite of the entreaties of the two other players, Adrien had to leave them after the next night's performance. All Saturday morning he had to spend travelling with Alfredo. They rehearsed in the train, arrived at four o'clock, made their entrée at eight and " pulled the place down." Now the ups and downs of his childhood began again. His dexterity in plucking cabbages and poaching pheasants came in useful when business was bad, and the hardness of his feet still saved his boots. The pair had to tramp to Bukharest to accept a six months' engagement with the Crateil Circus, a real gipsy concern with forty horses. The Alfredrieno, as the partners called themselves, were with this circus two years. Then Alfredo married—" There is always a woman," says Grock—and wanted his partner in life to be his partner in the ring. Adrien was turned adrift. He set out for Budapest with the germs of jaundice for companions.

Fortunately, as soon as he had recovered, he met a clown he had known in his childhood. As partners they set out for Berlin. But the clown disliked to part with his money. Every time Adrien wanted his share of their salary he had to use his fists. By keeping his partner short of money the clown thought he could make sure of not losing him. He reckoned without the mother wit that is learned while tramping the roads. While they were at Lubeck, Adrien went one morning to the circus—a permanent structure—and bore all the apparatus of their entrée into a lumber-room just under the roof. Then, exhausted by his efforts and by starvation, he went out into the street, heard a French accent and borrowed a mark. (He still speaks of the act of kindness with uncontrollable emotion). That night his partner called in the police. They asked a few questions and went away. Adrien heard there was a vacancy in the band. " I am a violinist," said Adrien. He was the first fiddle for two weeks. Yet, though seven marks a day was heaven, the smell of the ring was life. Therefore, when the miscreant clown returned, saying, " Here are your wages, now tell me where my stuff is," Adrien pointed to the loft. Then he leant against a pillar, holding his sides with laughter, while the other panted up the ladder and down with his belongings, returning each time more begrimed than the time before. Once his sense of justice was satisfied Adrien agreed to go on as before. They went to Hamburg. On the first night Adrien hurt his knee while tumb-

212

ling and could not put foot to stage. For a month he limped and hopped about the arena. Then they agreed to part. " Let me have my coat," said the partner. " You son of a gun," said Adrien, " I paid you thirty marks for it." He paid him—with a hiding.

Penniless, as before, he found his way to Cologne. At last his inquiries at circus doors led him to trace a showman who wanted a contortionist. " I am a contortionist," said Adrien. He put himself on a table and screwed his body about until the professional onlooker was satisfied. That engagement lasted six months. Then he joined a tumbler named Conche in a music-hall act consisting of somersaults while playing violins. But his partner had softening of the brain. After one or two spills, due to the other's inability to push hard enough, Adrien had to leave him though no other work was in sight. Another spell of idleness was unthinkable. So when the Baroceta, two Spanish clowns who performed in the open, offered him food and the shelter of their caravan in exchange for his services, he agreed. It was " a funny life," says Grock. On their arrival at a town they all marched through the streets playing brass instruments, halted, made a speech, tuned up again, marched, halted, addressed the throng, and so forth. Previously they had erected what looked like a nightmare ship. At one end was a tall mast with a ladder at the side for one clown to climb in order to reach a chair at the top. By means of a rope whose end he had carried with him, he pulled up a trapeze hanging from the cross bar of two great posts some distance in front. Grasping the trapeze, he would dive down between these posts and up into the air on the other side. At the extremity of the swing he had to let go with a leap that took him towards another pair of posts bearing a trapeze. Here the other clown was hanging head downwards with arms outstretched ready to grasp the clown who came hurtling towards him through the air, by the hands. From the chair to the inverted clown the distance was about fifty metres. The flight often took place at night time, in the flickering light of oil flares that added mystery to the feat by lighting up the swiftly flying body at one instant, half illumining it the next, allowing it for one brief second to be almost lost except for its outline against the stars, and then, when the clown was flung into the air by the released trapeze, making a dazzling patch of white where his costume caught the light and leaving the uppermost parts of him in shadow. The exploit over, the hat was taken round and tribute demanded before a repetition would be given. After the second flight, the hat went round again. And after the third flight. But when the third collection had brought forth the last reluctant sou, the forces of the caravan began to demolish the structure ready for the next day's trek.

During a prolonged stay in one of the larger towns Adrien amused himself by taking a seat in a café to listen to the concert. There was some delay. He overheard voluble expostulations that suggested that all was not well. He put a question to the waiter. The proprietor was ill. As he was also the pianist there was no one to play for the girls. " I am a pianist," said Adrien. He was the accompanist at that evening's concert. He was implored to come every night, until the proprietor was better, at ten francs a night. He said goodbye to the Baroceta.

The proprietor was recovering from his illness. Adrien made desperate efforts to find a job. After the concert he stayed at the café until morning, applying to showmen or writing band parts for entrées and acts he feared might never be performed. At an early hour one day two women knocked at the bolted door. Could they lodge there? All the rooms were taken, but the pianist offered to escort them to a house where lodging could be obtained. As he walked into the sunlight the younger of the two smiled at him and spoke his name. She was Franz Wetzel's youngest daughter—only fourteen when he had last seen her nine years ago. What brought her there? Had he not heard of the Swiss " international circus " that had just arrived? Her husband was the best entrée. So Adrien was taken to the caravan and introduced to an acrobat who said, " I know all about you—my wife has been speaking of you so many times." They took him to the proprietor. Alas, there was no room for an extra entrée in their performances. In fact, the only vacancy likely to occur was that of a cashier. " I am a cashier," said Adrien. Because he knew two languages he was welcome, since Schmidt, the proprietor, was a German

214

Swiss and did not know French, while the others knew no German. Adrien was, to use his own adjective, a " beautiful " cashier. He remained one for seven months, until Schmidt's brother-in-law was in need of work. By good luck there was now room for another entrée. He had only to find a partner. They told him that Brick was con- cluding his term of military service. The offer was made just at the right time. They rehearsed together one afternoon and went straight into the arena. Schmidt said they were very funny. " Wait but a week," said Adrien. But how should they be billed ? " Brick and Wettach " was dull. Adrien reflected. That day—it was the 1st of October, 1903—he thought how well " Brick and Grock " would sound. Grock was born.

Their partnership lasted three years. The " Famous Eccentric Brick and Grock " triumphed in France, Africa, South America, and Spain. They obtained music-hall engagements. They were able to save money. They mingled acrobatics, dancing and knockabout humour exactly to the public's taste. They were sure of the conquest of the earth. But—" There is always a woman." Brick fell in love in Spain. He was going to be married, he was going to Paris, he was going to have a wife for his partner in future. Therefore, " Brick and Grock " was dissolved. Adrien stayed on at Barcelona, intending to act alone, though clowns were expected to appear in pairs. The risk was all the greater because audiences in that part of the world are notoriously hard to please. " If you're good as a clown in Spain," says Grock, " you're good for all the world." Yet he succeeded. In fact, when Antonnet, having lost his partner, had witnessed his perform- ance, he decided that here was the only clown to take the vacant place. "You can do practically everything in our business," he said. Together Antonnet and Grock created a furore. They set out confidently on their travels through Europe. At Berlin, however, they caused a fiasco. Attracted by an offer of four thousand marks a week, they took their circus entrée on to the stage of a music-hall. It was so thorough a failure that the contracts were torn up. Antonnet and Grock set their teeth. Every night they changed their tricks to see what was best suited to their new environment. After a week of experiment they were acclimatised. New papers were brought for them to sign, but they said " Cross out four thousand and write five thousand." They were at the Winter Garden when the best British showman, Mr. C. B. Cochran, saw them. They came to the Palace Theatre in 1911 and 1913. There was, however, still the woman. For some such reason, Grock and Antonnet parted at the end of their second London season, after a partnership of seven years. No more would Grock be the partner. In future it must be " Grock and Partner." He engaged Lola (who has since appeared as " Lola and Her " with his wife, the sister who helped Adrien in his early struggles). They were part of a performance given in aid of those who suffered from the effects of the fire at the Chiswick Empire in 1913. Sir Oswald Stoll witnessed that matinée and gave them a contract. Later they went to Copenhagen. In 1914 they were in Russia. War called Lola back to France and soldiering. The managers thought a change of partners rendered Grock's value less. But Mr. Cochran agreed to his terms, and brought him to the Empire for six weeks. Ever since, in spite of one or two changes of partners,[1] he has gone on from strength to strength. As his funds increased he decided to have, in addition to his house in Paris and his flat in London, a villa in Italy. " I am an architect," said Adrien. Forthwith he designed a beautiful villa that he built on the top of a hill overlooking his own wide expanse of land and the Mediterranean.

Grock's homes and cars and dogs and chickens and vines and orchards seem to prove that the clown at last has the state due to his clownship. Is there a king who means so much to his subjects ? He is, to liken him again to Grimaldi, our familiar. To laugh at his anxieties, indignations and joys is like laughing at our own. He is a never-completely-exploded hoax upon our sympathies. When he stares at us with a face full of hurt surprise, trying to explain in a mumble that the violinist has hit him and that it hurts, his inarticulate reproof, too keenly felt to be put into words, moves us to shame, how-ever quickly we may laugh it away. All his ridiculous trials arouse

[1] In the spring of 1924 Grock suddenly " disappeared " from London. He reappeared at the Empire, Paris, in September, with Lola his partner once more.

216

GROCK WITH THE CLOWN OF THE MARIONETTES

From a photograph taken on the stage of the London Coliseum

our suspense, and all his triumphs our glad congratulations, as you may hear and see in those around you.   Emotion breaks out in gasps and applause during his tribulations with a violin bow.   He is about to play.   He throws it nonchalantly into the air.   With a movement expressive of the swagger of doing what is difficult with graceful ease, he gives a turn of his wrist, grasps at it as it falls, smiles at the audience —and misses.   He tries again and misses.   He omits the smile the next time, but again he misses.   A third and a fourth time he misses. He gives a jerk of elbow and wrist and a stamp of the foot to inform us that as a rule he can depend on his dexterity.   With despondent steps, with his violin drooping at the trail, he walks towards a screen. By the way his body is puckered with care we guess what he is about. And when the bow flies up above the screen time after time, the laughter is almost a cheer of encouragement.   Grock emerges without confidence : he has a hangdog look.   Naturally his anxiety produces the same series of failures.   Again he retreats behind the screen.   Again practises.   Again makes a grim, downcast appearance. But now he forgets his old worries in new problems.   First he comes out without his fiddle.   When he has fetched that, he has forgotten his bow.   When he has remembered both he holds them in the wrong hands.   Not only is he unable to play but he cannot imagine what is wrong.   He turns his back on the audience in the hope that this will restore the violin to its right side.   He places them on the floor and scratches his bald head to think things out.   He caresses his chin with- out hope of enlightenment.   Anyhow he must go on with it.   He turns round, picks up the bow and the fiddle—lo ! each is in the hand it should be.   Up flies the violin bow in elation, nonchalantly his hand goes out and catches it.   He prepares to play.   First, however, there is something to be thought over.   Though the audience are applaud- ing, he takes a second or two to realise that he has achieved uncon- sciously what he could not do of set purpose.   "A-a-h," he yells.   He is overcome with joy.   He wants others to share his joy.   His mouth opens wide with joy.   What a pleasant place the world is after all ! Yes we feel that, too, although we may laugh it away.

Grock's way of spending twenty-five minutes on the stage is

arranged as methodically, Mr. Agate points out, as a well-made play. His efforts to push the piano nearer to his chair, his pranks which cause the violinist to strike him, his seizure of the keyboard cover as a weapon of retaliation, his negligence in leaning it against the piano's side, his removal of his hat to a place where it slides down the slanting cover, his eager leap on to the piano's top and toboggan down the slope to retrieve it, have a cumulative effect similar to that of the events in Sardou if not in Greek tragedy. But there is still surer proof of his psychological dexterity in the way he teasingly doles out or withholds the sweetmeats of melody. There have been musical clowns even before Bottom desired the tongs and the bones, but never before has one been able to hold his subjects in trembling servitude by toying with their emotions as a cat manages a mouse. He knows the chords that reduce any audience to the state of the child who wants to be played a tune. At the moment of the greatest expectancy of joy, he lifts his fingers from the keys and clicks his tongue against the roof of his mouth with a resounding " Tick." Here, most notably, he is making his audience laugh not at him but at themselves, at their plaintive desire to have their souls tickled with mellifluous, sugary harmony. At last, he satisfies them. After blowing out the foot-lights and throwing himself backwards on to a chair, he gazes wistfully into the spot-light and plays Verdi on a conceitina with a volume of sound seemingly equal to an organ. The greatest musician might well envy the audience's veneration for this performance. The secret, however, has little to do with virtuosity or even the public's particular taste in music. Grock has satisfied their desire for the ridiculous, and they accept his idea of the sublime.

PANTOMIMES

ORIGINS OF PANTOMIME

When the Pantomime season comes round in each city, they leave all else and sit for whole days watching Titans and Corybantes, Satyrs and neat-herds.

LUCIAN.

Gian Farina.   Fracischina.

DEPARTURE OF THE ITALIAN COMEDIANS IN 1697

From a print after Watteau

YET why satisfy the desire for the ridiculous unless an idea of the sublime is to be revealed ? Since showmanship was cut off from religion, the clown has been swung out of his orbit. Even the romance of the Renaissance was not for him so fair a course as the sacred drama of the Middle Ages. No change from laughter to emotion on the stage has ever been as exhilarating as the transformation created in the Wakefield Nativity Play when the shepherds, straight from their horseplay of tossing the sheep-stealer, went in fear to the light over Bethlehem. After science had succeeded to poetry, Christianity became a matter of facts to be affirmed or denied. The Bible was taken from showman and clown, and given into the keeping of grammarian and historian. Puritans and atheists poisoned life with the antiseptic of science. Christ was taken from the living world of imagination into the cold cells of reason. The spirit that saw the shepherds offering their bob of cherries, bird and ball for tennis, was killed by logical respect for Holy Writ. The clown was forbidden to replace publicans and sinners.

The cleavage was widened by the rational wits of the classic revival. Sublimity, whether religious or profane, had to be separated from ridicule. The preposterous Heroick Play was the result. Being at a loss without an emotional setting, the clown was ousted by the Italian invaders. Even the Harlequinade, however, required the contrast. It was created by music, dancing and spectacle. These devices are " pantomime." Whatever its literal and academic meanings (the two differ), the term has always been used by the people to denote performances, associated with clowns, setting forth a legend by other arts than the living word.

What confusion a pretty lady can cause the world is shown in its etymology. Simply because of a charming blue-stocking's conceit,

223

the word has been so tangled for three centuries that even scholarship mistakes its obvious meaning. In 1706 the Duchesse du Maine, ever seeking some new thing to add to the glories of the *Nuits de Sceaux*, decided to present the fourth act of Corneille's "Horace" as a ballet by Mouret to be danced by Ballon and Prévôt. Out of literary conceit she called it "ballet-pantomime." Her claim was that dumb-show was an art belonging to the ancients. No *savant* pointed out that "imitator of all" does not signify speechlessness.[1] But French scholars have known what the word means. On the other hand the gallant lexicographers of England have, from that day to this, insisted that pantomime means dumb-show for no other reason than that the Duchesse du Maine said it was so.

In France the pantomimes were described as early as 1570 as those who imitate all things. Littré's dictionary of 1869 states they were actors who played all the parts in a piece and expressed themselves only by gesture. That the second qualification is incidental may be inferred by examining the word. Mime became a stage term in a roundabout fashion. In Greece it described prose dialogues, not meant for acting, which imitated scenes of everyday life. In Rome the actors, borrowing the word from Athens much as London does from Paris, used mime to denote either a type of entertainment which mimicked topical events, or else any kind of mimic. *Pantomimus* denotes not a performance but a performer. Therefore the distinction marked by the prefix, is between an imitator and, literally, an *imitator of all*, the explanation being that the *pantomimus* played not one but every part in the mythological legends he set forth upon the stage. There is no lack of evidence to support this view. Dr. Margarete Bieber's *Die Denkmäler zum Theaterwesen im Altertum* contains the photograph of a figure which carries, beside a lyre and a sword, a three-sided mask—a face placed horizontally above two others—made in the likenesses of a bearded man, a woman and a youth. Then there are the tales told by Lucian of the stranger who marvelled because

---

[1] But the mistake was older than the ballet. In *La Vie de Scaramouche* (1695), Constantini described Fiurelli as one of the most perfect pantomimes because *il jouait plus d'action que de parole*. The term was translated as "pantomimes or mimics."

PANTOMIMUS

From a photograph in Dr. Bieber's "Theaterwesen im Altertum"

there were five masks and only one performer, and of the dancer who aroused a philosopher to enthusiasm. In the English version of H. W. and F. G. Fowler, the latter runs :

> The time-beaters, the flutes, even the chorus were ordered to preserve a strict silence ; and the pantomime, left to his own resources, represented the loves of Ares and Aphrodite, the tell-tale sun, the craft of Hephæstus, his capture of the two lovers in the net, the surrounding gods, each in his turn, the blushes of Aphrodite, the embarrassment of Ares, his entreaties.

" 'Tis as if your hands were tongues," is the praise of the spectator. That has been unduly stressed. Another incident ends with the comment, " I observe that you have but one body ; it had escaped me that you had several souls," but this, though apter, has been quoted infrequently. Descriptive recitative played an important part. Lucian explains that the pantomime's mask had a closed mouth because :

> the dancer has plenty of other voices at his service. In the old days, dancer and singer were one ; but the violent exercise caused shortness of breath ; the song suffered for it, and it was found advisable to have the singing done independently.

This should dispel the illusion that the performance was derived from the dramatic dances of the Greeks, like those, described by Xenophon, between a man driving a yoke of oxen and a robber who fought until one or the other was led off in bonds. The story thus acted needed no explanatory song. But to the show of the pantomime the chorus was important as one may see from the complaint of Petronius that Trimalchio's whole household sang so that " you'd have thought yourself in a pantomime chorus." Apparently, the performances did not differ greatly from those described by Suetonius, when Nero sang and acted, with the aid of masks made in the likeness of his own face and women he loved, the tragedies of the Heroes and the Gods. He presented the story of Canace in child-birth, of Orestes slaying his mother, and of Œdipus plucking out his eyes. He dressed for the part and as Hercules was bound in chains which moved a sentry to run to his aid. Further details that help to reconstruct the show of the Roman pantomime can be found. All the same, Professor Hastings' statement in " The Theatre " that " when one of the characters of the

225

pantomime had to expiate a crime, the director borrowed a criminal from a neighbouring prison, who was tortured before the eyes of the public," is inaccurate. Martial certainly describes the death of a robber ordered by Domitian to be eaten alive by a bear to provide a Prometheus for the public's entertainment and also the end of an unhappy actor of Daedalus who had to don waxen wings and fall into a bear's clutches. But these performances took place in the circus : a pantomime, telling the same stories, would have had the advantage of representing the eagle as well as Prometheus, the sea as well as Icarus, the labyrinth as well as Daedalus. Such transformations were the essentials of his art. Lucian suggested that Proteus was probably a pantomime " liquid as water, rapid as fire," and the nearest approach to a Roman pantomime in the entertainments of to-day is described as a " Protean artist."

Blount's " Glossographia " in 1674 defined pantomime as " an actor of many parts in one play." In the seventeenth century that was the general interpretation. There were differences of application—Bacon used the word in " Sylva Sylvarum " in place of mimic, Puttenham in his " Poesie " and Middleton in " The Fair Quarrel " as synonymous with performer, and Jonson in " Love's Triumph " to point out that the manner of the old pantomimi was " antic gesticulation and action "—but there was no definite misconception. Elsewhere in the literature of that time " pantomime " and " mime " express their literal meaning. Thus in his " Strappado " (1615) Braithwait wrote,

In time no question but hee'l prove true pantomime to imitate all formes, shapes, habits, tyres, suiting the Court.

and in " Hudibras " Butler employed the term similarly in this fashion :

Not that I think those pantomimes
Who vary action with the times,
Are less ingenious in their art,
Than those who dully act one part.

As far as the English language is concerned, the error can be clearly traced to the dancing-master, John Weaver. His writings included letters to *The Spectator* in praise of dancing with one or two references to the pantomime " who is said to have given the audience, in dumb show, an exact idea of any character or passion," whereas, of course, the pantomime gave an idea of *every* character and passion.

To give a word a wrong meaning has ever been an effective way of making believe that you have a new idea. That is why the Duchesse du Maine dubbed her ballet, " pantomime." Otherwise she could not have asked her respectful guests to believe that dumb-show in action was her own discovery. Morals expressed in dumb-show heralded the Reformation in allegories so heretical that the authors dared not put what they wished to express into words. Plots were outlined in dumb-show in plays before Shakespeare's time. Dancing in dumb-show was a French art at the time of the Restoration when the Dancing Master in Davenant's " The Playhouse to be Let " declared

> I'm for down-right plain history
> Exprest in figures on the floor, a kind
> Of morals in dumb shows by man and beasts.

And if his explanation that " the audience now and then must be informed by choruses in rhyme " called forth the comment " Oh ! Dumb-shows with speeches," we need only point out that such was also the practice of the Roman pantomimes. Dumb-show without speeches was a very significant feature of entertainment in Paris just before the Duchesse du Maine devised the new kind of ballet. These were given by the Alards at the fairs of St. Germain and St. Laurent. The royal ordinance of October 21, 1680, which reunited the actors of the Hôtel de Bourgogne and those of the Théâtre Guénégand, gave to the new troupe the exclusive right to perform plays in Paris. But this affected neither the opera nor the Italians. When the latter were expelled in 1697, the Alards, states Maurice Albert in his book on the theatres of the fairs, claimed to be their legitimate heirs because they wore the costumes of Scaramouche and Arlequin. As all the dancers, tumblers and marionettes of the fairs had assumed the characters of the Commedia dell' arte, the authorities would not allow the claim. But the royal ordinance only referred to plays. To evade it, the forains invented vaudeville, monologues, revue and other forms of entertainment including dumb-show. Their first evasion of the law was to act detached scenes from comedies. When a specific ban was placed upon these, they measured out the words as if they were reciting Alexandrines on a pretence that the scenes were from tragedies. When these were forbidden, the Alards (in 1708) bought the right of the opera to present spectacles, songs and dances. The next year there were fresh restrictions. To overcome these each actor was provided with sheets of paper, bearing laconic statements in large print, which were rolled and placed in a pocket at the player's right hand. As the comedy progressed, each player at his cue drew forth a sheet of paper, unrolled it for the audience to read, and then put it in another pocket. When this was no longer legal, *écriteaux* (long strips of paper) were hung from the top of the scene to inform the audience who the character was and what he had to say, while the actor translated the words in actions which were called by-play in England, *lazzi* in Italy and *jeux de théâtre* in France. Another method was to exhibit placards bearing verses, post actors in the audience to sing the words, and so encourage the audience to join in. In 1716, however, the Italians returned to Paris, and two years later the forains were suppressed—but only for a time.

London fairs were invaded by dancing or tumbling Harlequins and Scaramouches before the turn of the century. They were all the more welcome when plays were forbidden at Smithfield by Lord Mayors between 1698 and 1702. At the same time the theatres began to engage the French *forains*. There was fierce theatrical competition between the two English companies, and the actors would sooner win the public with raree-shows than let them go to see their rivals' plays. In his epilogue to the " Ambitious Stepmother " at Lincoln's Inn Fields in 1700, Rowe complained :

> Show but a mimic ape, or French buffoon,
> You to the other house in shoals are gone,
> And leave us here to tune our crowds alone.
> Must Shakespear, Fletcher and laborious Ben,
> Be left for Scaramouche and Harlequin ?

During the season of 1701-2 the Sieurs Alard presented " an Italian Night Scene " at Drury Lane. Weaver claimed to be the first

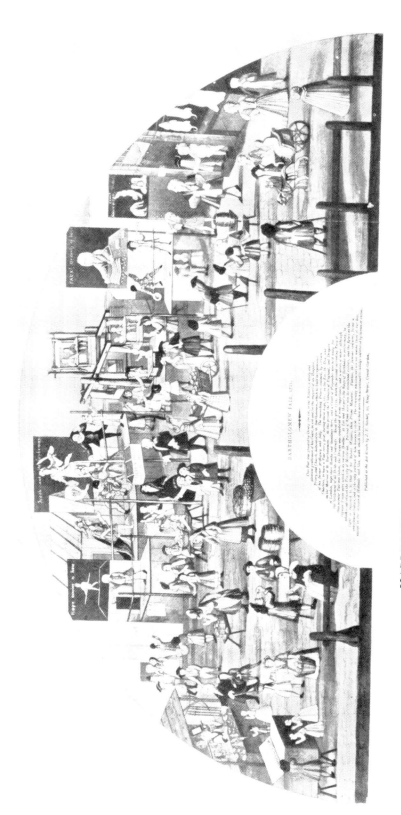

HARLEQUINS IN DROLLS AT BARTHOLOMEW FAIR

From a print in the possession of Messrs. Maggs of Conduit Street

Englishman to adopt the idea. In his " History of the Mimes and Pantomimes," he states :

> The first entertainment that appeared on the English stage, where the representation and story were carried on by dancing, action and motion only, was performed in grotesque characters, after the manner of the modern Italians, such as Harlequin, Scaramouche, etc., and was called

THE TAVERN BILKERS

composed by   Mr. Weaver

And first performed in Drury Lane Theatre, 1702.

Actually, however, Weaver was at Lincoln's Inn Fields in that year and the law forbidding actors to transfer their services had just been reinforced. As the statement was not made until twenty-six years later, we must be excused for doubting his word, especially as the evidence suggests a later date. Early in 1715, the *Daily Courant* files show, the Harlequin and Scaramouche dances included in the " Entertainments of Dancing " which generally followed the play, began to be elaborated. At Lincoln's Inn Fields on April 18 there was, besides a dance of two Scaramouches, " An Entertainment between a Harlequin and Two Punches," and on April 23 an " Entertainment betwixt a Countryman and a Harlequin." In the November there was an " Italian Night-scene between a Harlequin, a Scaramouche and a Punchinello." Meanwhile Drury Lane had offered the public an occasional dance between a Scaramouche and a Harlequin, but in the April of 1716 M. Sorin and Mr. Baxter—" lately arrived from Paris "—represented these two characters in stories such as " The Whimsical Death of Harlequin." Their repertoire also included " La Guinguette ; or Harlequin Turned Tapster," a subject much favoured. One of the *pièces à écriteaux* of the Sieurs Alard was *Arlequin à la Guinguette*, performed at Paris in 1711, and a booth at St. Bartholomew's Fair announced " A new entertainment between a Scaramouche, a Harlequin, and a Punchinello, in imitation of bilking a reckoning."

These Harlequinades, danced at the end of the play, received more attention in the spring of 1716. Two days after Rich had staged at Lincoln's Inn Fields, " a dance between 2 Punchinellos, a

Harlequin and Dame Ragonde," Drury Lane announced " a Mimic-Night-Scene after the Italian Manner, between a Harlequin, Scaramouche and Dame Ragonde ; being the same that was performed with great applause by the Sieurs Alard 14 years ago." Rich carried the idea further in the autumn by presenting " a New Italian Mimic Scene (never performed before) between a Scaramouche, a Harlequin, a Country Farmer, his wife and others," and in the January of 1717 this " last New Italian Mimic Scene " became " Harlequin Executed ; or, the Farmer Disappointed." Next came Weaver's " New dramatic entertainment of dancing, after the manner of the ancient pantomimes, called The Loves of Mars and Venus " on March 2, 1717. This, the first performance in England to make use of the word pantomime in its label, was probably inspired by Ballon and Prévôt who had become well-known in London. The composer would have us believe it appeared a year earlier, and Cibber, his manager, declaring it to be the explanation of " how our childish pantomimes first came to take so gross a possession of the stage," gives it special attention in his "Apology" :

> The fable of Mars and Venus was formed into a connected presentation of dances in character, wherein the passions were so happily expressed, and the whole story was so intelligibly told, by a mute narration of gesture only, that even thinking spectators allowed it both a pleasing and a rational entertainment ; though at the same time, from our distrust of its reception, we durst not venture to decorate it with any extraordinary expense of scenes, or habits ; but upon the success of this attempt, it was rightly concluded, that if a visible expense in both were added to something of the same nature, it could not fail of drawing the town proportionately after it. From this original hint, then (but every way unequal to it), sprung forth that succession of monstrous medlies, that have so long infested the stage, and which arose upon one another alternately, at both houses, outvying in expense, like contending bribes on both sides at an election, to secure a majority of the multitude. But so it is, truth may complain, and merit murmur with what justice it may, the few will never be a match for the many, unless authority should think fit to interpose, and put down these poetical drams, these gin-shops of the stage, that intoxicate its auditors and dishonour their understanding, with a levity for which I want a name. If I am asked (after my condemning these fooleries myself) how I came to assent, or continue my share of expense to them, I have no better excuse for my error than confessing it. I did it against my conscience ! and had not virtue enough to starve, by opposing a multitude that would have been too hard for me.

On April 2, 1717, Weaver composed a Harlequinade described as a " dramatic entertainment of dancing in grotesque characters called, The Shipwreck ; or, Perseus and Andromeda.   Perseus by Harlequin, Andromeda by Columbine, Monster by Crocodile . . .   Four Sailors and their Wives by the Comedians."   Once more Lincoln's Inn Fields set up rivalry with a Harlequinade called " The Cheats ; or, the Tavern Bilkers" on April 2, and "The Jealous Doctor; or, the Intriguing Dame " on April 29.   The next season the competition was more unscrupulous.   Thus when Drury Lane staged " Harlequin Turned Judge " on December 5, 1717, Rich at Lincoln's Inn followed six days later with " Columbine, or, Harlequin Turned Judge." Soon Drury Lane found the strain too great, and, as a pamphlet of the period declared, the actors " began to talk of shutting up shop." But Rich over-indulged his partiality for foreign performers, including the performing dogs of a German named Swartz which could dance the minuet.   His dancing-master, John Thurmond, went to the Lane and proved a resourceful rival.

Weaver's Harlequinade version of " Perseus and Andromeda " confused the public.   All dumb-shows were called pantomimes although one of the Harlequinades (" The Comical History of Dr. Faustus " in Dec. 1723) was announced as

> not in the least designed for an imitation of the ancient pantomimes, Harlequin, Scaramouche, Punch and Pierrot being of the present Italian theatre.

Thenceforward, the term was more and more loosely used.   The Harlequinades of the seventeenth century became known as "speaking-pantomimes " which moved Garrick to add a fresh one to the species. Though Hazlitt protested against " all dumb-show speaking," the pantomime with words increased.   To-day " pantomime " is used to imply either a state of affairs far removed from sanity or a representation of life that is far removed from reality.

TRANSFORMATION

Nature was out of countenance, and each day
Some new-born monster, shown you for a play.
But when all failed, to strike the stage quite dumb,
Those wicked engines, called machines, are come.
Thunder and lightning now for wit are played,
And shortly scenes in Lapland will be laid :
Art magic is for poetry professed ;
And cats and dogs, and each obscener beast,
To which Egyptian dotards once did bow,
Upon our English stage are worshipped now.

DRYDEN.

Trastullo.　　Sig. Lucia

WHILE all other arts of the theatre have at odd times waned, scene-shifting has waxed from age to age. The stage undertakers have a line of descent as unbroken as the Lord Mayor's. Actors may lose the traditions of their forebears and authors find the nib worn from Shakespeare's pen, but Drury Lane's spectacles are the result of the accumulated experience of the English theatre's three or four centuries of life. The tradition dates back even farther than Elizabeth's Office of the Revels which supplied the court with costumes of satin, velvet, damask and cloth of gold, with tinsels, and topasses and " stones called sitterines," with banners and fireworks, with hell and hell's mouth, with devices for thunder and lightning, with a castle having " pillers Arcatrye, frize carnish and the roofe gilt with gold and fine silver." The undertaker of the present piece at Drury Lane is joined, by generations of clasped hands, with the Master of the Revels who mounted " The History of the Knight of the Burning Rock " at Whitehall, using

> Ivy and Holly for the Rock.
> Aquavite to burne in the same rock.
> Rosewater to allay the smell thereof.
> A hoope and blewe Lynnen cloth to mend the clowde
> that was borrowed and cut to serve the rock.

These are the seeds of corruption. Lavish devices are well enough in revels, but not in plays. Because drama is an art that is both looked at and listened to, the undertaker argues that both senses should be indulged to the full. The mind, however, cannot fully exercise sight and hearing at the same time. Actors refrain from moving at the actual moment they are speaking for this reason. But of what use is their care if the undertaker is meanwhile supplying sweet sights and sounds to clog the playgoer's senses ? As long as the multiplication of " effects " and " properties " was confined to the court, no harm was done except that the debasement of taste outlawed Shakespearean tragedy.   But when the drama, tragedy no less than comedy, aroused an interest in James I., court and playhouse were merged.   The players profited little by being made royal servants.   Instead of lording it over rough, masculine audiences, they were the sycophants of effeminacy.   Soon the King called upon Jonson for " shows, shows, mighty shows."   Soon these were made less of words than of Inigo Jones's " Painted cloth, deal board, vermilion, lake or crimson " until the poet railed against those

> That do cry up the machine and the shows ;
> The majesty of Juno in the clouds
> And peering forth of Iris in the shrouds.

Such things were but toys, said Bacon, but he too felt that alterations of scenes were things of great beauty and pleasure.   Therefore, he, too, added to the knowledge of this preposterous science :

> Let the scenes abound with light, specially coloured and varied ; and let the masquers, or any other, that are to come down from the scene, have some motions upon the scene itself before their coming down ; for it draws the eye strangely, and makes it with great pleasure to desire to see that it cannot perfectly discern.   Let the songs be loud and cheerful, and not chirpings and pulings.   Let the music likewise be sharp and loud, and well placed.   The colours that shew best by candle-light are white, carnation, and a kind of sea-water green ; and oes, or spangs, as they are of no great cost, so they are of most glory.

Davenant took Jonson's place.   With Inigo Jones he set " Britannia Triumphans " before Charles at Whitehall in 1637.   To give coherence to the alteration of scenes, they introduced Merlin, forerunner of Harlequin-magicians and fairy queens.   These are scene-shifters' creatures.   To link them with Prospero who made the " strong based promontory shake " in poetry—or with Ariel because of his table-shifting exploit—is erroneous.   They resemble more closely the mountebank seeking to amaze his audience with spurious, dazzling wares.   In " Britannia Triumphans," Merlin changes a prospect of London into " a horrid hell, the further part terminating in a flaming precipice, the nearer parts expressing the Suburbs."   At another word from the magician, hell changes into a vast forest.   The earth opens and a " richly adorned Palace, seeming all of Goldsmith's workes, rises up." Britanocles comes out, addresses the king, returns, and the palace sinks. Fame rises on her wings singing till hidden in the clouds. The scene changes to a sea where Galatea rides on the back of a Dolphin followed by a great Fleet sailing before a prosperous gale. The verse is doggerel.

Moved by the profit to be found in " music, musical present-ments, scenes, dancing, or other the like," Davenant secured a royal patent for a special theatre to be built in Fleet Street, and only aban-doned the scheme on being made governor of their majesties' servants at the Cockpit. Now that the undertaker held the control that once belonged to Shakespeare, Burbage and Kempe—author, actor and clown—the drama was doomed. The Civil War all but saved the theatre by arresting its growth when development had taken the wrong direction. Davenant, however, survived engagements on land and sea, conspiracy against the Commonwealth and violation of the Ordinance that closed the theatres. By permitting him to perform his operas of " The Siege of Rhodes," " Sir Francis Drake " and " The Cruelty of the Spaniards in Peru," Parliament struck the drama a heavier blow than the Ordinance. Just as the companies were reviving the Shake-speare traditions, Davenant and Killigrew obtained from Charles II. patents and the suppression of all other companies. Though Dave-nant died in 1668, his policy had substituted " musical presentments " for the drama of emperors and clowns. Killigrew, though the King's jester, emulated him to the neglect of laughter. " Fairy operas " drained the theatre's funds and energy. Davenant and Dryden transformed Shakespeare into pantomimes. Following their ex-ample, Shadwell designed " The Tempest, or the Enchanted Island " to be staged with machines and lavish scenes of aerial spirits. His opera of " Psyche " was described by Downes, the prompter, as " set out specially in scenes the charge of which amounted to above £800." Dryden's chief effort to compete was " King Arthur ; or, the British Worthy," described by Jeremy Collier as " a strange jumble of Hotch Potch of Matters " :

> Here we have Genii, and Angels, Cupids, Syrens and Devils ; Venus and St. George, Pan and the Passions, the Hell of Heathenism and the Hell of Revelation.

237

This piece employed two magicians. Oswald, the Saxon, was assisted by Osmand whose attendant spirit was the gloomy Grimbald. Arthur was protected by Merlin who called the airy Philidel to his aid. When Osmand raised an enchanted wood and made Arthur believe his Emmeline was imprisoned in one of the trees, Merlin broke the spell.

Dryden's rival was Elkanah Settle, who had learned the trade of dumbfounding the public while arranging Pope-burning pageants, Lord Mayor shows, and drolls for Bartholomew Fair. " A Midsummer Night's Dream " served him for the plot of a droll. He also changed it into the opera of " The Fairy Queen." " Magnificent palaces " were included in the scenes. There was a river bridged by two great dragons, and a " Prospect of Terras Walks on eight several stages mounted one above the other," with an " Ascent of marble steps 24 ft. high," thirty-two pedestals and above fifty people on the terraces. The expenses of setting these out were so great that, though the court and the town were " wonderfully satisfied," the company got but little profit. Yet Settle's " The New World in the Moon " was on an unreduced scale. One scene was built in this fashion :

> Three grand arches of clouds extending to the roof of the house terminated with a prospect of cloudwork, all filled with the figures of fauns and cupids ; a circular part of the black clouds rolls swiftly away, and gradually discovers a silver moon, near fourteen foot diameter ; after which, silver moon wanes off by degrees, and discovers the world within, consisting of four grand circles of clouds, illustrated with cupids, etc. Twelve golden chariots are seen riding in the clouds, filled with twelve children, representing the twelve celestial signs. The third arch entirely rolling away, leaves the full prospect terminating with a large landscape of woods, waters, towns, etc.

Elaborate spectacles were shown even at the fairs. Settle's " The Siege of Troy " at Mrs. Myn's booth was, according to the advertisements, elaborately mounted. There was a wooden horse " 17 foot high to the top of his back," and forty soldiers with their officers came out of his sides. The temple of Diana, " a magnificent structure richly adorned," contained ten statues that were changed by Cassandra's magic wand in the twinkling of an eye from gold to black. The burning of Troy was " performed by illuminations and transparent paintings seen scattered through the scenes, both in the upper and

238

"THE SIEGE OF TROY" AT SOUTHWARK FAIR

From the engraving by Hogarth

lower town." Doggett (the comedian whose coat and badge are rowed for on the Thames) made a droll from " Friar Bacon " with " real conjuration, besides a flying shoulder of mutton, dancing and singing devils," and another from the " Distressed Virgin " with comic songs and dances and " machines never seen before." Pinkethman, Mills and Bullock acted the droll of " The Siege of Barcelona, with the Taking of Fort Mountjoy." It contained

> The pleasant and comical exploits of the renowned hero, Captain Blunderbus and his Man Squib. His adventures with the conjurer, and a surprising scene of the flying machine, where he and his Man Squib are enchanted.

The puppets followed suit. Their " little opera " of the " Old Creation of the World " showed fountains playing, the sun rising over Noah's Ark, angels ringing bells, Dives rising out of hell to speak to Lazarus in Abraham's bosom and machines " double and treble." Powel's " Heroick Love ; or, the Deaths of Hero and Leander," concluded with

> an extraordinary piece of machinery, after the Italian manner, representing the splendid Palace of Diana ; breaking into double and triple prospects, with all the changes of scenes and decorations belonging to the play.

Scenic splendour being commonplace, competition increased in extravagance. Though united against the rivalry of the puppets, the actors, now one company, were still unsuccessful. Colley Cibber tells how even the very handsome receipts of two operas, " The Prophetess " and " King Arthur," did not so far balance their expense as to keep them out of a large debt. But this, he says, was not all that was wrong. Every branch of the theatrical trade had been sacrificed to the necessary fitting out " those tall ships of burthen, that were to bring home the Indies." Christopher Rich, who had bought the share of Davenant and adopted his policy, was an able and unscrupulous attorney, caring little for plays or players. The extraordinary prices he paid to singers, dancers, tumblers and jugglers were deducted out of the sinking salaries of his actors. Only the jealousy of the "exotic performers " and the assurance of a bricklayer that the structure of the theatre would be endangered, prevented him from completing a deal for the exhibition of an elephant on the stage at Dorset Gardens.

239

When Betterton rebelled and formed a second company in the tennis court at Lincoln's Inn Fields, they were too late to save themselves. As " Mimic " in Motteux's " Farewell Folly " explains (while he is picking up " humours " at the fair) they had full audiences at both houses, but the " Painters, the printers, the chandlers, the singers, the fiddlers, the dancers, the renters, the doorkeepers, poundage and patentees " shared the money between them. There was another reunion in 1708. But when Rich tricked the actors of their " bene-fits," the company left Drury Lane and set up for themselves at the Haymarket. *The Tatler* of July 15, 1709, gave notice that " a magnificent palace, with great variety of gardens, statues, and water-works " was to be bought cheap in Drury Lane, besides several castles very delightfully situated ; as also groves, woods, forests, fountains and country seats, with very pleasant prospects on all sides of them ; spirits of right Nantz brandy, for lambent flames and apparitions ; three bottles and a half of lightning ; showers of snow ; a sea consisting of a dozen large waves ; a dozen and a half of clouds ; a rainbow ; a new moon ; a gilt coach with a pair of dragons ; elbow chairs and flower pots very expert in country dances. The actors, armed with a lease, lay siege to Drury Lane and entered the theatre by way of the building next door. Rich, however, had moved with all his palaces and castles into the old theatre in Lincoln's Inn Fields. Because of the trouble over his patent he was not able to open until 1714. A month before the first performance he died. His son, who referred to him in a prologue as a " Martyr," addressed himself to the same " good old cause.'

To understand the type of Harlequinade John Rich did so much to establish in London, the performances of the *forains* of Paris must be studied. Magic and transformations were important parts of their stock-in-trade. The great Zorastre himself had appeared with them in *Les Forces de l'Amour de la Magie* in 1678. It was, according to Albert's *Les Théâtres de la Foire*, a mixture of juggling, gymnastics and naïve comedy. At the time, Arlequin's wooden sword was merely a slapstick. The conjurer's *baguette* was seized as a novelty by the Italian comedians who exploited it in many pieces during the next

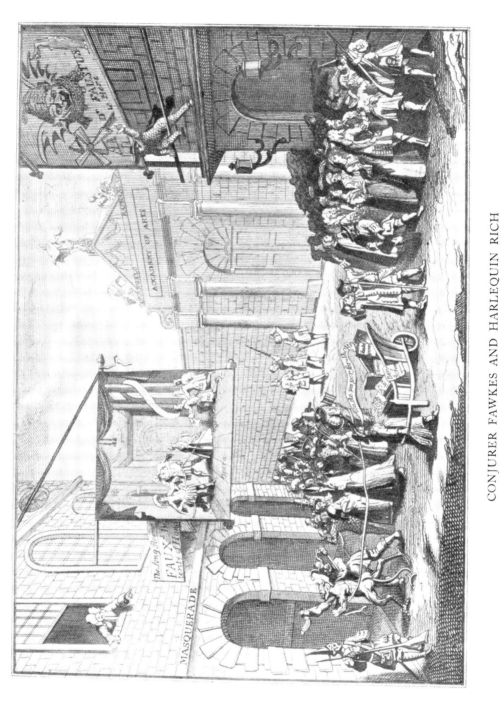

CONJURER FAWKES AND HARLEQUIN RICH

From Hogarth's "Opera and Masquerade"

twenty years. The magic wand, however, was only occasionally given to Arlequin. It was the perquisite of the immortals or magicians who generally used it themselves. Thus in *Des Souhaits*, Momus caused the scene to be transformed in order to offer Arlequin the choice of health, wit, good fortune, favour, merit, folly or riches. Because Arlequin, gazing covetously upon the symbolical figures, answered, " Rather than cause any jealousy, I'll take the whole shop," Momus waved his *baguette* and Arlequin went down the trap. Similarly in *Arlequin Jason* (1695), Medée struck the stage with the *baguette*, changed it into a garden of fountains which played and statues which danced. In *Ulisse and Circé*, the enchantress wielded it. In *Les Fées*, Arlequin received the wand from a fairy (after the fashion customary in English pantomimes of a century later). Meanwhile at the Paris fairs, magic was still developing. Constantine Octave, who took the place of the elder Alard on his death in 1711, invented transformation machinery which changed the entire scene in the twinkling of an eye.

When these ideas were brought to London by the *forains*, Fawkes —either at his booth on Tower Hill or in the old tennis-court in James-street, Haymarket, which he shared with Powel's puppets— was giving displays of " dexterity of hand, far exceeding all that ever performed in this Kingdom." Rich combined the ideas of conjuring and transformation. His magic wand changed palaces and temples to huts and cottages ; men and women into wheelbarrows and joint stools ; trees into houses ; colonnades to beds of tulips ; mechanics " hops " into serpents and ostriches. Wrote a scoffer in *The Crafts-man* :

> How artfully contrived was that incident of the wind-mill ! What a prodigious genius does it require to metamorphose man into woman, and women into laurel trees ! How does it raise our imagination to see some drawn up by wires to the top of the stage ; and sink it again, to see others let down to the bottom through trap doors ! Walking tables, and flying hobby-horses are become familiar to our eyes. The device of setting an old barn on fire discovered a vast deal of spirit ; but that masterpiece of raising the stage up into the air is inimitable.

There was little of the Italian buffoon in this magician. John Rich, who appeared under the name of Lun, was a dancing Harlequin after the fashion of the *foires*.   Instead of the mask of a black cat, he wore a vizard.   The only reference to the comic side of his performance is contained in a pamphlet which likens his methods of treating actors to the way he gave his clown, Hippisley, " a stroke on the shoulder with his Harlequin-sword, made him turn about to him, and then with a grin slapped the door in his face."   Lun was an accomplished dancer who could scratch his ear with his foot like a dog, and rapidly execute two or three hundred steps in an advance of three yards.   Like Carlin, he was always surrounded by cats ; but whether, like that Arlequin, he considered himself their pupil in the art of deportment there is no record.   Davies praises him for his grace :

> Mr. Garrick's action was not more perfectly adapted to his characters than Mr. Rich's attitudes and movements to the varied employment of the wooden sword magician.   His taking leave of Columbine was most graceful and affecting.   His consummate skill in teaching others to express the language of the mind by action, was evident from the great number of actors he produced to fill up the inferior parts of his mimic scenes.

Apart from the early specimens, Rich's pantomimes generally consisted of two parts.   The first, a story from Ovid's *Metamorphoses*, was meant to be serious.   It exhibited, said Fielding, a certain number of heathen gods and heroes, who were " certainly the worst and dullest company into which an audience was ever introduced ;   and, which was a secret known to few, were actually intended so to be, in order to contrast the comic part of the entertainment, and to display the tricks of Harlequin to the better advantage."   Between the three instalments of the classic tale—this pattern, however, was constantly varied —two comic scenes were performed.   These Fielding considered " duller than anything before shown on the stage," and only to be set off " by that superlative degree of dullness which composed the serious."

The courtship of Harlequin and Columbine was probably first introduced in the pantomime of January 24, 1718, called " Amadis ; or, the Loves of Harlequin and Columbine."   In the autumn, the Italian troupe from Paris arrived with their comic pieces, *Les Deux Arlequins*—in which one was constantly taken to task for the offences of the other—*Colombine Advocate* and *Arlequin Homme à*

Bonne Fortune. From 1718 to 1720 the life of pantomime was uncertain. Drury Lane went back to Weaver's classical ballets— " Orpheus and Eurydice " and " Cupid and Bacchus "—and Rich contented himself, apart from the mock-opera of " Harlequin-Hydaspes," with a revival of " The Cheats." But magic put new life into the entertainment. On March 16, 1721, a performance of " King Lear " was followed by " The Magician ; or Harlequin a Director "—of the South Sea Company. The results, according to a pamphlet by a George Rennell, were remarkable. Whereas before " everybody fled from a set of people who looked like real ghosts and who appeared in such frightful shapes as scared even parsons and undertakers from their house," Lincoln's Inn Fields now had a spell of prosperity because of " Puppet-Shows and Monstrous Tricks," which induced the vulgar to believe Mr. Rich was a real sorcerer. Drury Lane had cause to talk of " shutting up shop." But their rival's quarrels restored the balance.

Rivalry was still keener in 1723. Drury Lane came to grief with "Blind Man's Buff," for the feats of its eight Harlequins were hissed. Meanwhile Lincoln's Inn Fields had a part serious and part grotesque entertainment mixed with singing called " Jupita and Europa," with Jupiter (by Lun) in the character of Harlequin, Pluto as Punch and Hercules as Pierrot. That November Thurmond at Drury Lane staged " Harlequin Dr. Faustus : With the Masque of the Deities." A description of this was published—to save people the trouble of going to see it, commented Pasquin. Mephistopheles flew into the study of Faustus upon a dragon vomiting fire. Faustus received gold for his contract, but, running short of money, sold his leg to a usurer, whereupon the Devil waved his wand, " Legs of several colours, sorts and sizes " flew in, and a woman's leg attached itself to Faustus's stump. Harlequin, Scaramouche, Punch and Pierrot, during a quarrel between the salesman and his wife, robbed a shop and flew away upon four spirits in the shapes of a cat, a hog, a goat and an owl. When caught, Harlequin flew up through the ceiling, whereupon the mob seemed " very much surprised and went away." Harlequin and his companions took refuge in a barn. When the door was

243

forced they ran upon the roof and jumped into the chimney. The barn was set on fire. "A tune of horror" was played. The scene changed to the study, where two fiends seized the doctor and other devils tore him piecemeal. The gods and goddesses in a poetical heaven expressed their "Joy for the enchanter's death."

This pantomime was replaced at Drury Lane on December 10 by Thurmond's "The Escapes of Harlequin." Rich, however, borrowed Thurmond's previous idea. First he staged "The Comical History of Dr. Faustus," and then "The Necromancer; or, Harlequin Dr. Faustus." In addition, the Haymarket revived Mountfort's "Dr. Faustus." Apparently, the town could not be surfeited. Though occasionally varied with "Mars and Venus" or "The Escapes of Harlequin" at Drury Lane, and with "Amadis" at Lincoln's Inn, Faust held both theatres fairly regularly until the end of the season, and in spite of new pantomimes—"Harlequin Invisible in the Emperor of China's Court" and "The Robbers; or, Harlequin Trapped by Columbine" at Lincoln's Inn Fields in the spring of 1724—he was revived for many seasons, the theatres long rivalling each other in showing "the burnings of hell-fire."

Each house strove to out-do the other in ingenuity. Rich kept to magic. Booth, Cibber and Thurmond saw in the popularity of Faust a sign of the public's interest in crime. In the *Weekly Journal* of December 14, 1723, an announcement ran:

> By private letters from Drury Lane, we are informed that that theatre is preparing to revive several extraordinary entertainments in grotesque characters, as Bateman, or the fair Vow Breaker; shewing how Bateman hanged himself, how he appeared to his sweetheart as she lay in, with the merry humours of the gossips at the christening, as also the London Prodigal, the Creation of the World, the History of Friar Bungy, and also of Friar Bacon and his brazen Head to be performed by Keyber, and Punch by B——. In all the foregoing entertainments, the heathen gods and goddesses are to be introduced, in order to give the greater surprise, with scenes, machines, and decorations, proper to each entertainment, the whole to be managed and contrived by the three ingenious gentlemen, who were the inventors of blind Man's buff, and Harlequin Dr. Faustus.

Thurmond brought out on November 29, 1724, "Harlequin Sheppard," with "New Scenes Painted from the Real Places of Action." The first scene was the prison. Sheppard—Harlequin in

244

A Skip-shod Sibyl led his steps along
In lofty Madnefs meditating Song.
Dunciad, Book III.

CIBBER AND SETTLE

From "The Works of Alexander Pope", Vol. V., 1757

HARLEQUIN SHEPPARD

From the frontispiece to "Harlequin Sheppard", 1724

a skin-tight costume—found a small nail and unlocked the padlock of his fetters. The keepers surprised him and chained him down again. By means of a pie full of implements he escaped up the chimney. In the street the prisoners were singing a ballad of how Blueskin killed Jonathan Wild, who was brought on the stage with his throat cut. Sheppard came from the top of Newgate " upon the Turner's leads by the help of a blanket." Through the windows of a house Turner's maid was seen undressing for bed. Sheppard hailed a coach. When caught entering a cellar by a mob, he broke through an iron grate, tore down the shutter of a window, and threw himself " through the glass into the house." With the mob still in pursuit, he came out of another part of the house, threw himself " into a window up one pair of stairs of the next house," broke through the ceiling, got upon the roof and dropped tiles upon the people below. When they took shelter in the cellar he barred them in, knocking down one who struggled to get through the grating. He was seen in a butcher's shop by an ale-house boy and finally arrested while drinking with Frisky Moll, who ended the entertainment with a song full of thieves' slang.

Rich had intended to startle the town with a " Rape of Proserpine" on a lavish scale, but "some very necessary persons from abroad" failing him, he collaborated with Theobald (the Shakespeare commentator) in " Harlequin a Sorcerer; or, the Loves of Pluto and Proserpine," performed on January 21, 1725. Theobald's libretto directs that the opening scenes should show " dark rocky caverns by the side of a wood, illumined by the moon; birds of omen promiscuously flying, flashes of lightning faintly striking." Witches flew across. Harlequin, in a post chaise " swiftly flying after," was welcomed by them in a dance. After the comic scenes, while composing himself for rest on a couch, he was carried off by demons. As they disappeared a machine descended with Pluto and Proserpine. Dances alternated with songs, until the sorcerer's arrival in hell was announced. Proserpine sang a final tag:

> With utmost pleasure, now I see
> The monarch of my heart and me,
> No more great Pluto sues in vain,
> No more my anger I retain.

The " dark scene " of the opening, an idea which persisted, was paralleled in " Argentina ; or, the Sorceress," which the Italian comedians brought to the Haymarket in 1726. It began with a thunderstorm in a forest. The sorceress entered in a flying chariot drawn by monsters. Arlequin, set before a magic feast, was directed not to touch the macaroons.[1] When he fell to the temptation they flew into the air and he was swallowed up by the earth, table and all. In the end Argentina foreswore magic in order to marry him.

Thurmond's " Apollo and Daphne " at Drury Lane on February 23, included the metamorphosis of Daphne into the laurel tree. The next January Rich followed suit in " Apollo and Daphne ; or, the Burgomaster Tricked." But there was a temporary change on November 9, 1726, when Rich staged the first Arabian pantomime to be seen in London—a masque of music called " The Sultan "—with " all the scenes, flyings, machines and other decorations," as an afterpiece generally to operas such as " The Prophetess " and " Camilla." The flyings, a trick employed by the Italians in *Arlequin Phaeton*, were a dangerous form of entertainment. Mishaps were not uncommon. In a Faustus pantomime :

> One James Field who represented the Miller's Man fell from the upper stage in a flying machine by the breaking of the wires : he fractured his skull and died miserably : three others were much hurt, but recovered. Some of the audience swooned, and the whole was in great confusion upon the sad accident.

There were equally dangerous tricks in a sequel to Faustus staged at Drury Lane on December 31, 1726. Thurmond's " The Miser ; or, Wagner and Abericock," opened with Harlequin-Wagner in the study of Faustus. He turned a globe several times and out came Abericock " in the habit of a running footman." The spirit opened a large folio and showed the picture of a Quakeress. Harlequin, dressed as a Quaker, went to the house of the Miser where lodgings were to be let. The Miser's daughter was the Quakeress. Pierrot, the Miser's servant, was roasting an egg while his master counted his gold. When Harlequin entered, the scene changed to his apartment.

---

[1] It is not suggested that Ibsen was influenced by this incident when writing " A Doll's House."

To please the daughter Abericock was brought out of a portmanteau to conjure up a collation.   Pierrot, scandalised on peeping in, was withheld by the clown, Harlequin's servant, who showed him " the Provision on the Table."   While the moon passed " through the horizon," the Miser buried his jewels in the garden, but Harlequin stole them in order " to be gay with wine and woman."   The Quaker-ess made Abericock change Pierrot into a false Harlequin, but he was spirited away and dropped from the top of the house—the machinery failed one night and Pierrot was killed—which restored him to his proper habit.   Harlequin was followed to the fair by the Quakeress, who led him away from the booths and parades.   By restoring the jewels he gained the Miser's consent to their marriage.

In the January of 1727 Rich at last staged Theobald's " The Rape of Proserpine ; with the Birth and Adventures of Harlequin." It was in this that hell rose and heaven descended to dance on earth, and a cornfield was set on fire.   It provoked a special attack in Pope's satire on pantomimes in the " Dunciad."   Cibber, taken to the Elysian Shade, meets Settle, who points to " what Dulness and her sons admire."   Cibber sees

> a sable Sorc'rer rise,
> Swift to whose hand a winged volume flies :
> All sudden, Gorgons hiss, and Dragons glare,
> And ten-horn'd fiends and Giants rush to war.
> Hell rises, Heav'n descends, and dance on Earth :
> Gods, imps, and monsters, music, rage, and mirth,
> A fire, a jigg, a battle, and a ball,
> 'Till one wide conflagration swallows all.
>
> Thence a new world to Nature's laws unknown,
> Breaks out refulgent, with a heav'n its own :
> Another Cynthia her new journey runs,
> And other planets circle other suns.
> The forests dance, the rivers upward rise,
> Whales sport in woods, and dolphins in the skies,
> And last, to give the whole creation grace,
> Lo ! one vast Egg produces human race.
>
> Joy fills his soul, joy innocent of thought ;
> What pow'r, he cries, what pow'r these wonders wrought ?
> Son ; what thou seek'st is in thee ! Look, and find
> Each Monster meets his likeness in thy mind.

247

> Yet would'st thou more ?   In yonder cloud behold,
> Whose sarsenet skirts are edg'd with flamy gold,
> A matchless youth ! his nod these worlds controuls,
> Wings the red lightning, and the thunder rolls.
> Angel of Dulness, sent to scatter round
> Her magic charms o'er all unclassic ground :
> Yon stars, yon suns, he rears at pleasure higher,
> Illumes their light, and sets their flames on fire.
> Immortal Rich ! how calm he sits at ease
> 'Mid snows of paper, and fierce hail of pease ;
> And proud his Mistress' orders to perform,
> Rides in the whirlwind, and directs the storm.
>
> But lo ! to dark encounter in mid air
> New wizards rise ; I see my Cibber there !
> Booth in his cloudy tabernacle shrin'd,
> On grinning dragons thou shalt mount the wind.
> Dire is the conflict, dismal is the din,
> Here shouts all Drury, there all Lincoln's Inn ;
> Contending theatres our empire raise,
> Alike their labours, and alike their praise.

Though contemporary accounts, including " Harlequin Horace " which imitates Pope, are equally scornful, Lun's performance is praised by those who wrote after his death.   Jackson, the historian of the Scottish stage, saw him act, in his dining-room and upon the lawn of his house at Cowley, the scenes of catching the butterfly and of the statue.   When preparing his last revival of the " Sorcerer," Rich showed a new Harlequin how he was to be hatched by the heat of the sun.   " This," said Jackson,

> certainly was a master-piece in dumb-shew.   From the first chipping of the egg, his receiving motion, his feeling the ground, his standing upright, to his quick Harlequin trip round the empty shell, through the whole progression, every limb had its tongue, and every motion a voice, which spoke with most miraculous organ, to the understandings and sensations of the observers.

This strange old man with uncouth manners and coarse yet pleasant face had invented the Harlequin of fantasy.   Custom, as Theobald wrote, had " made it a sort of necessity, in order to give tricks some air of probability, that Harlequin should be a piece of a magician."   A myth who is the poet's constant joy was originally no more than a scene-shifter's creature.

248

SHAKESPEARE VERSUS HARLEQUIN

It is to humour the town that the Necromancer Harlequin has associated with tumblers and savages, to prophane the place, which, under proper regulation, would indeed be the school of wisdom and virtue.

"The Adventurer" (1752).

Evariste Gherardi.
dit Arlequin.

HARLEQUIN DRAWN BY DEVILS INTO COVENT GARDEN

From the engraving by Hogarth

"ARLEQUIN," said Gherardi, "has no marked character; he is whatever one wishes him to be." Originally he was the serving man in the Commedia dell' arte. When the Italians turned parodists, he represented all manner of men. Yet he was neither part nor player. He had on the stage the limitless licence *x* enjoys in mathematics. In the Hôtel de Bourgogne's version of "Le Misanthrope," for instance, Domenique was Arlequin and Arlequin was Alceste. Here was a subtlety of fascinating possibilities. In his "European Characters in French Drama of the Eighteenth Century," Mr. Harry Kurz states that Arlequin appears

> as a savage Indian from America, as a Dutch bell-ringer, a clown in the Polish court, a messenger for Spanish royalty, and even as an enchanted king of Naples. He figures prominently in Oriental plays; now he is a black slave in Bagdad, now a Turkish Hula or substitute-husband, later a deaf-mute Moor who is prince of Guinea, and again a king of Serendib in Madagascar. He rises to the supernatural when he poses as Mohammed before Tartars, or when he figures as an ass in Greece, or when he discourses upon love with Venus. His adventures do not end here, for Piron uses him in his *Arlequin Deucalion* (1723) to outwit the jealous Comédie Française which had forbidden dialogue in the Italian Theatre. Since the play had to be a monologue, Piron has Arlequin figure as the only survivor of the Flood.

Not only was the Harlequinade parody amusing in itself, but by leaving what Harlequin equalled to be worked out by the performance, the parody could be on occasion a satire too daring to be stated in plain terms. That was the possibility seen by London wits.

These Harlequinades, which were not in dumb-show, were in every way distinct from pantomimes. The first examples were not intended for the stage. One, published in 1724, was "The British Stage; or, the Exploits of Harlequin: A Farce. As it was performed by a Company of Comedians at both theatres with Universal Applause."

It is declared to be " Designed as an entertainment for the audiences of Harlequin Dr. Faustus and the Necromancer." There is a dialogue between a dragon who boasts of his singing, and a windmill who admires Harlequin's exploit of jumping over the moon without breaking his shins, but Punch fears that if they " don't excel the immortal Fawkes " they are undone. There is an ass to represent the public. The next satire, published in 1727, purported to be a new work by Thomas D'Urfey, who died at a ripe old age a few years before. It was not directed against Rich and Cibber. Its political significance was apparent in its title :

> The English Stage Italianised in a New Dramatic Entertainment called Dido and Æneas or Harlequin, a Butler, a Pimp, a Minister of State, Generalissimo, and Lord High Admiral; dead and alive again, and at last crowned King of Carthage by Dido. A Tragi-Comedy after the Italian manner ; by way of Essay, or First Step towards the further Improvement of the English Stage.

Parody appealed strongly to Rich as a method of drawing the public to his own theatre and damaging his rivals at the same time. In 1719 he ridiculed Nicolini Grimaldi and the Italian opera in " Harlequin Hydaspes," and in 1728, when the coronation of George II. was celebrated in Drury Lane's performances of " Henry VIII.," Rich announced, " A new grotesque farce called Harlequin Anna Bullen, it being a burlesque upon the coronation of Anna Bullen, and the ceremony of the champion in Westminster Hall as performed in the theatre at Drury Lane."

Then Fielding pulled Harlequin's wires. His first attempt was in " The Author's Farce ; with a Puppet-Show, called The Pleasures of the Town," performed at the Haymarket in 1729. The puppet-show, as the Jack-Pudding in the farce announced beforehand, consisted of

> the whole court of nonsense, with abundance of singing, dancing, and several other entertainments : also the comical and diverting humours of Some-body and No-body : Punch and his wife Joan, to be performed by figures ; some of them six-foot high.

That it was not merely an attempt to ridicule the changing of playhouses into booths and puppet-shows, was proved by Punch's " I'll

A JUST VIEW OF THE BRITISH STAGE, OR THREE HEADS ARE BETTER THAN ONE, SCENE NEWGATE, BY SND &

This Print Represents the Rehearsing a new Farce that will Include ye three famous Entertainments Dr Faustus, Harlequin Shepherd &c which will be added Scaramouch Jack Hall the Chimney Sweepers Escape from Newgate through ye Privy with ye comical Humours of Ben Johnsons Ghost concluding with the Hay-Dance Perform'd in ye dir by ye Figures A B C quidqued by Ropes from ye Mules Neck there are no Conjurers concern'd in it as ye ignorant imagine — ye The Bricks Rubbish &c will be real but the Excrements upon Jack Hall will be made of Chewd Gingerbread to prevent Offence. Vivat Rex.

HOGARTH'S PANTOMIME SATIRE

From a print, ascribed to Hogarth, representing Booth, Wilks and Cibber, the patentees of Drury Lane, contriving a pantomime. "Scene Newgate by MD-V-to," refers to Devoto, the scene-painter

turn great man, that requires no qualification whatever," the " Great Man " being a title bestowed upon Walpole. Lun also appears as " Monsieur Pantomime," referred to as the only votary of nonsense " that sets people asleep without talking." The Haymarket soon provoked Walpole's anger. When he was present at a pantomime performance called " Love Runs All Dangers " in 1733, one of the comedians " presumed to hint " at his intended Excise Act. After the fall of the curtain, Sir Robert went behind the scenes and demanded of the prompter whether the offensive words were written down. Being assured they were not, he gave the comedian a severe beating. Worse was in store for the statesman. Fielding installed " The Great Mogul's Company of Comedians " at the Haymarket. In the April of 1736 they performed " Pasquin " which hit equally hard politics and pantomime. After watching " The Election," Sneerwell attends a rehearsal of " The Life and Death of Common Sense," which makes him ask why pantomimes are called entertainments. Fustian marvels how creatures of human understanding, having been diverted foɪ three hours with Shakespeare, Jonson or Vanbrugh, can

> sit for three more, and see a set of people running about the stage after one another, without speaking one syllable ; and playing several juggling tricks, which are done at Fawkes' after a much better manner ; and for this, Sir, the town does not only pay additional prices, but lose several fine parts of their best authors, which are cut out to make room for the said farces.

Keen as were the thrusts in " Pasquin," those in " Tumbledown Dick ; or, Phaeton in the Suds," were still more so. It was " A dramatic entertainment of walking in serious and foolish characters, interlarded with burlesque, grotesque comic interludes, called Harlequin a Pick-Pocket." Ostensibly it was directed against Lun, " Vulgarly called Esquire," who was lauded in an ironical preface. After a scene between Machine, Fustian (an author), Sneerwell (a critic), and the Prompter, the curtain rises to disclose Phaeton, who complains to Clymene that the parish boys gibe at his doubtful parentage. He asks his father to clear his name. The Sun responds by ordering his watchmen to dance. Phaeton comments :

> Father, the dance has been very well done.
> But yet that does not prove I am your son.

253

The scene changes. In the King's Coffee House a song is raised in praise of gin. Harlequin is caught picking pockets, and the watchmen bind him in chains. But the Genius of Gin, coming out of a tub, cries :

> Take, Harlequin, this magic wand,
> All things shall yield to thy command ;
> Whether you would appear incog.,
> In shape of monkey, cat or dog ;
> Or else to show your wit, transform
> Your mistress to a butter-churn ;
> Or else, what no magician can,
> Into a wheelbarrow turn a man.

In the next scene a justice is being taught to spell by an old school-mistress. Columbine coaxes him to let Harlequin escape. Here Machine explains that, " Aristotle in book concerning entertainments, has laid it down as a principal rule, that Harlequin is always to escape." Harlequin hits the Justice a great rap upon the back, and runs off, but when Columbine tries to follow, Pierrot holds her. Harlequin enters a jar which is presented to Columbine. He carries her off to a barber's shop, where he prepares to shave her, blinds Pierrot with the suds, and turns the justice into a periwig-block. Pierrot takes the wig off the block, puts it on, and admires himself. While pretending to show him how " to powder it better," Harlequin throws him into the trough and shuts him down. The plot is taken to the country. When a rustic remarks, " It begins to grow a little lighter," Aurora crosses the stage with two or three girls carrying farthing candles. This rouses Fustian, but Machine quiets him with :

> Why will you not allow me the same latitude that is allowed to all other composers of entertainments ? Does not a dragon descend from hell in Doctor Faustus ? And people go up to hell in Pluto and Proserpine ? Does not a squib represent a thunderbolt in the Rape of Proserpine ? And what are all the suns, sir, that have ever shone upon the stage, but candles ? And if they represent the sun, I think they may very well represent the stars.

Jupiter with a pair of bellows blows out the candle of the sun, and remarks " I would not have you think I want suns, for there were two very fine ones that shone together at Drury Lane play-house." Phœbus replies that " You had better send for the sun from Covent

254

Garden house, there's a sun that hatches an egg there, and produces a Harlequin." Says Jupiter, " That egg was laid by an ass."

When " The Historical Register " added to the affronts of " Pasquin," Walpole decided to take action against the Haymarket. But as Fielding's plays were in high favour, he obtained the help of Giffard of Goodman's Fields Theatre, Whitechapel. As this manager was addicted to pantomimes—such a title as " Harlequin in the City ; or, Columbine Turned Elephant" suggests they were even more preposterous than Lun's—he had no reason to feel kindly disposed towards the Grand Mogul. In addition, he was promised a thousand pounds. For this he supplied the manuscript of a play called " The Golden Rump," remarkable for its scurrility, blasphemy, immorality and sedition. By reading extracts, Walpole induced Parliament to pass the Licensing Bill. Had this measure not become law, pantomime would probably have died like many another frivolous theatrical fashion. If it had been rigidly enforced, pantomime would have been the staple of dramatic entertainment. Apart from actors at patent theatres, players were " rogues, vagabonds, sturdy beggars and vagrants." The royal companies might exercise their calling only in Westminster or wherever else the King might reside. All their entertainments were prohibited unless a true copy were sent to the Lord Chamberlain. The wording of the Act was formidable— but only for actors. Rope-dancers, tumblers, jugglers, scene-shifters and singers were practically unaffected. While the Chamberlain was constituted licenser of all new plays throughout Great Britain, his power to grant licences for theatrical entertainments was confined to Westminster. True, there was no law to license the music-houses, but, affecting to be open under a magistrate's licence for " music, dancing and entertainments," they carried on. Even the Haymarket and Goodman's Fields which were shut immediately, did not remain long closed. Sadler's Wells seems to have ignored the Act altogether. At the time it became law, the performance there was " Harlequin in China ; or the Death of Columbine," and they staged new pantomimes, such as " Harlequin Proteus " in 1739, " The Birth of Venus ; or Harlequin Paris, concluding with the loves of

255

Zephyrus and Flora " in 1740, and " Harlequin a Captive in Spain ; or the Privateer Bit " in 1741. But at Islington admittance was free —to those who bought a pint of wine or punch.

Meanwhile Rich had opened his new theatre at Covent Garden. Hogarth's view of the removal from Lincoln's Inn Fields shows a barouche driven by Harlequin and drawn by seven devils ; Polly Peachum sits inside with one of the performing dogs which were reputed to have made the success of Lun's first pantomimes ; at the end of the procession is a cart bearing a box of thunder and lightning. Not long afterwards he engaged a young Harlequin to be " Lun junior." This title was borne by Henry Woodward, a Southwark tallow-chandler's son. His stage career began when Rich presented the public with a " Lilliputian " version of " The Beggar's Opera " in 1729, with little Peg Woffington as Polly and Woodward as the beggar. The boy went to Goodman's Fields where he became Harlequin in " Harlequin Contrivance ; or, the Jealous Yeoman Defeated " at a dancing master's benefit. After spells at May Fair and Tottenham Court Fair, he was engaged at Covent Garden. When Kitty Clive and Mrs. Cibber fell out over who should play Polly and who Lucy in " The Beggar's Opera," he wrote " The Beggar's Pantomime ; or, the Contending Columbines," himself playing Harlequin MacHeath.

Drury Lane passed into the hands of Fleetwood who, according to a pamphleteer, "brought all the inhabitants of Sadler's Wells upon his stage, and entertained the public with sights of tall monsters and contemptible rope-dancers," yet blundered in every expedition he attempted " in the service of dullness." He had the good fortune, however, to be the victim of a profitable riot during a pantomime in 1734. The public demanded to see a dancer who was at the Prince's ball. When Macklin, who was playing the clown, apologised on his behalf, the audience in a rage pulled up the benches, bridged the orchestra and stormed the stage. Macklin went up to the thunder-loft, and through a stenterphon ordered the servants of the theatre " to make the stage dark, to open the traps, to let loose hell, to roll the thunder, and to flash the lightning." At first the rioters were

256

WOODWARD THE HARLEQUIN

From an engraving in the Author's Collection

frightened, but they again advanced and hacked the scenery. Macklin was hiding under a property world. A noted duellist, seized by mistake, cooled the ringleaders with a challenge apiece. Also they had exposed themselves to a charge of treason by destroying the arms over the royal box. For these reasons they were in so repentant a mood the next morning that they submitted to humiliation and the theatre's demand for £2,000. With restored fortunes, Fleetwood came to an agreement with Rich in 1735 for the purpose of uniting against the claims of the actors. The terms though simple—they agreed to divide all moneys at both playhouses " Above fifty pounds share and share like for the remainder part of this season, and to pay each other so much money as shall be wanting to make up fifty pounds " —were looked upon by the members of their companies as an understanding between the managers to keep down salaries. If an actor should prove obstinate, then he would be left to join the rogues and vagabonds who acted at their peril in other places than the theatres royal. If the actors should unite, then Rich and Fleetwood would show them that the play could be dispensed with by the masters of pantomime. The scheme, in spite of a storm of protest, had every prospect of success. Both managers astonished playgoers out of their indignation with new pantomimes of particular ingenuity. Drury Lane staged Theobald's " Merlin ; or the Devil of Stone-Henge." At the rise of the curtain, Harlequin was dancing with other revellers on a desert heath. Amid thunder and lightning the ghost of Faustus appeared and warned them of the approach of Merlin. Harlequin flew but was followed by the enchanter, who changed his apartment to " A pleasant prospect of the infernal regions " and made him his. After Time had appeared and Harlequin been carried off by spirits, Merlin exclaimed, " The great Enchanter Faustulus is mine." It provided an apt occasion for satire. In *Weekly Essays* of February 1735, *Arlequin Chef D'Oeuvre* composes an entertainment called " The History of the Fall of the Tower of Babel," remarking " I have a fine scene of the Tower of Babel : which, if not like the said Tower, hath, at least with the prospect of Stonehenge at Drury Lane,

257

this to recommend itself that it is like nothing else." He
adds :

> I shall throw down the Tower of Babel on the stage, turn the stones
> whereof it was composed into sugar loaves which shall be eaten up by Har-
> lequin and Scaramouche : then I shall turn the whole stage successively into
> an orange-grove, a dog-kennel, a ship, a palace, a mountain, a windmill, a
> wheelbarrow, and conclude the whole with a pleasant prospect of Hell,
> according to the conclusion of almost all the modern entertainments.

Fleetwood's next piece was " Harlequin Orpheus ; or, the Magic
Pipe," which set a fashion in Orpheus pantomimes. Dr. John Hill,
the notorious Mayfair actor and apothecary, who had made numerous
" uncredited discoveries in moss, mites, cabbage-leaves, cherry-stones,
stinking oysters and cockle shells "—in the words of Woodward—
had submitted an opera of Orpheus to Rich shortly before he staged
" Orpheus and Eurydice "—three operatic interludes alternated with
three scenes of Harlequinade—at Covent Garden in 1739. Hill's
accusation of theft led to a series of pamphlets which helped to acclaim
the new show. It drew the whole town, partly because of a regular
growth of trees, " represented more like nature than what has yet been
seen upon the stage," and partly because of the mechanical serpent
which frightened the ladies.

But the managers' plan to overthrow the drama was thwarted by
the sudden success of Garrick. His arrival at Goodman's Fields was
heralded by the pantomime, to celebrate the monument lately erected
to Shakespeare in Westminster Abbey, of " Harlequin Student ; or,
the Fall of Pantomime with the Restoration of the Drama." Though
mainly a conventional Harlequinade—remarkable for the introduction
of the Beau and the change of a water plug into " a Hot Codlin
Woman's Stall "—it did usher in the restoration of the drama. Playgoers,
surfeited with the sweets of Rich and Fleetwood, were carried away by
the news that Shakespeare was being magnificently acted at Whitechapel. Notwithstanding the theatre's distance from the polite ends
of Westminster, the way between Temple Bar and Goodman's Fields
was covered with a string of coaches. The patentees threatened
Giffard with Walpole's Act. In the end they brought him to ruin.

But they could not destroy the town's enthusiasm for the new actor. Fleetwood, abandoning Rich's projects, offered him an unprecedented salary. But in the autumn of 1746 Rich drew him to Covent Garden. This was the time of the rebellion of '45, which inspired Drury Lane with " Harlequin Incendiary ; or, Columbine Cameron " (music by Dr. Arne). It showed the Pope and the Devil plotting the downfall of England and the entrance of the Pretender into a palace that changed into a prison.

Meanwhile Fleetwood had died, and Garrick, with Lacy as his partner, became proprietor of Drury Lane. The opening of his management was celebrated in a prologue by Dr. Johnson which, after showing how " Great Faustus " had laid the ghost of wit and confirmed folly in her sway with pantomime, exhorted the drama's patrons to let " truth diffuse her radiance from the stage." Prophetically, however, it suggested :

> Perhaps, if skill could distant times explore,
> New Behns, new Durfeys, yet remain in store ;
> Perhaps, where Lear has raved, and Hamlet died,
> On flying cars new sorcerers may ride ;
> Perhaps, for who can tell th' effects of chance ?
> Here Hunt may box, or Mahomet may dance.

That season proved the truth of the forecast. The public, having exhausted the wonder of the day, were easily drawn to Covent Garden by Rich. During a performance of " Perseus and Andromeda," the machinery failed, and the hero, instead of being whirled through the clouds by means of a large wheel, fell on the stuffed dragon. More than this, however, was required to ridicule the taste for pantomime. Even the most elegant playgoers were drawn by raree-shows, including the performing monkeys and other " animal comedians " at Mrs. Midnight's Oratory. In response to an announcement that a conjurer would disappear into a pint bottle, the Haymarket was crowded to the doors, only to find the conjurer " rendering himself invisible " for the entire performance. The hoax led to a riot, and was the talk of the town. Rich exploited it by advertising a Don Jumpedo, who would not only enter a bottle but jump down his own throat. By

259

such means he more than held his own against Garrick.   The audience at Covent Garden, says Doran,

> assembled at mid-day, and sometimes broke the doors open, unless they were opened to them, by three o'clock, and so took the house by storm.   Those who could not gain admittance, went over to Drury Lane, but Garrick found them without a heart for tragedy ; the grown-up masters and misses had been deprived of their puppet-show and rattle, and were sulky accordingly ; he had to exclaim :—" If you won't come to Lear and Hamlet, I must give you Harlequin " ; and he gave them the best the stage had ever had, save Rich, in Woodward.

Both houses at Christmas, 1748, revived " The Emperor of the Moon." Rich, now too old for motley, employed so poor a Harlequin that Covent Garden failed.   At Drury Lane, Woodward amazed playgoers by the way he was tossed, a seemingly perilous exploit made possible by invisible bands that held him to the blanket.   Pantomime came back to favour so rapidly *The World* suggested that managers should have done with tragedy and comedy, advising Garrick that he would have " fewer enemies by being the finest Harlequin of the age, than he has at present, by being the greatest actor of any age or country." Though not moved to accept the satirist's advice, he made ardent efforts to satisfy the desire to gape.   His season of 1750 opened with a prologue that informed the public :

> Sacred to Shakespeare was this plot designed,
> To pierce the heart, and humanize the mind,
> But if an empty house, the actor's curse,
> Shews us our Lears and Hamlets lose their force,
> Unwilling we must change the nobler scene,
> And, in our turn, present you Harlequin ;
> Quit poets, and set carpenters to work,
> Shew gawdy scenes, or mount the vaulting Turk.
> For though we actors one and all agree
> Boldly to struggle for our vanity,
> If want comes on, importance must retreat ;
> Our first great ruling passion—is to eat.

Woodward was particularly admired in a scene which recalls Riccoboni's illustration of what was meant by *lazzi*—Arlequin, with a hat full of imaginary cherries, would pretend to eat them and throw the stones into the face of Scapin.   Similarly Woodward,

Mr LEE LEWIS speaking a PROLOGUE
in the CHARACTER of HARLEQUIN.

WOODWARD'S SUCCESSOR

A COMPANION to the BOTTLE; or,
DON JUMPEDO in the Character of HARLEQUIN
Jumping down his own THROAT.

RICH'S HARLEQUIN FOAX

From the engravings in the Burney Collection of Theatrical Portraits

sitting by a bare table, would pick up a bunch of imaginary currants by the stalk :

> Then, holding high his hand, with the points of finger and thumb compressed, he seemed to shake the stalk, and to strip off the currants with his mouth.   In like manner he would appear to hold up a cherry by the stalk, and after eating it, to spurt the stone from his lips.   Eating a gooseberry, paring an apple, sucking an orange or peach—all were simulated in the same marvellous fashion.   In short, the audience perfectly knew what fruit he seemed to be eating by the highly ingenious deception of his acting.

This habit strayed into his acting of Mercutio, Bobadil or Ranger.   If he mentioned an undertaker, he flapped his hat, pursed up his brows, clasped his hands, and with a burlesque solemnity strode across the stage before resuming.   At the word waiter, he would mimic the wiping of a glass or the drawing of a cork, and would not say mercer until he had measured off several yards of cloth on the flap of his coat.   In " The Rosciad," Churchill described him as a " great master of grimace," who played to the eye with a mere monkey's art, twisting and turning and torturing every limb.   He had a shrug, a wink, a stare and a croaking voice ; in short, he " threw too much Harlequinade " (to quote another critic) into his work.   Yet that, it seems, was somewhat characteristic of the acting of the time.   The tragedians of the last age, stated *The Connoisseur* in 1754, studied fine speaking and neglected action.   The players of the new generation had run into a contrary extreme :

> Their gestures sometimes resemble those afflicted with St. Vitus's Dance ; their whole frame appears to be convulsed ; and I have seen a player in the last act so miserably distressed, that a deaf spectator would be apt to imagine he was complaining of the colic or the toothache.   This has also given rise to that unnatural custom of throwing the body into various strange ATTITUDES.   There is not a passion necessary to be expressed, but has produced dispositions of the limbs not to be found in any of the paintings and sculptures of the best masters.   A graceful and easy deportment is, indeed, worthy the care of every performer ; but when I observe him writhing his body into more unnatural contortions than a tumbler at Sadler's Wells, I cannot help being disgusted to see him " imitate humanity so abominably."   Our pantomime authors have already begun to reduce our comedies into grotesque scenes ; and if this taste for Attitude should continue to be popular, I would recommend it to those ingenious gentlemen, to adapt our best tragedies to the same use, and entertain us with the jealousy of *Othello* in dumb shew, or the tricks of *Harlequin Hamlet.*

"Attitudes" was a word borrowed from pantomime terminology. There is a curious volume of about this date in the King's Library called "A Chacoon for a Harlequin, With all the Postures, Attitudes, Motions of the Head and Arms and other Gestures proper to this character." F. Le Roussau, who dedicates this work to Louis Dupré because of the neatness of his attitudes, endeavours to express movements by means of a notation, various marks being used to show when the face should be straight forwards, turned to the left or to the right, and so forth. A curl directs that to stretch the arm forwards, draw it back, then stretch it forward again, is "the salutation of a Harlequin."

Woodward was known as the "attitude Harlequin." To the rhythm of the music he would perform a series of postures "according to the vicissitudes demanded by the various passions represented." To carry out the conventional routine of jumping through walls and windows a substitute was engaged. One night, by some blunder, the two Harlequins met in the centre of the stage which set the audience into a clamour of laughter. In addition to playing Harlequin, Woodward supplied Garrick with a new pantomime each year. "Queen Mab" was the most popular. He also wrote "The Genii," "Harlequin Fortunatus," "Proteus; or, Harlequin in China" and "Mercury Harlequin." Out of Ranger, the part in Wycherley's "Love in a Wood" which Garrick played, he made a Harlequinade with a scene that burlesqued Rich's pantomime of "The Fair," especially the performance of the Famous Turk who had caused Quin and Peg Woffington, conceiving it a degradation to perform on the same stage as wire-dancers, to refuse to act. But Rich won the day with a revival of "Harlequin Sorcerer" of so much added lustre that the cynical Foote was moved to admire a fountain, and other actors to admit they remembered nothing like the rage for this show. After Harlequin's interview with the witches, the scene showed bricklayers going to work in the early morning. From a balcony Columbine called to Harlequin, but Pantaloon and his servant espied them and gave chase. Coming to "a house half-built with real scaffolding before it," Harlequin, hiding Columbine behind a pile of bricks,

MUNDUS · TOTUS · AGIT · HISTRIONEM

RICH   WOODWARD   GARRICK

THE THEATRICAL STEEL-YARDS OF 1750

From an engraving in the Burney Collection in the British Museum

lured Pantaloon up a ladder, then descended and removed it.   The
scaffolding fell with all the men upon it.   Harlequin, dressed as an
old ballad singer, made mock of the song,[1] " I love Sue, and Sue loves
me," in " Harlequin Ranger."   Then there was " a most delightful
perspective of a farmhouse."   Columbine, caught dancing before a
barley-mow, was carried off by a constable to Pantaloon.   At his
house, the servant, with many dumb gestures, ushered in a large
ostrich.   When left alone with Columbine it changed into Harlequin.
Again they eloped to the farmhouse.   When Pantaloon and the
servant arrived, he changed into an old washer-woman, soused them
with soap-suds and drove them away.   The next scene showed an
equestrian statue about to be unveiled.   The horseman sneezed.
The servant, recognising him as Harlequin, climbed the pedestal,
only to be bitten, kicked and beaten to pieces by the horse.   Harlequin
was last seen disconsolately resting on a couch before being carried off
by devils.   Pluto and Proserpine descended.   When brought the
news that " Harly is trapped at last," the black-bearded monarch said
" everything shall be jolly."   The final scene was a fine garden where
Carmargo showed her historical desire to cast off the thraldom of
clothes and give her limbs free motion.   Ballet was becoming more
important in pantomime.   " A Parallel between an Evening spent at
the Playhouse, and the several Stages of Life " in *The Adventurer*
suggests that it was perhaps the chief attraction.   The account of the
pantomime runs :

> I gazed at the prodigies which were every moment produced before me
> with astonishment ; I was bewildered in the intricacies of enchantment ; I
> saw woods, rivers, and mountains, alternately appear and vanish ; but I knew
> not to what cause or to what end.   The entertainment was not adapted to
> my understanding, but to my senses ; and my senses were indeed captivated
> with every object of delight ; in particular, the dress of the women discovered
> beauties which I could not behold without confusion ; the wanton caresses
> which they received and returned, the desire that languished in their eyes,
> the kiss snatched with eagerness, and the embrace prolonged with reciprocal
> delight, filled my breast with tumultuous wishes, which, though I feared to
> gratify, I did not wish to suppress.   Besides all these incentives to dissolute

---

[1] Song-writers' fascination with the phrase " I love Sue," from that day to
this, is a sign of the theatre's abiding reverence for tradition.

pleasure, there was the dance, which indulged the spectators with a view of almost every charm that apparel was intended to conceal.

Garrick judged that " monstrous pantomimes " could be superseded by ballet unadulterated. Accordingly he engaged the Swiss ballet master Noverre in 1755 to enlist the best performers he could find for an exhibition called " The Chinese Festival." At this time feeling against France ran high, and the ballet—on the mere suspicion that the performers were French—was not allowed to be danced. Gentlemen of rank leaped out of the boxes to support the manager with their swords, but the rioters tore up the benches, broke the lustres, threw down the partitions of the boxes, and, mounting the stage, demolished the Chinese scenery. Garrick gave up the attempt and returned to pantomime. In 1758, however, Woodward, tempted by the managerial purple, left Drury Lane for Dublin. He arrived there safely. Another ship taking Maddox, the wire dancer, and Theophilus Cibber to perform in Dublin, foundered off the coast of Scotland. Benjamin Victor, who awaited their arrival, throws a light on the passion for pantomime in his lament :

> Poor Cibber ! he had long felt the blasts of adversity ; his life was tempestuous, and his fate ended it in a storm ! Our loss of Maddox was almost irretrievable ; because, with our Harlequin, went the music, and the business and plot of the pantomime ; as also among the geniuses, the man who played on the twelve bells, fastened to his head, hands and feet, etc., etc., etc.

Woodward's place was filled by Grimaldi and Delpini, but the first Harlequinade after his departure was written by Garrick, who also invented the machinery. While Rich was providing a double bill of pantomime consisting of " The Fair " and " Harlequin Statue," Drury Lane set out to show Shakespeare's victory over " the Smithfield group "—the arts of the fair. Garrick called his work " Harlequin's Invasion." It was originally written to serve the interest of a favourite performer of Bartholomew Fair, where it passed under a title designedly long and ostentatious, concluding " The Taylor Without a Head ; or, the Battle of the Golden Bridge." For the stage, it was labelled a Christmas gambol after the manner of the Italian comedy—not a pantomime because the personages had the

264

Fidele aux loix de la Cadence   *Originale dans ma danse*

MLLE. CAMARGO

From an engraving after Lancret in the British Museum

use of their tongues.   The piece was a success and was revived several times.   It was Lamb's first pantomime :

> The transformation of the magistrates into reverend beldams seemed to me a piece of grave historic justice, and the tailor carrying his own head to be as sober a verity as the legend of St. Denys.

Under the new title of " Shakespeare versus Harlequin " the piece was drastically reviewed by Hazlitt, who declared its essence to be " prosing stupidity remaining like a mawkish fixture on the stage." The heels, and wand, and motley coat of Harlequin were sacred to nonsense.   The words, the cap and wings of Mercury (the representative of Shakespeare) were worthy of a better use :

> The bringing Harlequin to the test of reason resembles the old story of hedging in the cuckoo, and surpasses the united genius of the late Mr. Garrick (to whom this dull farce is ascribed), and of the professional gentleman who has fitted the above productions of " the olden times " (viz., those of the late Mr. Garrick) to modern taste !   After all, though Harlequin is tried by three grave judges, who are very unnecessarily metamorphosed into three old women, no competition, no collision takes place between him and the genius of Shakespeare, unless Mr. T. Cooke's playing very cleverly on a variety of musical instruments, so as to ravish the heart of Miss Dolly Snip (Madame Vestris), can be construed into so many proofs of the superiority of Shakespeare's muse.   Again, Mr. Harley, as Harlequin, and Mr. Oxberry (as a country clown) get up into a tree to see the sport, from which it is as difficult to dislodge them as owls from an ivy bush ; and the sport is to see Joey Snip, the tailor, have his head cut off, and walk with it about the stage, and, unlike the sign of the good woman, talk without his tongue.   The slicing off a blackamoor's head or two with the stroke of a scymitar, provided the thing is done quickly, and instantly got out of sight, we do not much object to ; but we do not like to have a ghastly spectre of this sort placed before us for a whole evening, as the heads of the rebel Scotch lords were stuck on Temple bar for half a century.

Notwithstanding these defects, its first season in 1759 left Garrick over confident.   Two years later the coronation of George II. called for revivals of " Henry VIII." as an excuse for pageants.   The preparations caused a wit in the *British Chronicle* to report the imaginary " Proceedings of the Court of Claims held in the Green Rooms of both Theatres."   Some of the decisions were :

> The Harlequins at each House, claimed to open their mouths in any part of the Procession, in which they might speak without meaning.   Allowed —the Herald's Part that proclaims the King's titles.

The Horse in Perseus and Andromeda claimed to represent the Champion Horse. Not allowed, as a flying one.

The Horse in Harlequin Sorcerer claimed the same. Not allowed—as a standstill one.

The Trap door Engineers claimed to see the Procession, in their respective Offices under ground, especially as the Peeresses passed over their heads—with other liberties. Allowed the sight only.

For once Garrick was thrifty. He revived Cibber's pageant which Davies, his biographer, termed " the meanest and most unworthy of the theatre I ever saw." Too much reliance had been placed on the scheme of opening the back of the stage to show a real bonfire in Drury Lane itself, with a crowd stimulated to cheer for Queen Anne Bullen by means of free draughts of porter. But the smoke covered the stage. Dukes, duchesses, archbishops, peeresses, heralds and so forth were seized with colds, rheumatism and swelled faces, and driven from the stage with hooting and hissing. Covent Garden, on the contrary, exhibited a profusion of " velvet, silk, satin, lace, feathers, jewels, pearls and a variety of ornaments, as had not been seen on any stage," and the performance was repeated for " near two months together." Before the end of the run, Rich died. He deserved the epitaph he gave to his father. In the sense that his death took away the reproach from pantomime, he died " a martyr to this good old cause." Though the object of satire and contempt during his lifetime, pantomime immediately afterwards was spoken of in the tone of sentimental regret that has persisted ever since. When Horace Walpole found Sheridan's " Robinson Crusoe " incoherent, he added, " How unlike the pantomimes of Rich, which are full of wit, and carried on a story." In the prologue to the revival of " Harlequin's Invasion," Garrick likewise referred to Lun's " matchless art and whim " that gave " the power of speech to every limb." In Churchill's satires, the change is still more evident. " The Rosciad," published in 1761, sneers at pantomime :

Harlequin comes their chief !—see from afar,
The hero seated in fantastic car !
Wedded to novelty, his only arms
Are wooden swords, wands, talismans, and charms ;

> On one side folly sits, by some called fun,
> And on the other, his arch patron Lun.
> Behind, for liberty athirst in vain,
> Sense, helpless captive, drags the galling chain.
> Six rude mis-shapen beasts the chariot draw,
> Whom reason loaths, and nature never saw,
> Monsters with tails of ice, and heads of fire ;
> Gorgons, and Hydras, and Chimaeras dire,
> Each was bestrode by full as monstrous wight,
> Giant, dwarf, genius, elf, hermaphrodite.
> The Town, as usual, met him in full cry ;
> The Town, as usual, knew no reason why.
> But fashion so directs, and moderns raise
> On Fashion's mouldering base their transient praise.

Yet " The Ghost," published a year or so after Rich's death, sneers at the critics of pantomime :

> Coxcombs, who vainly make pretence
> To something of exalted sense
> 'Bove other men, and *gravely wise*,
> Affect those pleasures to despise,
> Which, merely to the eye confin'd,
> Bring no improvement to the mind,
> Rail at all pomp ; they would not go,
> For millions to a *Puppet-Show*,
> Nor can forgive the mighty crime
> Of countenancing Pantomime.

Of Rich himself, few kind things were said in his lifetime. Afterwards, financial strategies forgot, he was mentioned with affection. Tate Wilkinson gives a sketch of the old man in the last year of his life which shows the attractive side of his personality. Wilkinson had undertaken to mimic Foote who, hearing of the scheme, called to say, " If you want to engage that pug, black his face and let him hand the tea kettle in a pantomime." Otherwise, Foote would " instantly produce your old stupid ridiculous self, with your three cats, and your hound of a mime all together next week at Drury Lane." Rich was perturbed at " Master Futseye's " animosity towards his cats. Yet he went forward with his scheme, which had no evil results. He left Covent Garden to his son-in-law, the singer Beard, stipulating he should sell out when offered sixty thousand pounds (which occurred in 1767).

While continuing to revive " Harlequin's Invasion," Garrick would not dispense with pantomime. He also revived Woodward's " Queen Mab," and staged three new pieces—" The Witches ; or, Harlequin Cherokee," " The Magician of the Mountain " and " The Rites of Hecate ; or, Harlequin from the Moon "—between 1762-4. He declined a farce called " The Wishes ; or, Harlequin's Mouth Opened," which ridiculed pantomimes. Foote and Murphy showed their faith in the idea by taking a lease of Drury Lane in the summer of 1761 to stage it. For the greater part of the performance, the audience approved the story which consisted of the realisation of a series of wishes. In the last scene Harlequin, toying with his mistress on a couch, said " I'll be hanged." Immediately, a gibbet rose and drew him up by the neck in its halter. This was not to the audience's taste, and the piece failed miserably.

On the first day of 1763, Woodward returned from Dublin and was engaged at Covent Garden. Knowing the town's displeasure at his fickleness, he spoke a prologue that began, " Behold ! The Prodigal—returned—quite tame," and offered the excuse :

> Faith ! they put powder in my drink, d'ye see ?
> Or else, by Pharaoh's foot, it could not be !
> Belike Queen Mab touched me (at full o' th' moon)
> With a Field-Marshall-Manager's battoon.

His new pantomime on the subject of Faustus, and Beard's revival of the coronation spectacle, were not the only blows suffered by the drama. At Drury Lane, Garrick was browbeaten by a notorious personage named Fitzpatrick who from a box asked, " Will you, or will you not, allow admittance at half-price after the third act of every piece, except a new pantomime, during its run in the first winter ? " Garrick's agreement meant that " Harlequin was to frisk, frolic, and leap over the heads of the best writers of the age." At Covent Garden, however, Beard resisted successfully. He sued Fitzpatrick, who was warned that if a life were lost in a riot he would be held responsible. But Garrick had not surrendered his hopes of supremacy in scenery and costume. Emulating Sadler's Wells, whose Harlequinade in the summer of 1769 was " Shakespeare's Choice Spirits ; or, Falstaff in

268

Pantomime," he brought the jubilee pageant he had arranged at Stratford-on-Avon to Drury Lane.   Covent Garden had a rival procession which failed because, through lack of streamers with titles, half the spectators were ignorant what the tableaux referred to.   Foote opened the Haymarket for the summer with a " burlesque parody " of both pageants called " Drugger's Jubilee," and spoke a prologue satirising the managers' taste :

> Blasted the bay on every classic brow,
> Taylors are deemed the only poets now ;
> Hark ! what a roar at Lear's old surtout,
> Falstaff's stuff vest, and Pistol's hat and boot !
> To solemn sounds see sordid scene-men stalk,
> And the great Shakespeare's vast creation—walk.
> Can a lean wardrobe all his powers express ?
> Can his fine phrenzy creep into a dress ?
> E'en Roscius blushes at his own success,
> And feels some transient touches for his crime,
> To have sunk those scenes below a pantomime.

Then Woodward ridiculed Garrick's masterpiece in " Harlequin's Jubilee."   Antony and Cleopatra danced on and off, and a procession of pantomime properties, such as a walking windmill, a sack of flour, the sun and the egg from " The Rape of Proserpine," a skeleton and a magic box, paid all the adulation of Garrick's scene-men for Shakespeare, to a statue of Rich.   In response to their homage and chorus in honour of his memory, Lun descended from his statue.   Lamb, as a child, saw a revival of the piece :

> To my apprehension (too sincere for satire), Lun was as remote a piece of antiquity as Lud—the father of a line of Harlequins—transmitting his dagger of lath (the wooden sceptre) through countless ages.   I saw the primeval Motley come from his silent tomb in a ghastly vest of white patchwork, like the apparition of a dead rainbow.   So Harlequins (thought I) look when they are dead.

Rich's ghost was never laid.   In 1778 a mixture of his pantomimes (such as that given at the Prince of Wales's house in 1740) was presented at Covent Garden with the title of " The Medley."   In 1790 " Harlequin's Chaplet " repeated at that house scenes " selected from at least twelve of fourteen different pantomimes."   The tricks, recognisable as having descended without any alteration from " Harlequin Sorcerer," continue in use down to this day.

269

There can be no question that Garrick had become another of Davenant's heirs. Besides instituting the emblematical pageant which has remained in pantomime ever since, he revolutionised staging. De Loutherbourg, who came to England in 1770, found full employment for his ingenuity in scenery and " the picturesque of sound " at Drury Lane. He introduced the new method of making thunder by shaking a suspended sheet of copper ; the octagonal box full of shells, peas and shot to imitate the rush and wash of waves ; the cylinders of seed and shot to imitate rain ; the lamp behind the scenes to form a luminous moon ; the windlass to regulate the movements of clouds. Above all, he invented the " transparency." While Woodward had no employ, Garrick tried to substitute for pantomime a " masque " with a transparency of " the late naval review at Portsmouth." But the public were growing restive. Several riots broke out because entertainments were too light-headed. The comedies of Goldsmith and Sheridan were staged at Covent Garden during a spell of reaction against the scene-shifter's tricks. At the same time, pantomime returned in a new form with a strong moral flavour. Woodward's occupation was gone. When he reappeared as Harlequin at Covent Garden in 1776, he was told

> As he is not so young and active as he was formerly he would do well to heed his rank among the regulars, and not be scaling walls, leaping over hedge and ditch, and risking his neck among the hussars and pandours of the army.

The piece was not a pantomime but one of the topical skits called " occasional prologues," a fashion (set by Foote) that dramatised greenroom gossip. " News from Parnassus," as Woodward called his piece, contained references to the newspapers, the passion for real water at Sadler's Wells and the retirement of Garrick. He was brought on in a sedan chair, revealed his lozenges under his cape, was assailed by the rest of the company, jumped out of the window, and reappeared in the sedan chair which was transformed into an apothecary's shop. The next year he wrote a prologue during an illness :

> Let me not bear too grave a mien ;
> But if (a common case) I quit the scene,
> This parting is well made, the farce is o'er
> And Woodward's voice awakes your mirth no more.

DE LOUTHERBERG'S DESIGN FOR "A CHRISTMAS TALE"

From a mezzotint in the Burney Collection in the British Museum

In the April of 1777 he died, leaving it unspoken. Sheridan, who took his place as pantomime author for a space, followed his lead in breaking away from ancient mythology. He had contributed patriotic songs to Woodward's " Harlequin Fortunatus." One was about the sailor who

> when the fight's begun,
> Each serving at his gun

thinks only that should the day be won how 'twill cheer the hearts of distant friends to hear

> That their old companion he was one.

Another was about " Britons bold and free " whose watchword should be " Strike home ! revenge your country's wrong." The pattern has never altered.

Meantime, though the fever had shown some abatement at the theatres royal, pantomimes were the staple summer amusement throughout the land. Strolling players had a stock piece which appeared under such names as " Cupid's Holiday ; or, Harlequin at Richmond " or " Harlequin at Hounslow " according to what theatre or town-hall they hired. Every travelling show had its pantomime, forerunners of Richardson's immense booth where, at Greenwich or Smithfield, a melodrama (with three murders and a ghost), a pantomime, a comic song, an overture and some incidental music were, says Boz, " all done in twenty-five minutes." For fifteen minutes the principal tragedian would gaze on the crowd outside or converse confidentially with the Harlequin while four clowns engaged in a mock broadsword combat. Then the performance began again. Richardson's waggons took pantomime to all parts of the country. They came lumbering down at fair time to the dull little town in which Dickens " had the honour to be brought up."

> Our eyes open wide with wonder, and our hearts throb with emotion, as we deliver our cardboard check into the very hands of Harlequin himself who, all glittering with spangles, and dazzling with many colours, deigns to give us a word of encouragement and commendation as we pass into the booth ! But what was this—even this—to the glories of the inside, where amid the smell of saw-dust, and orange-peel, sweeter far than violets to youthful noses, the first play being over, the lovers united, the ghost appeased,

271

the baron killed, and everything made comfortable and pleasant—the pantomime itself began ! What words can describe the deep gloom of the opening scene, where a crafty magician holding a young lady in bondage was discovered, studying an enchanted book to the soft music of a gong !—or in what terms can we express the thrill of ecstasy with which, his magic power opposed by superior art, we beheld the monster himself converted into Clown. What mattered it that the stage was three yards wide, and four deep ? *we* never saw it. We had no eyes, ears, or corporeal senses, but for the pantomime. And when its short career was run, and the baron previously slaughtered, coming forward with his hand on his heart, announced that for that favour Mr. Richardson returned his most sincere thanks, and the performance would commence again in a quarter of an hour, what jest could equal the effects of the Baron's indignation and surprise, when the Clown, unexpectedly peeping from behind the curtain, requested the audience "not to believe it, for it was all gammon ! "

Summer pantomimes were given in London at the Haymarket, whose licence from the Lord Chamberlain did not extend to the winter months. Its most serious rival was Sadler's Wells, now engaging the best performers and engineers. Previously the standard of spectacle at Islington was " splendid peacocks strutting with the red-hosed legs of charity boys " and clumsy hobby-horses for steeds. " They must be easily pleased who go to Sadler's Wells for entertainment," was a newspaper comment in 1771. Two years later "The Whim Wham" reversed the opinion. It opened with a scene of a Barbary harbour. Harlequin and Columbine entered in a galley as Christian slaves, and were bought by " a Turk of eminence." Harlequin was set to work in the garden, but being detected in familiarities with Columbine was confined in a dungeon decorated with scenes of executions. A magician appeared. The cell was changed to a garden where Columbine stood on a pedestal. They were transported to a carpet warehouse in England, a tallow chandler's, a Holborn bird-shop, the rock in Marylebone Gardens, Vulcan's Forge " as exhibited by Signor Torre " and a temple of dance and song. " Harlequin Restored ; or, the Country Revels " in 1774 opened with a view of the tomb of Harlequin with his figure in sculpture. When brought to life by the magician, he was welcomed by Pantaloon, Pierrot and Punch, met Columbine and was pursued by enemies. A cottage changed into an elephant and castle, a country ale-house into a Chinese compartment,

272

"HARLEQUIN NEPTUNE" AT SADLER'S WELLS

From Pyne's "Microcosm of London"

the entrance of a castle into a representation of Turn-stile, Holborn, a dairy farm into a country market-place and a cavern into the Temple of Hymen. The next year " Harlequin Neptune " made use of the New River. After a storm, Tritons and Sea Nymphs heralded the approach of Neptune (in a naval car drawn by two white horses) who threw off his cloak and was revealed as Harlequin. The scene changed to the street where Pantaloon lived, the usual pursuit introduced the usual changes of shops until they all came to a dreary shore, a Triton put an end to the persecution of Harlequin, they passed through the Cave of the Winds, and in Neptune's Palace a " compromise was made." Besides these pantomimes the programme at Sadler's Wells included spectacles of topical events such as the encampment in Hyde Park or the latest war news. The glorious First of June was celebrated in " Huzza for Old England," which reproduced the engagements of the Fleets in the West Indies, showed a transparency of De Grasse delivering his sword to Rodney, and ended with " striking figures representing the Cardinal Virtues, and at the bottom France and Spain suing for peace." Having caught the fancy of the town as well as of Islington, Sadler's Wells offered a fresh programme every Easter and Whitsun. Astley's presented similar spectacles. Then the Royal Circus was opened in 1782 with equally dazzling fare. Four years later John Palmer built the Royalty at Whitechapel to replace Giffard's old theatre, with Delpini to stage ambitious pantomimes such as " The Four Quarters of the World," containing a procession of Europe, Asia, Africa and America, drawn by horses, leopards and tigers across the orchestra, round the circle and back to the stage. Covent Garden took alarm. Sheridan, Colman, and Harris, the proprietors, turned common informers. Because Palmer's performance was not in accordance with the terms of the Act of 1752 (for the proper regulation of pickpockets and music-houses), he had to close the second night. The theatre was reopened with pantomime. Delpini was the clown. He uttered the words " Roast Beef ! " without a musical accompaniment. In consequence, Palmer had to appear before the magistrates. They discharged him. The patentees caused them to be dismissed from office and fined £100 apiece.

That was the undoing of the theatres royal. The danger caused Sadler's Wells to petition to be granted a patent. The other music-houses did likewise. In consequence, they obtained special licences to perform pantomime. The Act of 1788 ruled that, though the ordinary music-houses should be permitted songs and dances only, Sadler's Wells, the Royalty, Astley's Royal Grove Amphitheatre and the Royal Circus might " continue exhibiting performances of singing, dancing, pantomime and music" on payment of double the usual penal sums and sureties. The licences were to last from Easter Monday to the fifteenth day of September. The only drawback was that the proprietors were forbidden " to sell, give or supply any spirituous liquors, wine or beer " during the time of any exhibition. A new era of prosperity began for pantomime.

LEGEND

Science has succeeded to poetry no less in the little walks of children than with men. Is there no possibility of averting this sore evil? Think what you would have been now, if instead of being fed with tales and old wives' fables in childhood, you had been crammed with geography and natural history.

LAMB (to Coleridge).

Sig.ª Lucretia. Pulliciniello.

PANTOMIME was once the mirror of society. While an entertainment for adults, it reflected each change of fashion in correct behaviour. Frivolity spiced with impropriety inspired Harlequinades until the turn of the eighteenth century. Afterwards an edifying tone became increasingly evident. Morals were pointed, patriotism incited, virtue lauded and useful information imparted. Industrial spectacles, scenes in shops, factories, warehouses and dock-yards, as well as tableaux in honour of commerce, anticipated the age of advertising. At length, however, the strain of mental improvement broke and was succeeded by knockabout burlesque. In between whiles, pantomime authors, exhausted by moral and scientific ingenuities, returned to Woodward's choice of a fairy story for the main-spring of the plot. Dramatised nursery tales were not a new thing. There is almost a link with Harlequin in Lucian's statement that the *pantomimus* had to tell of Deucalion, in whose days the whole world suffered shipwreck, of the single chest wherein were preserved the remnants of the human race, of the dragon's teeth from which the Thebans sprang up, and the transformation of Cadmus into a serpent. Ancient mythology, however, lacks the naïveté that distinguishes the fairy tale. Likewise, the legends of the Middle Ages have too prac-ticable an air for the nursery. When dramatised in the sixteenth and seventeenth centuries these were still offered as specimens of mature wisdom. Faustus, Fortunatus, Robin Hood, Valentine and Orson had not become changelings by Shakespeare's day.

More resemblance to the modern pantomime is shown in the accounts of Scala's plays. In the latter part of the seventeenth century he created a liking in Italy for enchanted maidens, heroes changed by wizards into the shapes of birds or beasts, and for transformation scenes occurring when magical blood burst into flames. Then came

277

the real fashion of the fairy tale. Perrault's *Contes de ma Mère l'Oye ou Histoire du Temps Passé, avec des Moralités,* published in 1697, prompted a host of imitations. Before the excitement had died down, Antoine Galland returned from his theological studies in Constantinople to publish *Mille et une Nuits, Contes Arabes, traduits en Français* between 1704 and 1717. They were followed by the posthumous *Contes et Fables Indiennes de Bidpai et de Lokman* in 1724. Meanwhile there was an insistent demand for the *Contes des Fées* of Marie Catherine Jumelle de Bernville, Comtesse d'Aulnoy. This mingling of native and Oriental stories possibly explains why " Barbe Bleue " became an Eastern potentate in time.

The craze took immediate effect on the Paris stage in burlesques. Yet a little of the romance survived. At the Hôtel de Bourgogne on March 2, 1697, the Italians acted *Les Fées ou Les Contes de Ma Mère l'Oye*. Pierrot is the valet of a fairy. He conducts the prince in a flying chariot to the spot where the princess is imprisoned—and demands a tip. A troop of ogres seize the prince with the purpose of eating him at the wedding feast of their master (Scaramouche) and the princess. They catch sight of Arlequin, the prince's valet, but are prevented from laying hands on him by a fairy. " My principal occupation," she tells Arlequin, " is to fly incessantly to the rescue of maidens in danger of losing their honour." He replies, " And sometimes you arrive a little too late, eh ? " She warns him that she is only able to save them up to the age of fifteen years and six minutes. As the princess's time limit is nearly up he must make haste. She gives him a magic wand. Arlequin, to save them from Scaramouche, changes the prince and princess into rocks. After further adventures he transforms the cavern into a magnificent palace, and liberates four persons who had been condemned, for apt offences, into a clock, a lantern, a snail and a butterfly. *La Baguette de Vulcan,* another piece of the company at the Hôtel de Bourgogne, was similarly inspired by the fairy tales. The scene is a dark cavern defended by a giant of enormous size. Arlequin Roger enters to the sound of drums and trumpets, overcomes the giant, cuts off his head and dismembers him. When he rests content with his victory, the limbs and the head

278

re-join the body, challenge Roger to fight anew, and are again defeated. The hero touches the cave with the *baguette* Vulcan fashioned for him. It changes into a pleasant garden where, surrounded by the figures of people in an enchantment, sleeps Bradamante on a bed of flowers. In the eighteenth century the forains of Paris adopted Perrault's tales for their pantomimes. At the same time Favart's fairy operas were popular in the theatres. Italian and English playwrights followed suit. Until the Terror awoke France out of its daydreams the polite world seemed absorbed in tales of magic.

Summing up the literary needs of the time, *The Adventurer* (for November 18, 1752) decided that nature was exhausted—" deserts have been traversed, Alps climbed, and the secrets of the deep disclosed "—and all the events of history had been passed in review. The resources of Art remained to supply what was " perhaps the most generally pleasing of all performances "—those in which supernatural events were every moment produced by Genii and Fairies. That frame of mind seemed to be world wide. In Venice, Gozzi staked his reputation on drawing more people together than Goldoni could do with his comedies, by simply putting the old wives' tale of " The Love of the Three Oranges " on the boards. During the carnival of 1761 the piece was presented with Pantaloon, Brighella, Truffaldino (a new Harlequin) and Smeraldina (a new Columbine) as the characters. There is a prince who goes to the country of a witch to fetch the three magic oranges. His servant Truffaldino cuts one of them. Out steps a beautiful girl, gasping with thirst. The servant cuts another to give her the juice. It contains another beautiful girl, and both die of thirst. The prince seizes the last orange and does not cut the rind until he reaches a lake so that the third beautiful maiden is saved. " The play," said the author (translated by J. A. Symonds), " wound up with that marriage festival which all children know by heart—the banquet of preserved radishes, skinned mice, stewed cats, and so forth." Gozzi also wrote " The Raven," " The King Stag," " Turandot," " The Woman Serpent," " The Happy Beggars," " The Blue Monster " and " The Green Bird." Meantime Goldoni had had to remove to Paris in despair of his public.

279

Dr. Hawkesworth, a director of the East India Company as well as editor of *The Adventurer*, was the author of the fairy play " Edgar and Emmeline," staged at Drury Lane in the season of 1760-1, wherein magic wands were waved to change the sex of the hero and heroine so that they might discover whether their love were stable. He also wrote the story of "Almoran and Hamet" which became a pantomime at the New Royal Circus. Garrick, who presented the public with Woodward's fairy pantomimes and a children's opera called " The Fairies " in 1755, borrowed a plot from Favart for his " A Christmas Tale " at Drury Lane on December 27, 1773. The hero, who had to show his honour, valour and constancy to win a fair lady, overcame a wicked and powerful magician. There were buffoons to supply comic relief, and also transformations, such as trees and flowers which altered their colour, and a palace which tumbled into ruins. Hawkesworth and Garrick, however, were of less interest to the lovers of fairy tales than James Ridley, Chaplain to the East India Company. His " Tales of the Genii ; or the Delightful Lessons of Horam, the son of Asmar," which came out in 1764, ran into many editions, and supplied plots for pantomimes throughout the nineteenth century. It was translated into French in 1766, and found a place in the *Cabinet des Fées ; ou Collection Choisie des Contes des Fées, et autres Contes Merveilleux.* This monumental work ran into forty-one volumes, thirty-seven published in Paris between 1785 and 1789, and four at Amsterdam in 1793.

Our native folklore had a different history. When the plays of the minor Elizabethan dramatists were no longer current, the legends of Dick Whittington, St. George and Robin Hood were handed over to the ballad mongers—whose favourite subject was " The Children in the Wood "—and the booths at the fairs. " How that idle thing do work upon the people that see it, and even myself too," was the comment of Pepys on the puppets' performance of Whittington at Southwark. Showmanship had left the theatres of the Court for the minor stage of the public. The puppets, who had Punch for their clown, possessed all the most appealing plots. They reached the height of fashion's favour at the beginning of the eighteenth century owing to

280

POWEL THE PUPPET SHOWMAN

From "A Second Tale of a Tub"

ARLEQUIN WITH BAT AND WAND

Frontispiece to "Les Fées"

the enterprise of Powel, a showman popular in France, Germany and Spain as well as England. This Shakespeare of the minor stage, according to a pamphlet ("The Second Tale of a Tub") of 1715, "melted a whole audience into pity and tears when he has made the poor starved 'children in the wood' miserably depart in peace and a robin bury them." Money coming in apace, he bought new scenes for the better acting of several incomparable dramas of his own composing, namely "Whittington and his Cat," "The Children in the Wood, "Dr. Faustus," "Friar Bacon and Friar Bungay," "Robin Hood and Little John," "Mother Shipton" and "Mother Goose," besides Biblical dramas such as "The Creation of the World" and "Susannah and the Elders." Punch played a part in all of them. Says Swift,

> Observe the audience is in pain
> While Punch is hid behind the scene,
> But when they hear his rusty voice,
> With what impatience they rejoice !
> And then they value not two straws
> How Solomon decides the cause ;
> Which the true mother—which pretender,
> Nor listen to the witch of Endor.
> Should Faustus, with the Devil behind him,
> Enter the stage, they never mind him ;
> If Punch, to stir their fancy, shews
> In at the door his monstrous nose,
> Then sudden draws it back again,
> Oh ! what a pleasure mix'd with pain !

He would mount St. George's dragon, clap himself on the Queen of Sheba's lap, run roaring from the Duke of Lorraine's sword, dance in Noah's Ark, disturb love scenes with his ribaldry, plague everybody, get soundly mauled, and offer indecencies towards the ladies. He was attended by kings, queens, waiting-maids, virgins, babies, noblemen, baboons, tumblers, aldermen, rope-dancers, geese, country squires, rats, lord mayors, footmen, sows, Indians, cats, conjurers, owls, priests, brazen heads, robin-redbreasts and elders. Before the performance, says Steele, "the puppet-drummer, Adam and Eve, and several others who appeared before the Flood, passed through the streets on horseback."

Drury Lane planned to steal one of his plots, but gave up the attempt for reasons described in *The Spectator*. A great quantity of mice had been got together for an opera of Whittington and his Cat, but

> Mr. Rich, the proprietor of the playhouse, very prudently considered that it would be impossible for the cat to kill them all, and that consequently the princes of the stage might be as much infested with mice, as the prince of the island was before the cat's arrival on it.

Though the stage neglected the opportunity, the flesh-and-blood actors of Southwark Fair realised the value of the puppets' plots. A fair-bill dated 1731 sets forth how Lee and Harper, a famous partnership, would perform the droll of " The True and Antient History of Whittington," with Harper to act the part of Madge, the cook-maid. While the ship's factor was receiving gold-dust and jewels for the cat, Dick was so cruelly ill-treated by her that he " resolved to return to the country." He fancied he heard a message in the bells, and returned to the merchant's, where he had not been long before the arrival of his treasure, " half of which he bestow'd for the City's use." Lee and Harper also performed an opera of " Robin Hood " at the fair.

Apart from Woodward's pieces and Covent Garden's " Mother Shipton " in 1750, pantomime authors ignored these stories. How unconscious the theatre was of their value was shown by the accurate, yet facetiously intended, forecast of *The Connoisseur* for December 19, 1754. To Macklin and others, who had been discussing whether the stage might not be made more conducive to " Virtue and Morality," the essayist pointed out that not only did pantomimes sin in " representing Heathen gods and goddesses before a truly Christian audience," but Harlequin was a wicked sort of fellow, who was " always running after the girls," endeavouring " to creep up Columbine's petticoats," patting her neck or laying his legs upon her lap. Pantomime writers were therefore recommended to take their subjects from

> some Old Garland, Moral Ballad, or Penny History Book. Suppose, for example, they were to give us the story of Patient Grizzle in dumb shew ; setting forth, as how a noble lord fell in love with her, as he was hunting ;— and there you might have the scene of the Spinning Wheel, and the song of

DELPINI MOURNING IN "ALADDIN"

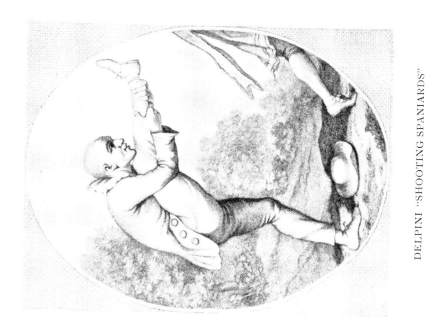

DELPINI "SHOOTING SPANIARDS"

From a Scrap-Book in the British Museum

the Early Horn ;—and as how, after many trials of her patience, which they might represent by machinery, this lord at last married her ;—and then you may have a grand Temple and a Dance. The other house have already revived the good old story of Fortunatus's Wishing-Cap ; and as they are fond of introducing little children in their entertainments, suppose they were to exhibit a Pantomime of the *Three Children in the Wood* ;—'twould be vastly pretty to see the pasteboard robin-redbreasts let down by wires upon the stage to cover the poor innocent babies with paper leaves. But if they must have Fairies and Genii, I would advise them to take their stories out of that pretty little book called the *Fairy Tales*. I am sure instead of ostriches, dogs, horses, lions, monkeys, etc., we should be full as well pleased to see the *Wolf and little red Riding Hood* ; and we should laugh vastly at the adventures of *Puss in Boots*. I need not point out the excellent Moral, which would be inculcated by representations of this kind ; and I am confident they would meet with the deserved applause of all the old women and children in both galleries.

There was a change of spirit, similar to that affecting the *Arlequinades* of the Italians in Paris, though not so fulsomely moral. Pantomime writers dramatised not the fairy stories but the still more popular volumes of sermons and travels. One of the first examples was " Harlequin's Frolick ; or, a Voyage to Prussia " at the Haymarket, which was followed in 1782 by " Harlequin Teague ; or, the Giant's Causeway " at the same theatre. This was one of the earliest pantomimes to create Harlequin by metamorphosis. According to Rich's convention, it opens with a gloomy view of the Causeway, where the imprisoned giant, who tried to join the two kingdoms, is about to be released by the genius of Ireland :

> On the departure of the *Genius*, Teague makes his appearance in the midst of a storm of thunder and lightning, during which the rock breaks asunder, and the Giant comes forth, a little boy. He immediately accosts Teague to know what had brought him to that part of the country ; to which he replies, that being very poor, he has vast inclinations to become rich, and hearing that London was the only place where a man stood a chance of gaining abundance for doing nothing, he was making the best of his way thither . . . upon Teague's declaring he means, notwithstanding his clumsiness, to play Harlequin when he gets to London, he is immediately transformed into that motley gentleman : the giant, after presenting the wooden sword, and enumerating its virtues, leaves him to pursue his journey.

After wishing himself to the Horns at Highgate, Harlequin meets Columbine and is pursued by Pantaloon and Pierrot to Drury Lane,

which is changed to a " Puff Warehouse," then to a floor-cloth manu-
factory and an anchor-smith's workshop.

Covent Garden had begun a series of topographical pieces in
1778 with Charles Dibdin's " The Touchstone ; or, Harlequin
Traveller " and " Mirror ; or, Harlequin Everywhere." Drury
Lane responded with " The Wonders of Derbyshire ; or, Harlequin
in the Peak." A year or two later, at Covent Garden, O'Keefe's
" Lord Mayor's Day ; or, the Flight from Lapland " fulfilled Dryden's
prophecy a century before. How incongruously morality abode in
these surroundings was shown in Messink's " The Choice of Harlequin ; or, the Indian Chief " at Covent Garden in 1782. After a
lengthy procession of sepoys, nishamdumdars and chataburdars had
conducted a bridegroom on an elephant and a bride in a palanquin, the
scene changed to a hotel. Harlequin, dressed in rich Oriental habit,
was confronted by Virtue and Pleasure, and chose the latter. Juno
left a huge grenadier in order to lure him to her garret. The grenadier
returned. At a wave of Harlequin's sword his head " hopped off."
Harlequin was taken to Bridewell, and then to a dark and gloomy cave
where Virtue gave him a new sword in order that he might enter Sir
Ashton Lever's museum—museums, then highly popular, were reproduced in several pantomimes.

" The Magic Cavern ; or, Virtue's Triumph," at Covent Garden
1785, was the work of Wewitzer, a comic actor noted for his acting
of Frenchmen, Jews and the learned Dr. Catterpillar in a Harlequinade museum scene. Another actor who helped to establish the
new type of pantomime was Wroughton, then manager at Sadler's
Wells, who composed " The Witch of the Lakes ; or, Harlequin in
the Hebrides." Harlequin's wand was used as a lecturer's cue to
point out the beauties of Scottish scenery, the lovers being pursued
from Edinburgh to a rocky cavern on the coast and thence to the
mountains. " The best pantomime since the days of Rich " was one
critic's verdict. Another wrote :

> The Circus boasts Delpini's " What you please,"
> And Astley glories in young Astley's ease,
> But that which most of all the public takes,
> Is Wroughton's treat, " The Witches of the Lakes."

Painted by Capriani and Richards   Engraved by Bromor

The PRINCIPAL SCENE in Harlequin every where.

Since amorous mythology was out of fashion in 1778, Charles Dibdin introduced
Prometheus, Tantalus and Sisyphus into his typographical pantomime.

From the Burney Collection in the British Museum

Delpini was an Italian. In 1776, at the time Woodward left Drury Lane, he was engaged by Garrick. Besides being a comic Pierrot he was the inventor of the Regency pantomime. While other authors were still making the bestowal of magic upon Harlequin the turning point of the story, he arranged that Harlequin should be formed out of another hero. Perhaps he was inspired by O'Hara and Dibdin's "Poor Vulcan" at Covent Garden in 1778, which showed the Olympians, after a matrimonial dispute, taking "the stage-cloud" to earth, where Vulcan became a blacksmith named Crump, Venus an ale-house wife named Maudlin, Jupiter a country squire, and Mars a recruiting sergeant. Adopting this principle of character transformation, Delpini, in 1781, arranged the dumb show of Sheridan's "Robinson Crusoe; or, Harlequin Friday" at Drury Lane, himself playing Crusoe to the Friday of the elder Grimaldi. He went to Covent Garden, where his "Aladdin; or, the Wonderful Lamp" was called "the bantling of the season" because of its brilliant scenery, excellent music and novel business. Delpini's pantomimes opened only with an incident or two belonging to the tale whose name they borrowed. The rest was the "common racing, hiding, seeking and stealing." Covent Garden followed this method the next year in "Blue Beard; or, the Flight of Harlequin." In 1792 "Harlequin's Museum; or, Mother Shipton Triumphant" restored the Lapland scenes, and showed a dockyard where a ship was launched and changed by Harlequin into a baker's shop. The next pantomime was "Harlequin and Faustus; or, the Devil will have His Own," and two years later "Robin Hood, or Merry Sherwood" introduced all the old ballad incidents but offered the public a Harlequin without a Columbine. On the other hand, "Harlequin and Quixote; or, the Magic Arm" in 1797 had a remarkably distorted plot. A persecuted Inca in a Peruvian Temple desired his son should marry the daughter of a Spanish grandee. As she was already betrothed to Don Quixote the Inca changed his son into Harlequin and conjured up the "Magic Arm" to guard him in danger. He appeared in the grandee's house in Granada, eloped with Columbine and hid in the Alhambra from her father, Don Quixote and Scaramouche. All arrived in "Old England,"

and the lovers were pursued until the Magic Arm came to the rescue. Here the Inca entered to assert his son's right to Columbine's hand. That matter settled, the scene changed first to the Great Wall of China, then to Tartary, and then to the reception of a British Embassy in a Chinese grand hall of audience. The moral was:

Let Amity's Voice
Bid great Nations rejoice.
And the Commerce of Britain
Spread under her wing.

From this time the Dibdins began to decide the pattern. Charles, the father, was born in 1745; the opera of " The Shepherd's Wedding," which he wrote and composed, was staged at Covent Garden sixteen years later. He had two sons. Charles Isaac Mungo, born in 1768, was given his third name after the negro part his father played. Thomas, born in 1771, appeared at the age of four years as Cupid to the Venus of Mrs. Siddons in a revival of Shakespeare's Jubilee at Drury Lane. In 1800, Thomas was the author of Covent Garden's " Harlequin's Tour ; or, the Dominion of Fancy." The scenes, " from views taken on the spot by several artists," were of " Regions of Fancy, Margate Pier, Dandelion, Road from Margate to Tunbridge, Tunbridge Wells, Charing Cross, Scarborough, Ullswater Lake, Bath, Weymouth, Forest Landscape and Fancy's Pavilion." Drury Lane set up in rivalry " Harlequin Amulet ; or, the Magic of Mona," which surveyed Wales. Pantaloon, an ancient gentleman of vast possessions in the Principality, had an ally in Morcar, Lord of the Mines in Mona, to destroy the Bards. In answer to their prayer St. David created Harlequin, who eloped with Pantaloon's daughter, gained his vast possessions and celebrated " The Festival of the Patron of Wales."

Six years previously " Penmaenmawr, or the Wonders of Wales " had presented at Sadler's Wells " a lively picture of the manners and localities of the Welsh, together with a varied view of the scenery of the country." Since then, however, Charles Dibdin the younger had become the author of the Islington theatre's pieces. He attached more importance to the plot than to the scenery, and his " Sadak and

Kalafradee " in 1797 told so coherent a story from the " Tales of the Genii " that the interposition of a Harlequinade midway was an incongruity. Thomas Dibdin also copied Delpini's idea in a version of " Mother Goose," but his manuscript was rejected by Kemble and Harris for five years running. Kemble's idea of a pantomime was very different. The suggestion he gave to Dibdin was this story of " King Arthur and Merlin and the Saxon Wizards," which was to be very short, very laughable, and very cheap :

> The pantomime might open with the Saxon witches lamenting Merlin's power over them, and forming an incantation by which they create a Harlequin, who is supposed to be able to counteract Merlin in all his designs for the good of King Arthur. If the Saxons came on in a dreadful storm, as they proceeded in their magical rites, the sky might brighten and a rainbow sweep across the horizon, which, when the ceremonies are completed, should contract itself from either end and form the figure of a Harlequin in the heavens ; the wizards may fetch him down how they will, and the sooner he is set to work the better. If this idea for producing a Harlequin is not new do not adopt it.

Dibdin did not. For the Christmas of 1805, he supplied " Harlequin Magnet ; or the Scandinavian Sorcerer." Harlequin, Pantaloon and Clown were created out of mystic inhabitants of northern regions, and chased each other not in London but through St. Petersburg and Moscow, shops being replaced by a frozen market. Harris, not satisfied with the box-office results, told his inventor he need bother his head no more. Six weeks before Christmas, he changed his mind and asked whether Dibdin had any odd sketches. Those that had been refused for five years running were then brought out. " Oh, what ? " cried Harris, " that d——d Mother Goose, you are so wedded to ! Let's have a look at her again : she has one recommendation, there's no finery about her," and Farley was told to commence rehearsals. Before the piece was ready, Drury Lane brought out on Boxing Day " The Enchanters ; or, Harlequin Sultan," a " Tale of the Genii " so imperfectly told that the audience could make nothing of it. " Harlequin and Mother Goose ; or, the Golden Egg " opened on December 28, and was the most triumphant pantomime of all time. Most of the praise was given to the " variety and ingenuity of the mechanical devices " of the Harlequinade, but the simple fable was not altogether negligible. Melancholy magicians and captive princesses had not a fiftieth part of the attraction of the jog-trot incidents of common life in " Mother Goose," and Squire Bugle with his fat face was " a much happier avant courier of fun " than a yellow dwarf. Here, plainly enough, was the proof that a clown in an emotional setting is of more account in showmanship than scene-shifting. Yet the lesson was disregarded. Thomas Dibdin's next pantomime, " Harlequin in his Element ; or, Fire, Water, Earth, and Air," revived the old model of allegorical and scenic ingenuity. The opening scene was a " beautiful garden with terraces, arcades, fountains, etc." Aurino descended on a light cloud and sang :

> Aquina ! Fountain Fairy !
> The genius of the air
> Invites thee here
> From springs so clear
> With love to banish care.

Aquina rose from the fountain. Terrena, from the earth, accused them of trampling on her and passed this sentence

> Water shall not rise
> Above her level ; Air shall keep the skies.

It thundered. Ignoso descended and threw fire from his wand upon the flowers which withered but were revived by the others. " Fire, why so hot ? " asked Terrena,

> Rather than quarrel let us use our powers
> And, gift with magic, aid some active sprite
> To foil the guardian and the girl to right.

whereupon she declared " This clod to form shall grow " and Harlequin was produced from a bed of parti-coloured flowers. After giving him the magic sword

> Ignoso sinks. Aquina strikes the fountains ; they begin playing. Terrena strikes the ground ; a bed of roses appears. Harlequin surveys everything and runs round the stage. Earth sinks into a bed of roses, and Water in the fountain. Air ascends in the car. Columbine enters dancing ; is amazed at the sight of Harlequin, who retires from her with equal surprise ; they follow each other round the fountain in a *pas de deux*. They are surprised by the entrance of Columbine's Guardian, who comes in preceded by servants in rich liveries. Clown, as his running footman, enters with a lap dog. Old

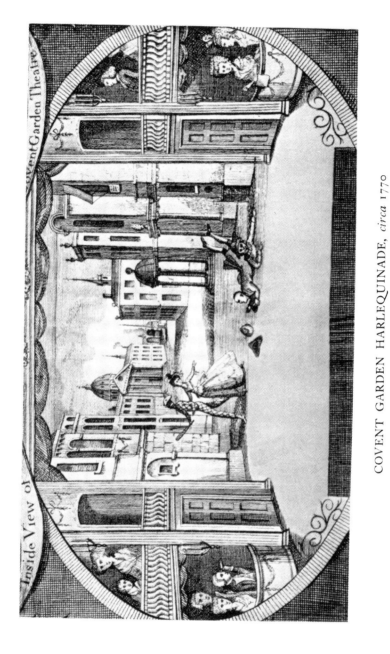

COVENT GARDEN HARLEQUINADE, *circa* 1770

From Mr. A. M. Broadley's Collection: reproduced from "Polly Peachum" by Charles E. Pearce
by kind permission of Messrs. Stanley Paul & Co.

Man takes snuff—views himself in a pocket-glass. Clown imitates him, etc. Old Man sees Harlequin and Columbine, and pursues them round the fountains, but the lovers go off, followed by Sir Amoroso and servants.

The pursuit continued through " Code's Artificial Stone Works " and " Dodd's Paper Mill at Cheyney, near Rickmansworth," and ended in " The Temple of the Elements."   Later in the season, the piece gave place to a revival of " Mother Goose."

Similarly, Drury Lane relied on machinery in " Furibond ; or, Harlequin Negro," a failure though Laurent was Clown.   The idea was taken from " Harlequin Mungo ; or, A Peep into the Tower " at the Royalty in 1789, which was named after the elder Charles Dibdin's part in " The Padlock."   The new pantomime aimed at celebrating the liberation of slaves.   Furibond was rescued from hanging by a snake which he gratefully placed in his basket.   A large passion flower burst forth and from this the Fairy Benigna emerged. After changing Furibond into Harlequin, she drew his attention to a transparency showing " Harlequin relieving distressed objects." Furibond begged for the release of his fellow slaves.   Britannia with her lion descended from the flies and a chorus sang

> She bears just England's blest decree
> That stamps the Negro's Liberty.

The scene changed to London, where Harlequin and Columbine were pursued from Greenwich Park to Charing Cross.

Pieces of this stamp do not agree with Planché's description of the Christmas pantomimes of his boyhood :

> A pretty story—a nursery tale—dramatically told in which " the course of true love never did run smooth," formed the opening; the characters being a cross grained old father, with a pretty daughter who had two suitors —one a poor young fellow, whom she preferred, the other a wealthy fop, whose pretensions were of course favoured by the father.   There was also a body-servant of some sort in the old man's establishment.   At the moment when the young lady was about to be forcibly married to the fop she despised, or on the point of eloping with the youth of her choice, the good Fairy made her appearance, and, changing the refractory pair into Harlequin and Columbine, the old curmudgeon into Pantaloon, and the body-servant into Clown ; the two latter, in company with the rejected Lover, as he was called, commenced the pursuit of the happy pair, and the " comic business " consisted of a dozen or more cleverly constructed scenes, in which all the tricks and

changes had a meaning, and were introduced as contrivances to favour the escape of Harlequin and Columbine, when too closely followed by their enemies. There was as regular a plot as might be found in a melodrama. An interest in the chase increased the admiration of the ingenuity and the enjoyment of the fun of the tricks by which the runaways escaped capture, till the inevitable " dark scene " came—a cavern or a forest in which they were overtaken, seized, and the Magic Wand which had so uniformly aided them snatched from the grasp of the despairing Harlequin, and flourished in triumph by the Clown. Again at the critical moment the protecting Fairy appeared and, exacting the consent of the father to the marriage of the devoted couple, transported the whole party to what was really a grand last scene, which everybody did wait for.

Early in the autumn of 1808 Covent Garden Theatre was destroyed by fire. Nothing was left but " the King's Arms, a Roman Eagle, Mother Goose, a few other pantomimic devices and pieces of mechanism, and some pikes, halberds, etc." The company, when established at the Haymarket, put on " Mother Goose " for the third time. Half-way through its successful run an additional scene was introduced showing the ruins of Covent Garden which, touched by Harlequin's wand, were transformed into " a prophetic picture " of the new theatre. When it opened in September, 1809, the " O.P." riots against increased prices hampered Kemble and Harris, but " Harlequin Pedlar ; or, the Haunted Well " and another revival of " Mother Goose " brought them success. Meanwhile, Drury Lane had been burned down and the company gone to the Lyceum, where at Christmas they performed " The White Cat ; or, Harlequin in Fairyland " by Kirby, the clown. The theatre obtained a licence for pantomime, and in 1810 staged the first Cinderella pantomime. Thomas Dibdin kept to the old style, supplying " The Colossus ; or, Harlequin and the Seven Wonders " to the Lyceum in 1811, and his brother to the old sentiments, exhibiting the " deleterious effects of wealth without wisdom " at Sadler's Wells in 1808 by means of " Thirty Thousand ; or, Harlequin's Lottery." But the fashion had definitely changed to fairy tales. Morality was generally satisfied by performing either " George Barnwell " or " Jane Shore " before the pantomime at the first performance, a custom instituted by Garrick in 1759. Between 1806 and 1820 most of the stories known to children

were pantomimed. But no return was made to the simplicity of
" Mother Goose." In 1814, when Drury Lane staged " The Valley
of Diamonds ; or, Harlequin Sinbad," Covent Garden followed
" George Barnwell " with a version of " Harlequin Whittington,
Lord Mayor of London," that served as a companion picture to the
tragedy of " the bitter fruit of passion's detested reign." With
a " very clever little dog " to perform the part of the cat and Grimaldi
to act Dame Cicely Suet, the tale should have been well told. But
the god in the machine was the Fairy Bizybæa, Genius of Industry.
Also the scene painter had been restored to the place of honour. A
view of Holloway " where Whittington's stone now stands " was
declared to be the best the stage could boast :

> The gradual clearing up of the atmosphere after a thunderstorm, with the
> sun appearing in all his splendour, presents to the eye a beautiful and ex-
> tensive landscape, is finely managed, and produced a delightful effect. The
> ascent of Bizybæa, the Genius of Industry, in a splendid temple, from the
> centre of the mile-stone, was executed with much adroitness.

Likewise in " Baron Munchausen ; or, the Fountain of Love " at
Covent Garden in 1818, spectacle displaced the story and the clown.
The scene was a snowscape. In the distance Etna burst into eruption,
the burning lava melted the mountains of snow and revealed a village
underneath. Munchausen waked to find his horse hanging from a
steeple and cleft the bridle with a pistol shot to bring it down. He
eloped with the heroine to a cavern in Etna where Vulcan granted their
admission to the bower of Venus. " Harlequin and the Ogress ; or,
the Sleeping Beauty of the Wood," at Covent Garden in 1822, was
equally distorted. The Fates, after spinning and winding a ball of
golden thread in a cavern under the Pyramids, gave it to Grim Gibbet,
porter of the castle, to attach it to the wrist of the sleeping princess.
Grim, however, fell asleep directly he entered her chamber. The
rescuing prince failed similarly and was condemned to wander in
search of happiness as Harlequin. In addition to spectacle, there was
always an endeavour to provide a sensation. One of the most popular
tricks of this kind was a balloon which ascended from the stage into
the thunder loft, descended from an aperture in the ceiling of the

auditorium and floated back to the stage. Roller-skating upon oil-cloth was introduced into " The House that Jack Built " at Covent Garden in 1824. At the end of the performance :

> A prodigious fat man makes his appearance ; when a race is called for, he, of course, tries his prowess, when the ice cracking beneath the heavy weight assembled on it gives way with a heavy crash, and " Fatty " is consigned to a watery bed. Assistance is immediately tendered, when, by Harlequin's power, a lean and shrivelled spirit of the deep rises from below to the great alarm of the beholders, and whose limbs continue to expand till his head touches the clouds.

During Grimaldi's prime Harlequin was kept in the background. The cause, however, was not so much the importance given to Clown as the passion for raree-shows. Peer Patch in Thomas Dibdin's " Harlequin Hoax," the skit given by Liston at the Lyceum in 1814, says :

> Harlequin the hero ? bless your unpractised head. Harlequin ! no. Who thinks of Harlequin, while there's a chimpanzee, a bear, a reindeer, a cat or a goose to be got.

and Liston commented

> I have been too long on the stage not to know that Harlequin is the worst part in a pantomime—a thing of shreds and patches, without a single point to get applause except when he jumps and that is always done by someone else.

Yet after Grimaldi's retirement, Ellar's fascination was considerable. As a child E. L. Blanchard could always be induced to go to bed by his mother's command " Change into Harlequin," whereupon he took off his clothes and jumped through the dimity curtains. After Woodward, the Harlequin at Covent Garden was Lee Lewes, who copied his attitudes. Boyce came next. When Harlequin had to pretend to be a statue, in accordance with the stock pantomime episode, he would imitate a clock-work figure. These attitudes became known in the nineteenth century as the " animations " which expressed Admiration, Flirtation, Thought, Determination and Defiance. His mask became recognised as a sign of invisibility and the colours he wore became emblematical, red indicating temper, blue love, yellow jealousy, and brown (or mauve) constancy. This interpretation, however, was not traditional. Verses

HARLEQUIN'S "ANIMATIONS"

From an engraving in the British Museum

in the *Annual Register* of 1761, to honour the memory of Rich, draw
a different moral:

> Hear, critics, hear! and spare your jest,
> Life's but a motley garb at best;
> He wore it long with grace and ease,
> And ev'ry gesture taught to please
> Where (some few patchwork foibles seen
> Scattered around—blue—yellow—green)
> His constant virtue's radiant hue
> O'er all superior shone to view.

From the time of " Harlequin Shepherd " at the latest, the skin-tight
costume of lozenge-pattern was familiar. A print entitled " The
Theatrical Steel Yards of 1750," which shows Garrick outweighing
his rivals while Woodward regards the downfallen Rich, proves that
the Italian jackets and trousers had not been discarded altogether.
Byrne, according to the Grimaldi *Memoirs*, introduced " an entire
change " of costume and acting when he played Harlequin in
" Harlequin Amulet; or, the Magic of Mona" at Drury Lane in
1800:

> His attitudes and jumps were all new, and his dress was infinitely improved:
> the latter consisted of a white silk shape, fitting without a wrinkle, into which
> the variegated silk patches were woven, the whole being profusely covered
> with spangles, and presenting a very sparkling appearance.

Many other alterations were made to Harlequin's appearance during
the Regency. He wore a high cocked hat with a chin strap, a deep
black velvet mask, and a full lace frill round his neck. A broad black
velvet band encircled his waist, formed a " V " for his neck, continued under his body and along the spine. Instead of lozenges, his
colours were in triangles arranged to form squares and saltires for the
lines of spangles. Instead of a slapstick he was armed with a willowy
magic sword. Byrne and his son acted at Drury Lane in 1804 a short
piece called " Old Harlequin's Fireside." He was the old Harlequin
sitting in an inglenook while Time rocked a cradle. A little Harlequin
boy appeared and passed rapidly through all the stages of life by means
of ingenious contrivances. The old Harlequin, descending into the
grave, handed his sword to the child who was told by the protecting
genius " always to exert his power in the cause of virtue."

While acting in the provinces Edmund Kean had to undertake Harlequin, and was no mean performer in the part. At Dublin he even copied " the lion's leap " of Bradbury, the clown. After he had made his name in town he announced that he would give an exhibition of his skill in pantomime. Owing to an accident while dancing he had to give up the attempt. Hazlitt, risking his limbs in the crush, felt the disappointment keenly :

> Good reader, it was not the jump through the trap-door that we wished liter-ally to see, but the leap from Othello to Harlequin. What a jump ! What an interval, what a gulf to pass ! What an elasticity of soul and body too —what a diversity of capacity in the same diminutive person ! To be Othello, a man should be all passion, abstraction, imagination : to be Har-lequin, he should have his wits in his heels, and in his fingers' ends ! To be both, it is impossible, or miraculous.

Byrne was at Covent Garden in 1805, but was succeeded the next year by John Bologna, the son of Pietro Bologna who made his first appear-ance at Sadler's Wells in 1786. Three years later Master Bologna gave a performance on the tight rope, and in 1792 there were " Ex-traordinary Exhibitions of Postures and Feats of Strength by Signor Bologna and his children." John Bologna played Harlequin at the Royal Circus from 1795 to 1802. Then he became a regular member of Sadler's Wells in the summer, performing many remarkable feats with Grimaldi, including the one described in " Joseph's Lament " :

> Never shall old Bologna—old, alack !
> Once he was young and diamonded all o'er,
> Take his particular Joseph on his back
> And dance the matchless fling, so loved of yore.

Harlequin had undergone strange changes at this house. In 1789 " The Mandarin " revealed him as Harlequin Widower. In " The Savages ; or, Harlequin Wanderer "—a combination of An-drocles and Crusoe—he was rescued by a ship whose commander was his son. In " Sadak and Kalafradee " he was derived from a faithful eunuch. The part was of so much importance that when a Harlequin, finding the scene changing too soon, slapped it with his hand instead of his sword, there was an uproar. At Covent Garden in 1805 Pietro was the Pantaloon. The next year, in " Mother Goose," he gave up

COSTUMES OF THE REGENCY HARLEQUINADES

From a Scrap-Book in the British Museum

this part to his son Louis, and John was the Harlequin.   Kemble, watching John Bologna play Oscar in " Oscar and Malvina," a ballet founded on Ossian, said " If that man could speak as well as he acts pantomimes, I would never appear again on the stage."   Like all his fellows he was the victim of the stage carpenters' carelessness.   Once there were no arms ready to catch him as he leapt through a clock case and he broke his collar bone.   Following Woodward's example, he had another Harlequin to take the leaps.   This was Ellar, the Harlequin Bluff of " Harlequin and the Swans ; or the Bath of Beauty " in 1813, whose leaps caused any specially agile feats to be termed " à la Ellar."   After jumping through the moon, he, too, was let fall and broke his wrist.   There was malice in the negligence, but he would make no complaint because " the fellow had half-a-dozen children." Evidently, such " mishaps " were a recognised form of reprisals against slights, real or imaginary, received by stage-hands from Harlequin.   Barnes, the Pantaloon, says as much in a story of his travels in France :

Monsieur le Directeur made his objections in strongly-urged French whispers to our Jew interpreter at the idea of the carpenters sitting down with us.   Ha ! ha ! ha !   Little did the Parisian manager know of the state of affairs in requesting the Harlequin (for such I have before mentioned the Jew-Frenchman was), to ask anything unpleasant of, or to do anything disagreeable to the persons upon whom his pantomimical existence depends. To explain this ignorance on the part of the French Director, I must tell you that when Harlequin jumps through a hole, a picture, or a window, he is always caught safely in a carpet at the back of the scene by the carpenters. If these men were to be remiss in their duty, the public would see no more of Harlequin for some time, for, from the velocity with which he takes his leap through the aperture—*sans ses amis avec le tapis* (dictionary), he would go to immortal smash !

So the Harlequin was afraid to say anything disagreeable to the stage-carpenters, and he asked me to break the unpleasant business to them. Lord, I didn't care a brass farthing.   I, Pantaloon, never go through the hole. I always stick in the middle, with my face to the audience.   I am not to be caught by the carpenters.   So I went to them in the most delicate way I could, and told them that they must not take their meals with us again, but that I would take them to a café, where they would have what was necessary.

Ellar continued to perform dangerous feats.   In the ballet of " Robinson Crusoe ; or, the Bold Buccaneer " at Easter, 1817, he

" flew from the back of the gallery to the extremity of the stage."   In the adoration of boyhood Blanchard noted how, when he walked, his heel was never less than an inch above the stage.   And, directly he changed to Harlequin, he would finish his series of attitudes by spinning his head round with remarkable velocity, " as if the masked face was only a whirling teetotum revolving on the centre of his frilled neck."   This curious and " rather unpleasant accompaniment " he had

> learned from old Bologna, who originally adopted it to show the effect produced upon the brain by the bowl of arrack-punch he had ordered in a scene representing Vauxhall Gardens, and from which he only recovered by the Columbine taking the bat and making him spin his head in the opposite direction.

Having obtained a " humble appointment on the theatrical staff " of Covent Garden, Blanchard was behind the scenes during ' Harlequin and George Barnwell " in 1836, and saw Ellar close to as he threw off the " slip-dress " of Alfred Trueman when changed by the Fairy Industry into the glittering Harlequin.   Ellar was then fifty-six. His face was discoloured by mercury poison administered by a jealous woman.   One evening in February, says Blanchard,

> he smote his wand upon a scene intended to represent the enlargement of every newspaper consequent on the removal of the stamp duty, and fainted in my arms before the stage-carpenter could reveal the size of the tremendous broad-sheets supposed to be the result of the potential bat.

Though his strength, too, was failing, Ellar lent for life many a sovereign to his old companion, Barnes.   When the old Pantaloon died in 1838, he wished all he had left of the funds raised by a special performance to go to Ellar, but there was no will and Harlequin received a scanty bequest.   He still seemed active and performed with John Bologna, Norman and the Leclercqs in a melodrama pantomime of " Robinson Crusoe " at Astley's.   A year or two later his livelihood was gained by playing the guitar after nightfall in fashionable squares, or dancing at miserable music-halls in the East End. Thackeray wrote :

> Our Harlequin Ellar, prince of many of our enchanted islands, was he not at
> Bow Street the other day, in his dirty, faded, tattered motley—seized as a

Miss F Dennett as Columbine

From a print in the Author's Collection

law breaker for acting at a penny theatre, after having well nigh starved in the streets, where nobody would listen to his guitar ? No one gave him a shilling to bless him : not one of us who owe him so much.

At last a benefit was arranged at the Victoria in 1840, when it was noticed that time had indeed " exhibited his power on the once active frame of poor old Ellar." When he died two years later (at Mount Row, Lambeth), his wife and child were totally unprovided for. Bologna lived to the age of seventy-one. He was at one time a teacher of dancing and at another assistant to the " Wizard of the North." Like Ellar, he was not helped by the Theatrical Fund, and died at Glasgow in poverty.

Leigh Hunt has left a portrait of Ellar in his description of a pantomime, shortly before the craze for topical allusion began to turn the Harlequinade into a political satire :

> In comes Harlequin, demi-masked, party-coloured, nimble-toed, lithe, agile ; bending himself now this way, now that ; bridling up like a pigeon ; tipping out his toe like a dancer ; then taking a fantastic skip ; then standing ready at all points, and at right angles with his omnipotent lath-sword, the emblem of the converting power of fancy and lightheartedness. Giddy as we think him, he is resolved to show us that his head can bear more giddiness than we fancy ; and lo ! beginning with it by degrees, he whirls it round into a very spin, with no more remorse than if it were a button. Then he draws his sword, slaps his enemy, who has just come upon him, into a settee ; and springing upon him, dashes through the window like a swallow. Let us hope that Columbine and the high road are on the other side, that he is already a mile on the road to Gretna. . . . Now the lovers dine indeed ; and having had no motion to signify, join in a dance. Here Columbine [1] shines as she ought to do. The little slender, but plump rogue ! How she winds it hither and thither with her trim waist, and her waxen arms ! now with a hand against her side, tripping it with no immodest insolence in a hornpipe ; now undulating it in a waltz ; or "caracoling" it, as Sir Thomas Urquhart would say, in the saltatory style of the opera ;—but always Columbine ; always the little dove who is to be protected ; something less than the opera-dancer, and greater ; more unconscious yet not so ; and ready to stretch her gauze wings for a flight, the moment Riches would tear her from Love.

Columbine had long, short-waisted, tight-fitting petticoats reaching

---

[1] Miss E. Dennett was " Mellisent afterwards Columbine " in " Harlequin and Friar Bacon," which was probably the pantomime Leigh Hunt had in mind. Three years before, when Miss F. Dennett was Columbine, there was a *pas de trois* by the sisters.

down to her ankles. When she supped with Harlequin she was dressed in the evening fashion of the day, with long white kid gloves drawn up over her elbows. In the 'forties, when the lovers were a pair of dancers, her skirts shortened. In the " Glitter Scene " at the end of the pantomime she stood on the centre of a wheel with Harlequin, Pantaloon and Clown round her. This would revolve while the dazzling columns of the palace whirled about. When this machinery was lacking they would form " a sort of human pyramid," with Harlequin as the base, Columbine the apex, and Pantaloon and Clown as the sides. Then the dusty green baize curtain fell, and Joey would thrust out his head underneath to invite the audience to " see us all to-morrow night." In 1859 the pantomime of "Goody Goose" at the Royal, Marylebone, had the glitter scene half-way. Instead of a dismal " cat scene " for the changing of the characters, the Harlequinade in future was heralded by a process of scene-shifting, limelight changing and chorus parading. At first a few fairies manœuvred before a mass of flowers, or seaweed or astral bodies. The central part lifted to show a transparency of some fairy realm. After the gauze had been withdrawn, some more fairies would appear. The new scene would be struck—and so on until the back of the stage had been reached. Then all the bands of the fairies would unite to march up and down with the twitching limp peculiar to pantomime. A few dancers would destroy any illusion of fantasy with their terrestrial desire for applause. The fairy queen would deliver a speech, a whistle would blow, and a front-cloth shop scene come between the audience and the glories of canvas worlds too intricate to mean anything to the imagination of child or adult.

Though the " opening " of pantomime increased until it was much more than half the performance, the " transformation scene " remained in the middle. To precede the Harlequinade a glitter scene with a pageant was introduced. Harlequin dwindled even more rapidly than Clown. In the twentieth century he was sometimes played by a female dancer. One of the last Harlequins was Fred Leoville of the Britannia. In January, 1922, he was playing in the Harlequinade after " Aladdin " at the Liverpool Olympia. One morning his wife fell from her chair at breakfast—dead. Leoville tried to perform each night. At first he collapsed. Then he rallied. But it was not many days before he died.

Of living Harlequins, the most notable is Tom Coventry, who lives at Ealing. Though sixty-eight he has a fresh colour, bright eyes and hair only slightly streaked with grey. There are no more Harlequins for him to play, but his knowledge of the art of dumb-show qualifies him more than most of the actors of the old stock companies to act for the films.

Cucuba.   *Cap. Babeo.*

BURLESQUE AND EXTRAVAGANZA

Now to the Drama turn—oh ! motley sight !
What precious scenes the wondering eyes invite !
Puns, and a prince within a barrel pent,
And Dibdin's nonsense yield complete content. . . .
Gods ! o'er those boards shall Folly rear her head,
Where Garrick trod, and Kemble lives to tread ?
On those shall Farce display Buffoon'ry's mask,
And Hook conceal his heroes in a cask ?
Shall sapient managers new scenes produce
From Cherry, Skeffington, and Mother Goose ?
While Shakespeare, Otway, Massinger forgot,
On stalls must moulder, or in closets rot ?
Lo ! with what pomp the daily prints proclaim
The rival candidates for Attic fame ?
In grim array though Lewis' spectres rise,
Still Skeffington and Goose divide the prize.
And sure *great* Skeffington must claim our praise,
For skirtless coats and skeletons of plays
Renown'd alike ; whose genius ne'er confines
Her flight to garnish Greenwood's gay designs ;
Nor sleeps with " Sleeping Beauties."

BYRON.

Fritellino.   Franca Trippa.

Mr. BANNISTER Jun.r in the CHARACTER of WALTER in the CHILDREN in the WOOD

"Your whole conscience stirred with Bannister's performance
of Walter in the Children in theWood". . . . *Lamb*

From an engraving in the Burney Collection of Theatrical Portraits

NURSERY tales were no more than a formal preliminary in the Harlequin pantomimes. When told for its own sake, the dramatised fairy story was a very serious affair. Colman's "Blue Beard, or Female Curiosity," for instance, was one of the "penny-dreadful" dramas that raged at Drury Lane from J. P. Kemble's "Lodoiska," in 1794, to "Feudal Times; or, the Banquet Gallery," in 1799. The most successful was "Monk" Lewis's "The Castle Spectre," notable for an incident thus described in the stage directions:

> Osmond, drawing his sword, rushes upon Reginald, who is disarmed, and beaten upon his knees; when at the moment that Osmond lifts his arm to stab him, Evelina's ghost throws herself between them. Osmond starts back and drops his sword.

These led to the introduction of melo-drama, performances in dumb-show. Penny-dreadful plots were still used, but songs replaced dialogue. The first was Thomas Holcroft's "Tale of a Mystery," staged in 1802 at Covent Garden, where Henry Siddons' "A Tale of Terror," and Thomas Dibdin's "Valentine and Orson" soon followed. Drury Lane adopted the new style. "Robinson Crusoe" in 1800 was a ballet, but Skeffington's "Sleeping Beauty" in 1805 was a melo-drama in the costumes of England in the time of "ancient chivalry." Drury Lane's spectacle of "Cinderella; or, the Little Glass Slipper" in January, 1804, united the methods of ballet and melo-drama. This piece, the first to bring Cinderella into the theatre, made a critic think the English stage had never exhibited a more captivating entertainment of its kind. Yet the story was strangely perverted. The triumph of the heroine was not due to her fairy god-mother but to Venus, in order to introduce a ballet of Loves and Graces in the island of Cytherea. There was a part for Grimaldi, who was, however, eclipsed by scenery. Covent Garden, which now presented a nursery-tale ballet every Easter, staged Cinderella in 1820. When Miss Dennett, the youngest and tallest of three sisters who were popular dancers and Columbines, was transformed by a little hump-backed fairy from a poor housemaid to a bright princess, she inspired Hazlitt to write :

> This is a consummation more devoutly to be wished than the changing of a pipkin into a sign-post, or a wheelbarrow into a china shop. A Fairy Tale is the true history of the human heart—it is a dream of youth realised ! How many country-girls have fancied themselves princesses, nay, what country-girl ever was there that, some time or other, did not ? A Fairy Tale is what the world would be, if all had their wishes or their deserts—if our powers and passions were equal. We cannot be at a loss for a thousand bad translations of the story of Cinderella, if we look around us in the boxes. But the real imitation is on the stage.

Spectacle triumphed over the dramatised fairy tale as over pantomime. In Farley's " Aladdin ; or, the Wonderful Lamp," at Covent Garden in 1813, the mysterious lamp, the jewelled fruit, the service of plate springing up in a hovel, the procession of Aladdin's gifts to the Cham, and the flying palace, overcame Grimaldi's gaiety. But the craze for extravagance was carried to greater excess. In February 1811, Colman's " Blue Beard " was revived in the circus manner owing to the large profits made by Astley's " Blood-Red Knight." Early in the second act of " Blue Beard," says Boaden,

> Sixteen most beautiful horses mounted by spahis suddenly appeared before the spectators, and were received with immense applause ; their various and incessant action produced a delightful effect upon the eye ; and when they were afterwards seen ascending the heights with inconceivable velocity, the audience were in raptures as at the achievement of a wonder. Subsequently, however, they seemed still more astonished at the sagacity, or recollection, of the noble animals before them ;—in the charge, some of the horses appeared to be wounded, and with admirable intuition fainted gradually away. One of them, who in the anguish of his wounds had thrown off his rider, and was dying on the field, on hearing the report of a pistol sprung suddenly upon his feet, as if again to join, or enjoy, the battle ; but his ardour not being seconded by strength, he fell again as if totally exhausted.

" This splendid novelty," to use Boaden's description, was looked upon by the *Dramatic Censor* as " a black epoch for ever." But the public were so well pleased that Covent Garden two months later presented " Monk ". Lewis's " Timour the Tartar " in a similar fashion. In 1833, Bunn, manager of both the patent theatres, engaged Ducrow to arrange the equestrian spectacle of " Saint George and the Dragon; or, the Seven Champions of Christendom " at Drury Lane.

When legend was no longer used in melo-drama, it increased in favour with opera librettists. From Arne's " Robin Hood " in 1741 to " The Children in the Wood " in 1793, opera occasionally anticipated pantomime. In 1807 Rossini composed " Cenerentola " —performed at Covent Garden in 1830 as " Cinderella; or, the Fairy and the Little Glass Slipper "—in which Dandini and the Baron first came into existence. " Don Giovanni," a pantomime at Drury Lane in 1817-8 when Byron wrote :

> We have all seen him, in the pantomime,
> Sent to the devil somewhat ere his time.

was described by Keats (dramatic critic of *The Champion*) as " having been wire drawn for many years past at the neighbouring theatres, made a pet of at the Surrey, and fiddled away to hell at the Italian Opera." In 1826, Bishop's " Aladdin " at Drury Lane brought one of the first principal boys into a nursery story because of the fashion for making operatic heroes " breeches parts." In addition to opera, there were the fairy plays of Planché such as " Abudah; or, the Talisman and Oromanes " (one of the " Tales of the Genii ") at Drury Lane in 1819. Planché saw the fairy comedy of *Riquet à la Houppe* at Paris in 1821, and fifteen years later this inspired him to write his first fairy extravaganza.

Meanwhile pantomime discarded the fairy tale. Separated from the Harlequinade, it had no need to set forth how Harlequin became possessed of his magic wand. Instead of the operatic scene customary since the shows of Rich, the " opening " developed into a burlesque in dialogue. Thus the use of words in an entertainment supposed to be dumb, became general. The history of this tendency is involved. After Aphra Behn's " The Emperor of the Moon " and Garrick's " Harlequin's Invasion," the next speaking-pantomime was " Doctor Hocus-Pocus; or Harlequin Washed

305

White," at the Haymarket in the summer of 1814. It was described in the play-bills as " an anomalous, multiloquacious, ludrico-magico, absurdo-ratiocinatico pantomimical entertainment." In 1818 Planché wrote a speaking Harlequinade, with songs for Columbine, called " Rodolph the Wolf ; or, Little Red Riding Hood." It was, by the way, staged at Astley's old theatre in Wych Street, the Olympic. At the first performance " every trick failed, not a scene could be induced to close or open properly, and the curtain fell at length amidst a storm of disapprobation." Afterwards, says Planché, " all the culprits assembled on the stage in front of one of the scenes in the piece representing the interior of a cottage, having a door in one half and a latticed window in the other." Elliston harangued them in grandiloquent language, then, pointing in a tragic attitude to his wife and daughters and bidding the men look upon the family they had ruined, buried his face in his handkerchief to stifle his sobs and passed slowly through the door in the scene. The next moment the casement in the other flat was thrown violently open, and thrusting in his head, his face scarlet with fury, he roared out, " I discharge you all ! "

" Speaking-pantomimes " introduced dialogue into the Harlequinade. The experiment was dropped in favour of dialogue in the " opening." The first to be spoken (instead of sung) was written by Mark Lemon for " Harlequin Fat and Harlequin Bat ; or, the Giant's Causeway " in 1830 at Covent Garden. The new style was followed by Drury Lane in " Harlequin and Old Gammer Gurtch ; or, the Lost Needle " in 1836, " Harlequin and Jack Frost ; or, Old Good Hearty" in 1838, and so forth. Describing this " ingenious method of dovetailing extravaganza and pantomime," Planché wrote :

> Instead of the two or three simple scenes which previously formed the opening of the pantomime, a long burlesque, the characters in which have nothing to do with those in the Harlequinade, occupies an hour, sometimes much more—of the evening, and terminates with one of those elaborate and gorgeous displays which have acquired the name of " transformation scenes," and are made the great feature of the evening ; and, consequently, after which the best part of the audience quit the theatre, and what is by courtesy called the " comic business " is run through by the pantomimists in three or four ordinary street or chamber scenes. The usual number of curiously dressed

people stream in and out of exhibitions or cross the stage ; the usual number of policemen are bonneted ; the steps are buttered ; the red-hot poker is exhibited ; the real live pig let out of the basket ; and then, *à propos de bottes*, a portion of the transformation scene is suddenly discovered, sufficiently shorn of its beams to escape recognition by the two or three score of persons who have courageously sat out the performance, and are too much occupied in putting on their coats and shawls to think of anything but their beds or their suppers. The " transformation scene " is, however, declared every year to be unparalleled. That is the object of attraction, and all the rest is " inexplicable dumb show and noise."

Artists of some renown were employed. " Pantomimes," it was said, " are now virtually extinct ; Stanfield and Roberts have made picture galleries of them." In 1829, the Drury Lane pantomime concluded with Stanfield's diorama of the Falls of Virginia Water with thirty-nine tuns of real water. At Covent Garden, Roberts exhibited a moving diorama of the Polar Expedition, representing the progress of the *Hecla* and *Fury* in their endeavour to discover the North-West Passage. But as the audience had (*Chambers' Journal* stated) " just been exposed to the pitiless pelting of a snow-storm, or stumbling over huger blocks of ice encumbering the streets," Drury Lane won. Everything was sacrificed to spectacle. A version of " Gulliver " in 1845 was described as depending solely on the scene of the floating island.

Planché's fairy extravaganzas incited managers to still further extravagance. Under the management of Vestris (at this date Mrs. Charles Mathews) they were embellished by William Beverley. On the Boxing Day of 1849, " The Island of Jewels " at the Lyceum contained, says Planché, a scene where " the novel and yet exceedingly simple falling of the leaves of a palm tree which discovered six fairies supporting a coronet of jewels, produced such an effect as I scarcely remember having witnessed on any similar occasion up to that period." Year after year Beverley's powers were tasked " to outdo his former out-doings." The most complicated machinery, the most costly materials, were annually put into requisition. Planché was " painted out " by a new invention. Scenes were covered with thin glue and then plastered with gold or silver leaf :

> Nothing was considered brilliant but the last scene. Dutch metal was in the ascendant. It was no longer even painting ; it was upholstering.

Mrs. Charles Mathews herself informed me that she had paid between £60 and £70 for gold tissue for the dresses of the supernumeraries alone, who were discovered in attitudes in the last scene of "Once upon a Time there were Two Kings."

Besides the mechanical tricks and cumbersome "properties," the mise-en-scène included gigantic masks. These had been worn at Covent Garden's "Harlequin and the Swans; or, the Bath of Beauty" in 1813 by the rival factions of round bellies and long heads—an allusion to two farces at the rival houses in the previous season. At Drury Lane in 1842 the masks were the most important part of "William Tell." They continued in fashion for forty years, nearly twice as long as pantomime burlesque.

This was not a new style of entertainment. The methods of Brough, Burnand, H. J. Byron, A'Becket and Blanchard were anticipated by the mock romanza in Davenant's mask of "Britannia Triumphans." After a Giant had expressed his intentions of making the damsel dress his whale and fry his tripes, the Knight declaimed,

O master vile, thou mighty ill-bred Lubber,
Art thou not mov'd to see her wane and blubber? . . .
Though not to scuffle given now I'll thwart thee,
Let Blowze thy daughter serve for shillings forty.

Davenant, however, did not possess the utter abandonment to the pleasures of punning which is the distinctive feature of the Victorian burlesque. In Blanchard's "Harlequin Hudibras," a fairy, pointing to the Crystal Palace at Sydenham, said:

Behold my treasures here, there's nought forbidin' in 'em.
And all will be revealed though now it's hid in 'em.

In "Whittington and His Cat; or, Harlequin Lord Mayor of London," the Cat entered with a leather case of shaving tackle, which provoked his Master to say:

Why, Puss, the folks will say to see this stored,
You've been a-shaving 'stead of being aboard.

In "Harlequin Sinbad the Sailor; or, the Great Roc of the Diamond Valley and the Seven Wonders of the World," the outstanding example was "Sea-faring man, be plain, no deck-oration." But this was exceeded in Byron's "The Lion and the Unicorn," by the answer

308

to " Are those hares ? "—" Which they hair." In their everyday burlesques, examples such as the following were common enough :

> Descend, ye hailstones, bumpers, thumpers, frizzers ;
> It cuts you like a knife, doesn't it Nar-scissors ?
>
> I must Ganymede to earth to fly—
> Ganymede, brin-g an immed-iate supply.
>
> Now sing, as Sirens did before us ;
> We lure all here with tooral looral chorus.
>
> Sultan of Egypt, this pathetic tear
> Proves you've one faithful Vizier left—viz. here.

At Sadler's Wells the burlesque pantomimes included " Harlequin and Poor Richard ; or, Old Father Time and the Almanack Maker," at Christmas, 1840. Father Time sent his hour-glass to poor Richard, to be employed upon the lady who had neglected him. Her mask was changed for one with grey hair and a long nose. She gazed into a sham looking glass of gauze ; behind it a similar figure copied her movements. Her accepted lover left her. Richard, having won her heart, gave her back her beauty. The next year, " Harlequin and Cinderella ; or, the Little Fairy and the Large Glass Slipper," burlesqued Perrault's story by means of grotesque masks " ludicrously identified with the characters of the piece." After a number of nursery tales had been similarly treated year by year, Greenwood (Phelps' partner) invented in 1858 a piece with the title of " Harlequin and Old Isaac Walton ; or, Tom Moore of Fleet Street, the Silver Trout and the Seven Sisters of Tottenham." The opening scene was the " Muddy Mountains of Old Father Thames," where the god of the river uttered " Jeremiades on the impurities of his waters." Rejecting the medical aid of the Board of Works, he consulted the River Lee, who regretted the loss of her fish owing to Old Isaac. To change his occupation they proposed to marry him to the Fair Maid of Tottenham, " Maude the Milkmaid, youngest of the Seven Sisters," but she preferred Tom Moore, Walton's apprentice. At last, however, all the difficulties were solved by a fairy fish and an elfin jackdaw.

Both the length of the title and the complicated character of the plot were according to the custom of the minor theatres. Probably the longest title and most involved plot were invented at the Royal Victoria Theatre (the " Old Vic ") in 1856. The Christmas bills announced " Harlequin William the Conqueror and King Vice of the Silent City ; or, War, Wine and Love, and Queen Virtue in the Vistas of Light and Glitter." The first scene was " The Cavern of Vice " :

> A gloomy cavern, with arched roof, formed of faces, displaying the passions of man—skeletons, etc.—serpents and dragon with large eyes—Jack Sheppard in his cell in chains—the gin fiend—gamblers quarrelling, shooting one another—four satellites of Kantharadies, the agent of vice on earth, discovered with four attendant sprites.

Kantharadies desired Silenza, who had three other suitors. One was shown half-drunk, the other rushing into a cannon's mouth, and the third, Prince Pinafore-Belly, eating a lollypop. In the Silent City King Muddlewit and Queen Fuddlewit, the parents of Silenza, slept. The Queen of Virtue restored the city to life and bustle. The suitors arrived. The Princess chose Billy, who for her sake decided to be a man. Kantharadies, however, seized princess and suitors and threw the city back into its trance. The Queen of Virtue changed Billy into a knight in armour. He found his enemy in the Forest of Good, Bad and Indifferent. At the word war, the scene changed to Inkerman. Billy lost his way in the Valley of Flowers, lured on by the mirage of Silenza. He fell into the sea of gold, reached a rock and was protected by fairies. Then in the Hall of Vice, Death sent two of the suitors down traps. Billy defied him, only to be conquered by Kantharadies. But Daydawn changed the scene to the " Bower of a thousand lights in the world of stars," where Billy became Harlequin and Silenza Columbine.

Even Thackeray's fanciful account of an imaginary " Harlequin Conqueror " was not as fantastic as this. The turning point of his plot is that, at the Battle of Hastings, William is on the point of being defeated by the Sussex volunteers, " very elegantly led by the always pretty Miss Waddy (as Haco Sharpshooter) " when a shot from the Normans kills Harold. The fairy Edith comes forward and finds the body, which straightway leaps up a live Harlequin, whilst the Conqueror makes an excellent Clown, and the Archbishop of Bayeux

310

a diverting Pantaloon.   At the " Theatre of Fancy " Thackeray also
saw " Harlequin Hamlet, or Daddy's Ghost and Nunky's Pison."
In the scene of the ramparts of Elsinore by moon and snowlight, the
freezing of the nose of one of the sentinels is " very neatly and dexterously arranged."   Hamlet's umbrella is whirled away in the storm.
He and his friends stamp on each other's toes to keep them warm.
Hamlet's mother also loses her umbrella and retires " screaming in
pattens."   Then

> The cabs on the stand in the great market-place at Elsinore are seen to drive
> off, and several people are drowned.   The gas-lamps along the street are
> wrenched from their foundations, and shoot through the troubled air.   Whist,
> rush, hish ! how the rain roars and pours.   The darkness becomes awful,
> always deepened by the power of music—and see—in the midst of a rush,
> and whirl, and scream of spirits of air and wave—what is that ghastly figure
> moving hither ?   It becomes bigger, bigger, as it advances down the plat-
> form—more ghastly, more horrible, enormous !   It is as tall as the whole
> stage.   It seems to be advancing on the stalls and pit, and the whole house
> screams with terror, as the GHOST OF THE LATE HAMLET comes in, and begins
> to speak.

Thackeray adds, " After the usual business, that Ophelia should be
turned into Colombine was to be expected ; but I confess I was a
little shocked when Hamlet's mother became Pantaloon, and was
instantly knocked down by Clown Claudius."

Blanchard sought to separate pantomime from burlesque.   As
a child he was taken to the theatre each Christmas, and therefore remembered the fairy tale entertainments.   At sixteen he wrote a pantomime to be played by amateurs at Rodney House, Old Kent Road,
and was himself the Columbine.   Ten years later he wrote the pantomimes for the Olympic and the Victoria.   " Miserable and Christmas
Day at home, solus," is the entry in his diary for 1846.   For Boxing
Day the entry is " Pantomimes produced : both hits and houses
crowded."   He followed the prevailing mode until the second year at
Drury Lane.   From 1853 to 1857 he took his subjects from the
nursery.   The first, " Harlequin King Humming-Top and the
Land of Toys," was the story of an enormous humming top whose son
suffered from low spirits until restored to happiness by means of

311

marbles, football and hop-scotch. Of " Jack and Jill ; [1] or, Harlequin King Mustard and Four and Twenty Blackbirds Baked In a Pie," Henry Morley wrote :

> No doubt he is justified by diligent research among the nurseries of England in asserting that Jill was so far wanting in domestic education as to be unable to make a pie, that this was the cause of her misfortune, that the making of a pie was its remedy, and that the pie she made was the well-known pie of blackbirds mentioned in the Song of Sixpence. . . . We are busied among visions of good things, jams of all sorts, sauces, spices, pickles, and we are refreshed in a temple of salad.

Among Blanchard's rivals this year were the Adelphi's " Zigzag ; or, the Adventures of the Danube and Pruth in Search of Truth," with a naval combat represented by ladies and gentlemen dancing with ships on their heads, the Princess's " Blue Beard," with the finale of the deck of a man-of-war going into action, the Haymarket's " Little Bo-peep Who Lost Her Sheep," with the transformation of a ballroom into a coach and horses, and the Olympic's " Yellow Dwarf," a Planché fairy extravaganza. When Blanchard's " Hey-Diddle-Diddle ; or, Harlequin King Nonsense and the Seven Ages of Man " was at Drury Lane in 1855, Covent Garden made its first effort to compete for eight years, under the direction of " The Wizard of the North." Raising the highest expectation by a system of puffery little short of the marvellous, " Professor " Anderson presented the public with " Ye Belle Alliance ; or Harlequin and the Field of the Cloth of Gold " by George Augustus Sala. Morley considered it " the dullest that has anywhere been seen in London for a good many seasons past." After preparing the public for " two hundred young women, none under the height of six feet two," Anderson had produced four masks as chambermaids with clogs and caps, his dioramas had turned out to be two small and bad transparencies, and his " great tournament after Holbein," a lump or two of armour upon hobby-horses. His " Great Gun Trick " was burlesqued at Drury Lane by Charles Mathews as " Wizard of the South-South-West-by-East." Anderson's reply,

---

[1] Originally a way of saying " a lad and his lass." The play of " Jack and Jill " performed at Elizabeth's Revels is, therefore, not to be included in a study of the influence of the nursery upon the stage.

" Twenty Minutes with an Impudent Puppy," was a fizzle that induced the Strand to make further fun of him in " A Plague on both your Houses." Failing to make profit as a producer of plays, Anderson arranged for himself a Carnival Benefit which burned Covent Garden Theatre to the ground.

After imitating Blanchard's choice of subjects in " The Three Bears" and "Little Bo-peep," the Haymarket constructed their pantomime in 1858 by joining a fairy extravaganza to a Harlequinade. "Undine ; or, Harlequin and the Spirit of the Waters" was, apart from the concluding mixture of patriotism and advertisements, as serious as the plays of Lord Lytton. There was even an unhappy ending. In consequence, when Sir Hulbrand (Mrs. Leclercq) and the Lady Bertalda (Miss Fitz-inman) were changed to Harlequin and Columbine, Undine (Louise Leclercq) was ordered to watch over her faithless lover until time should restore her peace of mind. This was a clumsy device, since an exalted treatment of the story could not be reconciled with a finale of shop scenes. Therefore, the burlesque style of pantomime was occasionally revived. Blanchard's " Peter Wilkins ; or, Harlequin and the Flying Woman of the Loadstone Rock " was almost the last. Then it was discovered that the feminine grace of the extravaganza blended well with domestic horseplay. At the Royal English Opera, Covent Garden, " Bluebeard ; or, Harlequin and Freedom in her Island Home " had Miss Craven for the hero. The next year, in " The House that Jack Built ; or, Old Mother Hubbard and her Wonderful Dog," Miss Hunt was Jack at Drury Lane. But the principal boy was not yet safely installed. In " Faw Fee Fo Fum ; or, Harlequin Jack the Giant Killer " at the Lane in 1867, Jack was played by Joseph Irving.

A year or two later, however, the Vokes came to stay at this theatre. From " Beauty and the Beast ; or, Harlequin and Old Mother Bunch " in 1869, to " Bluebeard " in 1879, they set the claims of the fairy tale high, and made an attempt to keep the humour within its limits. Take " Whittington and His Cat ; or, Harlequin Lord Mayor of London " for example. There is no need seriously to consider Blanchard's claim to have revised the story " in strict

313

accordance with authentic records, newly discovered " because the cat—in the old tale a she about to kitten—is a tom. But there is some attempt to create in the scenery, music and lyrics, an atmosphere of the past. The knockabout business in the kitchen scene arises out of the story. When Dick is dismissed his cat seizes the joint from the spit, and during the chase crockery is smashed. Even the final procession—recorded in the " penny plain, twopence coloured " sheets still sold in the toy theatre shop at Houndsditch—is appropriate. Blanchard's directions run :

> Music. Enter in grand procession after the style of the Lord Mayor's Show, Zanzibar guards to clear the way. African prince with barrow painted emerald green, white, and gold, labelled " Meat for the Cat," six milkmaids, two-and-two, bearing milkpails, each milkpail labelled " Milk for the Cat," bearers with white wands marshalling handsomely dressed page bearing on crimson cushion handsome collar, inscription on banner above " Collar for the Cat," a Chinese bearing a large china cream jug on silver salver labelled " Cream for the Cat," two cooks bearing large tray—tablecloth on tray and rich tureen—steam from tureen—attendants with lighted candles on each side and banner inscribed " Lights for the Cat," four bearers with handsome basket with blue and white satin coverlid, banner " Cradle for the Cat." When in centre of stage, one pull of bearers sends up the head and shoulders of half-a-dozen kittens, second pull brings down from bottom of basket richly ornamented pincushion inscribed " Welcome, Little Strangers." Great flourish, and Cat enters magnificently decorated, followed by servants with rat-shaped heads, small powdered wigs, and cocked hats, and their tails trailing on the ground. Sovereign of Zanzibar, Whittington, Alice, Fitz-warren, and Cook now enter followed by grand palanquin—curtains to draw —banner " Comfort for the Cat." Curtains drawn. Discovery of White Cat in bridal dress.

This change of taste was due less to Blanchard than to the remarkable family who performed his pantomimes at this time. Frederick Vokes and his wife were makers of " Grand Fancy Costume Ball, Theatrical and Historical Dresses," with a shop at 19 Henrietta Street, Covent Garden. He advertised himself as the only histrionic costumier to receive the Prize Medal of 1851 and be " personally complimented by Her Majesty and the late Prince Consort." In 1869 he became " Producer of all the grand dresses at the Theatre Royal, Drury Lane " because of the sudden success of his children as a troupe. Mr. H. G. Hibbert in "A Playgoer's Memories " tells how

314

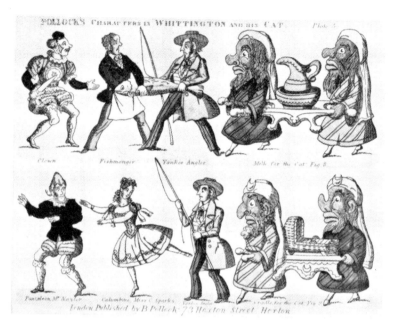

MASKS IN "WHITTINGTON AND HIS CAT"

By permission of the Toy-Theatre Shop in Hoxton

Papa Vokes, not thinking much of the stage as a vocation, made his son Fred into a skilful tailor.   But the boy managed to be Phelps' call-boy and assistant to the " Wizard of the North," being vanished beneath tin cones, discovered in portfolios and so forth.   Each of the other children took to the stage in turn, until their play at home prompted an aunt to form them into a troupe.   " Their little comedies," said Mr. Hibbert, " never lost that charm of spontaneity and childish improvisation."   They made their formal début at the Lyceum in the pantomime of " Humpty Dumpty " at Christmas, 1868, and the next year went in a body to Drury Lane.   Jessie and Victoria Vokes completed the troupe that year, and Kate Santley was their ally.   In " The Dragon of Wantley," the pantomime of 1870-71, Fawdon Vokes brought their number up to five.   They appeared in Alhambra ballets and also in the Drury Lane pantomimes of " Tom Thumb " and " The Children in the Wood," but were absent in America when " Jack in the Box " was given in 1873-4.   They resumed their sway over the next six pantomimes though Rosina left to marry Cecil Clay, author of " A Pantomime Rehearsal " which she acted here and in America many times.   At the troupe's final appearance at the Lane, they again numbered five by the addition of Mrs. Fred Vokes. That was Augustus Harris's first pantomime (Chatterton having crashed the year before).   Dreading the tyranny of the Vokes, Harris reciuited a new staff from the music-halls, while they went over to Covent Garden where Chatterton in 1800-1 staged Burnand's " Valentine and Orson " with Beverley to paint his scenes. But the Vokes were only in one pantomime at Covent Garden.   Chatterton was not successful, and went to Sadler's Wells to design, with the aid of Frederick Evans, the clown, a pantomime that should show " delicacy and refinement, as a contrast to the commonplace vulgarity and daring audacity which some people indulge in."   The Vokes family dwindled. Jessie died in 1884, Fred in 1888, Rosina and Victoria in 1894—all before they were middle-aged.   Fawdon, who played in " Dick Whittington " at Drury Lane in 1894-5, alone lived to a good old age, dying in 1904.   Another Jessie Vokes was Whimsical Walker's Columbine in the Drury Lane Harlequinade of 1917-1918.

Before Harris is held accountable for " vulgarising " influences, it should be noted that pantomime had been declining rapidly. In 1866, the Haymarket under Buckstone (who wrote pantomimes) and the Lyceum under Fechter dropped out of the competition. Other managers followed suit, until in 1880 *The Times* had to report that " Save for its two strongholds in Drury Lane and Covent Garden, which still defy the assaults of fashion and the sap of change, pantomime may now be considered as wholly relegated to the suburbs of London." Even if Harris had been solely responsible for the coarse fun and—to quote Leopold Wagner—" extravagant ballet scenes, with the lime-light directed upon an army of palpably naked thighs which decency required should be covered with skirts," he could have justified himself—when Covent Garden housed a circus at Christmas 1884 and 1885, and tried vainly to restore the tradition with " Jack and the Beanstalk " in 1887—by the results. Incidentally, he had the wisdom to abolish the curtain-raiser which had persisted as a relic of the time pantomime was preceded by a full-length play. There was no reason for its existence. From the days when unruly apprentices interrupted the performance of " George Barnwell " in their impatience to see the Harlequinade, the first piece had been received with lessening respect until in the 'seventies the gallery felt in duty bound not to allow a word of it to be heard.

There can be little question that Harris found the most amusing performers of the day for his pantomimes. On the other hand, he was incapable of appealing to the public's emotion by any other means than scene-shifting. Under his management Blanchard was author only in name. His pantomimes were " grossly interpolated." Harris directed members of his company practically to re-write the book ; in fact, Harry Nicholls was the actual author of the new versions of " Dick Whittington," " Aladdin," and " The Babes in the Wood " which appeared as the work of Blanchard. The veteran librettist complained that as he was crushed out by the music-hall element, the good old fairy tales would never again be " illustrated as they should be." Harris substituted engineers for authors. In " Beauty and the Beast " he brought upon the stage a huge ship, so heavy he had to

316

provide tramway lines to move it along. Cinderella went to the ball in an " electric automotor." Aladdin's magic palace was built by myriads of tiny British workmen who put up a hoarding bearing the words " Gussaris Builder and Decorator " and set to work behind it with trowels, hammers, steam cranes, scaffoldings and all the paraphernalia of the building contractor until myriads of tiny wives brought myriads of dinners. For " Sinbad," the back wall was taken down and the stage doubled in size to make room for the chief scene. This was introduced in the following fashion. The young Khedive was warned that Sinbad, whom he was pursuing, was a great favourite in London. " What is London ? " asked (in effect) the young Khedive. The Diamond Prince then conjured up a vision of the Tower of London with a procession of the Kings and Queens of England since the Conqueror, this leading to " Harry Jackson's Marvellous Representation of Napoleon I " and " a review of the troops after their return from Egypt." The natural effect of Harris's policy occurred when Sinbad was carried away by the gigantic bird. What happened on the first night has been related by Mr. James Glover, the musical director of many a Drury Lane pantomime :

> The roc filled the entire stage and was only supposed to move a few feet just to lift Sinbad off the ground. The front scene dropped and there was ten minutes to set the next scene. The curtain was down for an hour and a half, because the roc had stuck ! Twelve carpenters had to saw and hammer it away, and smash it to pieces, before the pantomime could go on. £1,000 gone in two hours ! Coming in front of the curtain Augustus Harris said : " I must claim your indulgence—this is a very heavy pantomime." And the gallery boys shouted back " Yes, Gus, it is ! "

This obsession with barbaric splendour was shown in Harris's choice of " principal boys." The most characteristic was Harriet Vernon. An obituary notice in *The Era* of July, 1923, described her as " a magnificent creature," who was willing " to show her ample figure as generously as the conventional tights and ' trunks ' of her day allowed—or, should one say, encouraged." She affected immense hats, and many feathers, carrying a decorated stick when the part allowed. She only stayed two years, possibly because her pride and extravagance made her demand a salary " as immense as her

317

figure," and Drury Lane's audiences were consoled the next year in "Beauty and the Beast" with Lady Dunlo and Vesta Tilley.

What would have been the effect on pantomime if Vesta Tilley had set the standard for principal boys? She had an inborn gift for swaggering in man's apparel—which would have given meaning to the fairy-tale hero's inversion of sex. At five years she was "a male impersonator" at a Nottingham hall whose chairman was her father. Ten years later she was Pertiboy in "Beauty and the Beast" at Birmingham. The next year, 1882, Harris made her Captain Tra-la-la in his "Sinbad," but she only returned once to Drury Lane. There was more than imitation in her mannerisms. There was more than caricature. She was always a very ordinary youth, but she represented him in an extraordinary manner. Men were constantly startled by the sensation that this was how they appeared in the eyes of a laughing woman. The momentary discomfort before the laughter may still be felt merely by seeing the words of her songs :

> Jolly good luck to the girl that loves a soldier !
> *All* good boys are we !
> *Girls*, if you want to love a soldier,
> You can *all* love *me*.

or again :

> I joined the Army yesterday,
> So, the Army of to-day's all right.

The lines conjure up her weedy, immaculate youths, strutting, swaggering, smoking cigarettes with an air. They were never unkindly depicted, even when they belonged to the seaside promenade type. And when the Tommy Atkins in Brodrick and scarlet tunic was replaced by the boy in khaki and kit-bag, clumping up and down the stage in ammunition boots, one felt that Vesta Tilley must have cried before she copied him.

"It would be futile," wrote Mr. Archer in the early 'nineties, "to look to Drury Lane for the regeneration of pantomime. The traditions of the theatre and its size are equally unfavourable to any experiments in the direction of literary grace and artistic refinement." There were other protests of the same kind. Therefore, Harris made "a certain effort in the direction of coherence." His "Cinderella" of

1895 was described by *The Times* as a return to the fairy extravaganza. That was the beginning of the modern pantomime which, in design, was better than any model that had gone before. Tradition, however, was a handicap. Rich's gloomy opening scene, Sheridan's patriotic songs, Garrick's processions, the Victorian army of limping girls and so forth, all remained to hinder the story. Whenever economy had to be considered, clownship was reduced. When Harris was re-formed, he did without Marie Lloyd and Little Tich. When the limited run of pantomime would not balance the high expenses of 1914-18, the number and quality of the comedians were again reduced. But wherever a fairy tale has been performed with the aid of a competent clown, there the people have gathered. Now that this perverse idea we call the pantomime, after wandering illogically about the mind of our race for two centuries, has at last become coherent, is it to be dropped as of no more account than a jig-saw picture that has been completed ?

Cap° Cocodrillo. Cap? Csgangarato.

PANTOMIME'S POSSIBILITIES

What we should do, then, is to pool our legends and make a delightful stock of religious folk-lore on an honest basis for all mankind. With our minds freed from pretence and falsehood we could enter into the heritage of all the faiths. China would share her sages with Spain, and Spain her saints with China . . . All the sweetness of religion is conveyed to the world by the hands of story-tellers and image-makers. Without their fictions the truths of religion would for the multitude be neither intelligible nor even apprehensible.

GEORGE BERNARD SHAW.

Metzetin   Riciulina

SO much emotion and so little thought go to the making of legend that it is the meet and proper setting for the clown. The origin of the fairy tale is more primitive than reason ; its simplest form is the joy and fear in the mind of a dog when he finds the slipper of a long-lost master. All legend seems related to the original fable that belongs to the very dawn of thought, the fable of the Nile. Because its waters took away life when they rose, gave deliverance when they subsided and left life behind them in the irrigated land, the river was worshipped as a trinity of dragon, sword and benefactor. Though changed from Apollo and the Python to Jack and the Giant, the tale has retained the same emotional appeal. Other tales, outwardly dissimilar, bear a certain resemblance. The sword may be a beanstalk, a cat, a magic lamp, a goose laying golden eggs, a glass slipper or " open sesame," but it still represents the means of deliverance. Likewise, the dragon may be a giant, ogre, wolf, magician or even stepmother, yet still be the persecutor ; and the benefactor may be a prince, princess, simpleton or apprentice, yet still be the same deliverer. What need is there to trace particular coincidences when there are so many ? Resemblances between legends can be explained by the principle that governs resemblances between clowns. A tale is made in a certain pattern to conform to human needs. The gamut of emotion must be played upon. There must be an object of pity, an object of disgust, cause for anger, an object of wonder, causes for fear, admiration, contempt and joy. Here is the " plotology " of fairy tales. The legend is born in a fact such as the Nile flood or the Lord Mayor's fortune. The story teller understands how to improve it in the telling : he adds the objects or incidents truth has not supplied. The pantomime author, descendant of Perrault's Mother Goose, behaves similarly.   By joining the stories of the Babes in the Wood and Robin Hood he completes a gamut.   Robinson Crusoe, his gun and the savages ; or Goody Two Shoes, the brazen head and the wicked squire ; or (perhaps in future) the beamish boy, the worple blade and the Jabberwock, may show the process of legend-making still continuing.

After a century of hack work, the nursery tales, fairy stories and legends have been rough-shaped for the stage.   That they are material worthy the hand of a master dramatist is evident even in the pinchbeck couplets of the librettists of to-day.   In fact, there can be little doubt that were an Elizabethan dramatist to set up in practice in the contemporary theatre he would find congenial employment in pantomime alone.   It is the only form of modern drama where poetry would not be self-conscious, the only form free from the restrictions of verisimilitude, the only form able to match the ridiculous with the sublime.   Moreover, it is the only drama that is constructed by collective effort.   The pantomime playwright labours for the common good, for, until perfection is reached, his efforts will become part of the stockpot from which he has borrowed.   Shakespeare made his name with Part I. of " Henry VI." though, according to Sir Sidney Lee, he wrote no more than 300 out of the 2,600 lines " at the most generous computation."   His company bought the old plays of " Titus Andronicus," " The Taming of the Shrew," " King Lear " and " Hamlet " for his raw material.   For the rest he could lay his hand where he chose on histories, poems and romances.   There was, indeed, a conspiracy between the man and his time to create genius. To-day the same conditions await a poet able to master the trade of a dramatist.

These possibilities of pantomime are not newly discovered.   In the 'nineties Mr. William Archer pointed out the opportunities in its "infinitely flexible, expansive framework" for all sorts of "ingenious and delightful developments," including the "most penetrating criticism of life":

The ideal pantomime should charm the senses, stimulate the imagination, and satisfy the intelligence.   It should be an enchanting fairy-tale to the young, to the old a witty, graceful, genially satiric phantasmagoria. It has this immense advantage over burlesque, that it does not necessarily involve the degradation of anything noble and beautiful. The nursery folk-lore in which it finds its traditional subjects presents just the requisite blending of the graceful with the grotesque. It is painful to see Lancelot and Guinevere, Faust and Margaret, grinning through a horse-collar; but the grace and pathos of the Babes in the Wood and Cinderella might quite well remain intact, while the Wicked Uncle and the Robbers, the Cruel Stepmother and the Proud Sisters, might be handed over to Fantasy as butts for its most impish humours.

Nothing, however, can be changed until managers learn wisdom. At present the frenzied finance of the theatre makes development impossible. Scenic competition is carried so far that occasionally the highest possible receipts would not equal the expenditure. This ridiculous state of affairs is the hereditary curse bequeathed by the courts of the spendthrift Tudor sovereigns to the theatre. Davenant's heirs have constantly intensified the obsession of scene-shifting. To-day the boon of electricity is turned into a burden upon the back of the playwright. Strangely enough, pantomime suffers comparatively mildly from the blight of spectacle. In spite of its array of chorus girls and transformations it pays its way more frequently than most spectacular shows. Nevertheless, the limitations of the holiday season, which bring the run of performances to a close at the end of the third month, cause in managers an unwillingness to speculate on a restricted success. The way out of this problem would be found were emotion created by the living word instead of by excess of painted canvas. If light and colour were deemed sufficient for the scene, expenses would be diminished and the pantomime be held in such respect that adults might attend at other times than the children's holidays.

The need of witty lines is not so great as the need of poetry. Clowns as a rule are capable of providing their own fun. When they fail it is generally because an emotional setting is lacking. Clownship is more concerned with actions than speech. "*Practical* absurdity," as Hazlitt said, is the essence of pantomime. Shocks and surprises, violations of probability, common sense and nature, must keep the brain and senses in a whirl too violent for words. There-

325

fore, the comment of Mr. Bernard Shaw (on a pantomime thirty years ago) has only a measure of truth :

> The spectacular scenes exhibit Mr. Collins as a manager to whom a thousand pounds is as five shillings. The dramatic scenes exhibit him as one to whom a crown-piece is as a million. If Mr. Dan Leno had asked for a hundred-guinea tunic to wear during a single walk across the stage, no doubt he would have got it, with a fifty-guinea hat and sword-belt to boot. If he had asked for ten guineas' worth of the time of a competent dramatic humorist to provide him with at least one line that might not have been pirated from the nearest Cheap Jack, he would, I suspect, have been asked whether he wished to make Drury Lane bankrupt for the benefit of dramatic authors.

Acting in accordance with this advice, Mr. C. B. Cochran employed the witty pen of Mr. Hastings Turner, author of comedies and revues, to write a version of " The Babes in the Wood." The result was not encouraging. If he could obtain the rare mixture of mellow humour and golden fancy that, say, T. W. H. Crosland possessed, the experiment of putting an author in control might well succeed. Gusto is needed. Wit is too delicate. " Georgian poetry " is too aloof. The pantomime author will not come from a university. He will arrive at the moment the opportunity offers itself, in the guise of an assistant stage-manager or minor actor in touch with the genuine needs of pantomime audiences who are more interested in food prices than epigrams. Yet the signs of a revolution of dramatic taste will not have to wait till then. In his recent works Mr. Bernard Shaw has, both in theory and practice, championed the " The legends, the parables, the dramas," which he declares are among " the choicest treasures of mankind ":

> People will have their miracles, their stories, their heroes and heroines and saints and martyrs and divinities to exercise their gifts of affection, admiration, wonder and worship, and their Judases and devils to enable them to be angry and yet feel they do well to be angry.

The pity is Mr. Bernard Shaw did not shape his " Metabiological Pentateuch " on these lines, following the hint in his preface concerning " the legend of Noah's Ark, with its funny beginning about the animals and its exquisite end about the birds." Instead of striving to achieve the impossible task of expressing an intellectual ideal in terms of emotion, he might have given us a logical exposition of mankind's aim and direction in a dramatised version of the Old Testament, with a better clown—Nebuchadnezzar or Jeremiah—than the Napoleon who blows a police whistle in " Back to Methuselah," to represent the voice of the present in the past.   There is no doubt Mr. Bernard Shaw is too good a showman not to appreciate the importance of the clown.   The more emotional his subject the more boisterous the comic relief.   In the second act of " Androcles and the Lion " the crescendo of emotion, created by Latvinia's determination to die, and crested by the slaughter of the torturers by Ferrovius, is followed by wild horseplay :

> Androcles holds out his hands to the lion, who gives him both paws, which he shakes with enthusiasm.   They embrace rapturously, finally waltz round the arena amid a sudden burst of deafening applause, and out through the passage. . . .   The place is emptied with magical suddenness.
>
> Androcles (naïvely) : Now I wonder why they all run away from us like that. (The lion, combining a series of yawns, purrs, and roars, achieves something very like a laugh.)

When he returned to legend Mr. Bernard Shaw was more discreet and less effective in the comic scenes.   In its emotional appeal " Saint Joan " is the greatest English drama since Shakespeare.   Its humour, however, merely makes plain that the dramatist realised his need of clownship without being able to bring in the clown.   In consequence, while the intellectual and emotional cravings are satisfied, the pent-up feelings find no safety-valve.   " Saint Joan," with all its mental vigour, tends to depress.   Because our need for the ridiculous has not been satisfied we fall short of the sublime.

After the theatre's constantly recurring play of mothers and fathers, ever the same however changed since the day we were instructed in its construction by our nursemaids, legend has the wide horizon that the world possesses for a child just released from the nursery.   After the titled nonentities and soulful peasants of the contemporary theatre, the hero of the nursery tale is as tall as a grown-up standing among dolls.   After the confines of cottages and drawing-rooms, shipwreck and inaccessible castle are as invigorating to the brain as ocean and mountain air to the lungs.   The ideals of an age notable for the bursting of the limitations of a cramped scientific code can only be expressed in the drama of unfettered imagination. The drama of marital dispute has been exhausted. Once the shutting of real doors became commonplace, managers had no other hope than that the letters dropped into real fireplaces could be burned in real flames instead of being thrust behind a sham electric fire. When this great aim of realism has been achieved, audiences will yawn the season through in vain, because there is no prospect that discussions between husbands and wives over acts of infidelity will ever satisfy the playgoer's desire to enlarge his experience of life in laughter and emotion. Crude as it is, and silly as its conventions are, the pantomime is more inspiring. However desperately encumbered with songs about various parts of the United States and other benumbing irrelevancies, the story will generally be given at least one moment to stir emotion and provoke the mind into contemplations of the secrets of the impossible. A simple scene in one of last year's pantomimes, "Jack and the Beanstalk," made one wonder at the courage of the hero who struggled up miles of beanstalk, clambered thigh-boot deep over the clouds, whirled among planets, took a flying leap through relativity and stormed a castle beyond the moon for love of a lady he had never known. That adventure cannot be staged in detail. But just the glimpse of the Lyceum's principal boy scrambling to her feet where the scarlet runners ended in space, to gaze, bewildered but eager, across the planets to where the giant's castle gleamed white in the milky way, suggested enough to make us believe a poet could suggest far more by rousing us from the lethargy of taking life for granted. Wild as it is, the tale is made of tame things. "It is impossible," says Mr. Chesterton,

> to picture plainer or simpler things than a cow and a beanstalk and a bag; everything about them is commonplace except what happens to them. It is obviously a tale made up by peasants out of their daily needs.

Those needs are not monopolised by peasants. Human beings are naturally led in quest of the sublime by immortal longings (or a will to improve the species) common to all. This generation, in particular, understands the virtue of being credulous. Like the Elizabethans, who believed in a race of men whose heads did grow beneath their shoulders, we are willing to recognise spooks rather than own to the

328

folly of scepticism.   Three hundred years ago the fool was known by his denials ; to scoff at El Dorado was to run the risk of seeing its gold and princes on London wharves the next morning.   To-day while we contemplate the Fourth Dimension, the restrictions of past, present and future, and of length, breadth and depth seem unreal. Herr Einstein has restored mankind's sense of wonder.   The incomprehensible once more joins earth to heaven.   There are no impossibilities now.   And that is what the theatre needs to show— yet how, if not in the legends of pantomime ?   The Jacob's ladder, however, must be balanced on earth by a clown, sitting on the lowest rung, who, like George Jackley at the Lyceum, eats bread and cheese out of a spotted handkerchief and yearns for nothing more than an onion.

Cucurucu.   Razallo.

ACKNOWLEDGMENTS

are due to the Editors of *The Nineteenth Century and After*, *Quarterly Review*, *Fortnightly Review*, *Daily Telegraph*, and other journals whose acceptance of articles on the subject of Clowns and Pantomimes has enabled the author to continue his studies ;

also to Professor Gilbert Murray for certain classical references, and to Mr. James Strachey for advice in psychology—though the author alone must be held responsible for the theories set forth upon these matters ;

also to Messrs. John Parker, C. B. Cochran, C. R. W. Nevinson, Arthur C. M'Lachlan, Ivan Patrick Gore, and to the late Mr. H. G. Hibbert and others whose assistance is indicated in the foregoing pages ; also to Mr. Michael Sadleir who has untiringly fostered this volume through the press.

INDEX

To Persons Real and Fictitious Mentioned in this Volume.

335

342

I N D E X